# John Evelyn and his World

# John Evelyn
# and his World

A BIOGRAPHY

## John Bowle

Routledge & Kegan Paul

LONDON, BOSTON AND HENLEY

*First published in 1981*
*by Routledge & Kegan Paul Ltd*
*39 Store Street, London WC1E 7DD*
*9 Park Street, Boston, Mass. 02108, USA and*
*Broadway House, Newtown Road,*
*Henley-on-Thames, Oxon RG9 1EN*

*Set in 11/12 Singer Baskerville by*
*Computacomp (UK) Ltd*
*Fort William, Scotland*
*and printed in Great Britain by*
*Thomson Litho Ltd*
*East Kilbride, Scotland*

*British Library Cataloguing in Publication Data*

*Bowle, John*
*John Evelyn and his world.*
*1. Evelyn, John – Biography*
*2. Authors, English – Early modern, 1500–1700 –*
*Biography*
*I. Title*
*828.4'03      PR3433.E5Z/*

*ISBN 0-7100-0721-3*

*To the memory*
*of*
*Wyndham Ketton-Cremer*

# Contents

# Illustrations

# Preface

When I was asked to write a biography of John Evelyn, I was encouraged in the attempt by the knowledge that in 1956 a definitive edition of his *Diary* had at last become available in the superb six volumes edited by Mr E. S. de Beer. Without this monumental and elaborately annotated work and the permission of the Trustees of the Evelyn Estate and of the Delegates of the Clarendon Press at Oxford to quote from it, an adequate biography would have been impossible. I am grateful to the Trustees and the Delegates for the permission accorded.

It has not, in these circumstances, been my objective to make further research into manuscript material already fully investigated, still less to attempt new discoveries in a specialized literary field; rather I have endeavoured, as an historian, to recreate the personality of John Evelyn in the context of his times both for readers who know him well and for those to whom he is still only a celebrated name. I have therefore taken account not only of the able and thorough *Sylva, a Discourse of Forest Trees* and *Gard'ner's Almanack* which in 1664 won him fame in his lifetime, but also of his many and varied writings: *The State of France* and *The Character of England*, for example; the *Fumifugium* against the London smog; the lively *Tyrannus or the Mode*; and the entertaining *Discourse of Sallets*. The *Life of Mrs Godolphin*, unpublished until 1847, also has touching interest, while his launching of the translation of de la Quintinye's treatise on gardening (*The Compleat Gard'ner*), following up the *Gard'ner's Almanack*, had wide effect. And these are only a selection of the indefatigable and versatile publications which, apart from the *Diary*, reflect the sharp observation and insatiable curiosity of a born writer.

Along with the *Diary* and correspondence, they build up a picture of an attractive, talented, yet representative character whose quality and development, spanning the evolution of later Jacobean England into the very different realm of Queen Anne, I have endeavoured to present.

My thanks are also due to the Master and Fellows of Balliol College for permission to examine the pocket books kept by Evelyn as an undergraduate; to Dr Mason of Christ Church, Oxford, who arranged for me to see parts of the Evelyn manuscripts there; to Sir Edgar Williams for kindly reading the proofs; and to Mrs Templeton who has given me so much expert help by typing the book.

John Bowle
Oxford

# Acknowledgments

The author and publishers would like to thank the following for permission to reproduce the illustrations: Mr Patrick Evelyn (plates 1, 2, 3 and 8); the Ashmolean Museum (plate 6); the Geffrye Museum (plates, 4, 5 and 7).

# Sources of the *Diary*

The main source of Evelyn's *Diaries*, which are in fact based on contemporary notes supplemented by memoirs, is the bound manuscript *Kalendarium*, which covers his life from 1620 to 1697, and the loose sheets which continue until 1706. It was written retrospectively in 1660 up to the end of Evelyn's visit to Rome in 1645. It was then continued in 1680–4 from 1649 up to 1684, and it is only after that that the narrative becomes a contemporary diary.

How the first selection from the *Kalendarium* came to be published makes an entertaining and representative story. In April 1813 a certain Mr Upcott, librarian and collector, conversing at Wotton with Lady Evelyn, widow of Sir Frederick Evelyn, great-great-grandson of the diarist, remarked, since his hostess was embroidering a 'tippet of birds' feathers', 'We all have our hobbies, I perceive, my lady'; whereat Lady Evelyn replied 'What are yours?' The librarian answered that his were 'collecting manuscripts and autographs'. 'Autographs,' she replied, 'what do you mean by autographs? Surely you don't mean old letters such as these?', and she opened a drawer of papers, some of which had recently been used to cut out patterns for a dress. Among them Upcott discovered two letters to 'Sylva' Evelyn, as the diarist was known in the family from the title of his book 'of Forest Trees', from Sarah, First Duchess of Marlborough.

He was delighted, whereupon Lady Evelyn remarked with the grand casualness of her kind 'Oh, if you like papers like that, you shall have plenty, for *Sylva* Evelyn and those who succeeded him kept all their correspondence, which has furnished the Kitchen with abundance of waste paper.' She at once summoned a housekeeper and commanded 'Take the key to the ebony cabinet in the billiard room; procure a basket, and bring down some of the bundles which are tied up and put away.' Upcott wisely accompanied her, secured the basket, carried the bundles into the dining room, and at once there examined them. Next day, he discovered the bound manuscript of the *Kalendarium*. 'Bless me!', exclaimed Lady Evelyn, 'if here isn't old Sylva's Diary; why I haven't seen it for years! I once sent it to Lord Harcourt, to Lord Liverpool, and to Mr Bray, [a local antiquary] who wished me to print it. But I don't think it would interest the public, nor prove of sufficient importance to repay the expense of printing.'[2] Under pressure from Upcott, William Bray renewed his request, and before her death in 1817 Lady Evelyn had consented that a selection should be published with Bray, aged seventy-nine, as editor and with Upcott as his assistant. Hence publication, in two volumes, in 1818.

The book was an immediate success; so much so that Lord Braybrooke, hereditary Keeper of the Library at Magdalene College, Cambridge, had Pepys's diary then first deciphered and published in a uniform edition with Evelyn's. Meanwhile with the death of Lady Evelyn, the Wotton property had passed to an Evelyn cousin.

'Sylva' Evelyn was already well known to a considerable public. *Sylva or a discourse of Forest Trees*, had been so comprehensive and practical that it was still in use, and a sumptuous annotated edition had appeared, edited by Hunter in 1776. But Bray, omitting any entries that might shock the sort of readers described by Jane Austen, now presented a new Evelyn: a high-minded and model gentleman, who proved much to the taste of those already moving away from Hanoverian raffishness towards early Victorian morality. 'These papers,' he wrote, 'may not be important enough to appear in the pages of all Histories of the Kingdom', but they 'may give some hints to biographers, or at least gratify the curiosity of those who are inquisitive after the mode in which their ancestors conducted business, or passed their time'. They still do, and much more.

So, following a chance conversation in Lady Evelyn's drawing room, the first edition of the *Diary* was launched. It was bound up with other papers at Wotton and entitled *Memoirs Illustrative of the life and writings of John Evelyn ... comprising his Diary for the years 1620–1705–6 and a selection of his familiar letters, to which being joined the private correspondence between King Charles I and Sir Edward Nicholas also between Sir Edward Hyde afterwards Earl of Clarendon and Sir Richard Browne*. A revised edition was edited by Upcott in 1827, reprinted in 1879 with a life by H. B. Wheatley. Upcott in 1825 also edited a selection of Evelyn's *Miscellaneous Works*. In 1906 Austin Dobson produced an edition of the *Diaries* in three volumes.

The other source of the *Diary*, supplementing the *Kalendarium*, is the *De Vita Propria* (*On his Own Life*), a short fair copy of 76 pages written in 1697, which revises and amplifies the *Kalendarium* up to 1644. There are also pocket books at Balliol College, Oxford, sparsely kept by the young Evelyn, but they are neither ample nor particularly revealing.

All previous editions have now been superseded by the thorough and definitive *The Diaries of John Evelyn*, edited by E. S. De Beer in six volumes, based on the full text of the original manuscript and explained by elaborate and comprehensive notes.

# Introduction

For every hundred readers familiar with the diaries of Samuel Pepys, there are probably no more than ten who have read the diaries of John Evelyn, and fewer who have read even *Sylva*, his *Discourse of Forest Trees*, let alone his many other writings. And this contrast is all the more ironical since it was only Evelyn's own diaries, themselves unpublished until 1818, that first brought Pepys's diaries to public notice. Yet Evelyn's record, extending over most of a long life from 1620 to 1706, and spanning such an important period of English history, is far longer than the record of Pepys, which covers only nine years, from 1660 to 1669.

Why is it, then, that Pepys has become a beloved companion to generations of readers, a household word throughout the English-speaking world, and John Evelyn, who covered so much more ground and much more time, has remained the possession of relatively few admirers, most of them already enthusiasts for historical memoirs, or for gardening and forestry?

There are, I submit, two principal reasons for the discrepancy. First, that Pepys was an ardent extrovert, a man of rather humble origins keenly on the make, who set down plainly his inmost thoughts and sexual adventures and repentances with disarming candour, as well as being a man of immense and untiring ability, one of the main founders of the administration and authority of the Admiralty and so of the Royal Navy.

Evelyn, on the other hand, while very observant and with a power of phrase occasionally reminiscent of his acquaintance John Aubrey, was very much the gentleman, the virtuoso, the amateur; the younger son of a landowner of substantial property which he inherited in old age, he was strictly conventional, concerned with the advancement of his family in the traditional way, mainly through judicious marriages. He was also, though a fervent Anglican, haunted – unlike Pepys – with Puritanical guilt and secretive, prudish and evasive about sex. Pepys was ordinary, with a concentrated energy that gave him

1

genius: Evelyn was a detached aesthete with a streak of unbounded and versatile curiosity which won him a more limited fame. Pepys rushes at his readers and lays his heart at their feet; Evelyn is guarded, ubiquitous and perceptive. Pepys is the vigorous and amiable spaniel; Evelyn like a detached and self-sufficient cat.

This contrast is further emphasized because all Pepys's work is an immediate uncensored day-to-day record of events, trivial or public, carried forward on the tide of a plebeian vitality, eager for pleasure and obvious success. Evelyn wrote his diaries from his childhood to 1645 retrospectively after a long interval, in 1660–4, and the next part again not until 1684: it was only in his declining years that the diary became contemporary.

Neither, of course, wrote for publication; but where, one suspects, Pepys would have enjoyed his fame, Evelyn would surely have been rather pained by his. Yet, as much as Pepys, he deserves the thanks of posterity. For he was versatile, untiring, watchful and he knew everybody. He was a good family man, who, in spite of the loss in the seventeenth-century way, by illness or miscarriage of seven out of eight sons, and two out of three daughters, managed to carry on the Evelyn line and preserve and enhance the family property at Wotton, Surrey. As a young man he was an observant, sometimes, in retrospect, overwhelmingly observant, traveller in the Netherlands, France, Italy and Switzerland, and always a connoisseur of architecture and painting. He was a pioneer of English gardening and he wrote far the best treatise on forestry of his day, so good that it still remains valuable. He was also a courtier who, having frequented the circle of Charles II in exile in Paris, had the personal friendship of the restored king, and who, in the absence of a regular civil service, undertook important and ill-rewarded responsibilities for the care of wounded and prisoners of war during the Second Dutch War, sat on the important Committee for Plantations and Trade and in 1674 wrote a pamphlet on the subject. A Balliol man, he did well by Oxford University, procuring valuable antiquities and books, and being awarded an Honorary Doctorate at the first Encaenia celebrated in the new-built Sheldonian. He was also a main founder of the Philosophical Club, reconstituted in 1662 as the Royal Society, which, amateurish in its day, has since become a pillar of the scientific world. He discovered and launched the genius of Grinling Gibbons. Though singularly without ambition, and essentially a private person who refused honours when they came his way, Evelyn did the state much service.

Though not as compulsively sociable as his friend Pepys, he was immensely perceptive, useful and energetic. He was also vulnerable; under what Virginia Woolf considered a slightly smug self-regard, he was haunted by an incalculable and ferocious God. His diary becomes increasingly cluttered up with elaborate and tedious accounts of sermons, interspersed, as old age makes him drowsy, with apologies to the Creator for falling asleep. His often elaborate and heart-felt lamentations at the deaths of his children, whom he deeply loved, conclude with a hasty and apologetic exclamation 'Thy will be don', as though as he wrote, his God was looking over his shoulder.[1] He lived always, like most of his contemporaries, under this shadow, and under the expectation of immediate reward or punishment in a future life. In spite of this obsession, his insatiable curiosity made him enjoy the present one.

In the perspective of history, he is particularly representative of the blend of the 'Ancient' and 'Modern' outlooks so characteristic of his time. His hard-hitting prose, as in *Sylva* and his pamphlet *Fumifugium* against the London smoke, is modern, foreshadowing the style of Dryden and Swift, lucid and conversational; but when he gets the chance, he lets his pen run away with him into labyrinths of pedantic classical learning in the manner of Burton's *Anatomy of Melancholy* or the coruscations of erudition in the works of Sir Thomas Browne. Though he was a casual and dilettante undergraduate, much of the strict Balliol Classical scholastic discipline must have stuck, and all his life he was a tiger for reading and had early mastered French and Italian. The older Evelyn became extremely learned, while always curious about the elementary scientific experiments then being conducted and about any kind of rare and exotic beast and bird that he had the chance to observe and record in accurate detail.

On balance, save in his religious obsessions, the 'Modern' in Evelyn predominates over the 'Ancient', and here he is again representative, while, being English, he spans the centuries by constantly recording the vagaries of a capricious climate, then even worse than it is now, and unmitigated by modern methods of heating, air conditioning or sanitation. It is indeed unlikely that Evelyn or any of his contemporaries often washed, and he records how, with exceptional enterprise, he *once a year* rinsed out his hair, first with warm water, then with cold water from a spring, and that the risky experiment turned out well.

Yet sundered as Evelyn may be from us by his gloomy seventeenth-century religion, his complacency, his reserve and entire acceptance of the values and prejudices of his class, he has an eye so observant and a pen so memorable that he can still recreate the life he knew. For he had a great feeling for England; he wrote his most famous book, *Sylva*, at the request of the newly refounded Royal Society, and the Commissioners of the Navy, to promote the planting and preservation of timber for the fleet on which the strength of this famous and flourishing nation was bound to depend, and he included a panegyric on the english oak, which yields 'far the most lasting timber', so that in ancient times men, indeed, had '*hearts of oak*' – an early use of the expression. And he praises the elm, 'a tree of comfort, sociable, becoming long walkes and Avenues', while the willow of all trees yields 'the most chaste and coolest shade'.

Like everyone at that time, Evelyn was a countryman, and where his rather priggish connoisseurship of art and architecture follows a now obsolete fashion, he still speaks to us directly of the gardens and woods he loved. It is perhaps his passion for gardening and forestry which brings him closest to us, and touches him to the rare and casually poetic phrase – 'I planted the *Ortchard* at *Says Court, New Moone, wind West.*'

# CHAPTER ONE

# Origins and Upbringing

'I was borne,' wrote John Evelyn, with astrology in mind and particular care,[1]

at about 20 minuts past two in the morning, on Tuesday, being the XXXI and last of October *Anno* 1620, after my Father had been married about 7 yeares, and that my Mother had borne him 3 Children, viz Two Daughters and one sonn, about the 33ᵈ Yeare of his age and the 23ᵈ [in fact 22nd] of my Mother's.

His elder brother George inherited the family estate at Wotton in Surrey, and a younger brother, Richard was born in 1622.

The Evelyns had originally been farmers at Stanmore and Harrow in the late fifteenth century, and John's great-grandfather had perhaps been Keeper of the Wardrobe to the young Edward VI. But it had been George Evelyn, John's grandfather, who had founded their wealth. He had been a pioneer in establishing gunpowder mills in England; by 1565 he had mills at Long Ditton and Godstone in Surrey, and when, in 1589, after the shortage of shot against the Armada had forced the Elizabethan government to reorganize the supply, George had obtained a major patent to make gunpowder over most of England. Then, under James I, George's son, John, had further developed the business.

Until the accession of Elizabeth I all gunpowder had been imported, mainly through Antwerp in the Spanish Netherlands, but as an English supply became urgent, in 1560, two years after the queen's accession, her government had paid £300 to a German, a Captain Gerrard Hendrick, to teach the 'trewe and perfect art of the making of saltpetre to grow in cellars, barns and quarries'. This repellent substance, native to India and Iran, in Europe had to be manufactured; composed, the Captain had revealed, of earth, animal excrement – preferably pigeon droppings – lime and ashes, the mixture being then soaked in urine. So contractors were empowered to collect loose earth in pigeon houses, outhouses and barns, and out of six parts of saltpetre (nitrate of potash) added to one of sulphur and one of charcoal they would make the explosive.[2]

George Evelyn had gone into the business at just the right time. For by 1564 Elizabeth I's Lieutenant of Ordnance had written, 'I see no reason to seek for powder beyond the seas if it may be made in a good cheap way at home', and various contractors had set up powder mills in Surrey, a county with easy access to London, yet separated from the capital by the Thames, an advantage since the Londoners disliked having stinking and dangerous powder mills in their suburbs. Moreover, there was plenty of timber in Surrey, convenient for the ironworks of the Weald.

In 1673, writing to John Aubrey, who was then compiling his *Natural History and Antiquities of Surrey*, John Evelyn would claim 'not far from my brother's house [at Wotton] across the streams and ponds since filled up and drained, stood many powder mills erected by my ancestors, who were the very first who brought the invention into England; before that we had got our powder out of Flanders.' Whoever had been the pioneers, by 1589 the Evelyns had outdistanced all competitors; for their patent allowed them 'to dig and get saltpetre in our Kingdom of England and Ireland, save for two miles round London walls and in the five most northern counties'. They were soon employing a thousand workpeople, underselling the foreign product, and making additional profits out of restoring 'decayed' powder: in 1589 they had already used up 583,583 lbs of saltpetre in six months.

Having established his fortune, John's grandfather George had retired to look after his many estates and numerous progeny. In the course of his strenuous career he had not only built up the business: he had married twice, sired twenty-four children and outlived all but six of them. John, his son by his first wife, carried on the powder mills, and would inherit property at West Dean near Salisbury and at Everley on Salisbury Plain, renowned for its hare warren, where in 1604 James I would ride up from Wilton House for the hare coursing. Robert inherited the mills at Godstone and Abinger Hammer, but sold them to John and in 1610 emigrated to North America. It was Evelyn's father Richard, George's only son by his second wife, who inherited John's birthplace, Wotton – an ample estate. John Evelyn the virtuoso aesthete with the long sensitive face depicted by Nanteuil, was the grandson of a tycoon of the armaments industry, whose wealth had derived from roaring and sulphurous mills that had made the 'black powder' to fight off the Armada and to supply the fleet after it, and which may even have been indirectly the planned instrument for Guy Fawkes' treason and plot.

After grandfather George's retirement, Evelyn's uncle John carried on the business until Charles I characteristically ruined it. In 1625 that ill-advised monarch by Prerogative Royal brought the entire manufacture of gunpowder under Commissioners of the Crown, and though the English had wisely then been 'careful to keep the manufacture thereof' from the native Irish, the king had even tried to increase the supply from Ireland. Charles also ordered the East India Company to import saltpetre in ballast from India, and during the personal rule of the late 1630s infuriated a widespread interest by allowing government contractors to carry off earth from pigeon houses without the owners' consent and to commandeer carts cheaply to carry the stuff to the king's main store at Southwark. Representatively, down in Wiltshire the rector of Knoyle, father of Sir Christopher Wren, presented a bill against the contractors for disturbing the rectory grounds and outbuildings.[3]

The height of the Evelyn prosperity was now over; though the immense investments of the founder in land remained. But Evelyn's father, Richard, was by then no longer directly concerned in the unsavoury business, on which the patent had now run out; still less was John Evelyn, his son.

They were well out of it: forty years later Aubrey would write of Chilworth near Guildford,

Tis a little commonwealth of powder makers who are as black as negroes. ... Here is a nursery of earth for the making of saltpetre; there is also a boiling house where the saltpetre is made; a corning house [for making the best gunpowder] and finishing houses, all very well worth seeing of the ingenious.

Evelyn himself recalled that 'a mill near Shere had blown up and shot timber through a cottage which had taken off a poor woman's head', and that the best gunpowder used to be made of 'dog-wood coals'; otherwise he would serenely and piously cultivate his tastes and hobbies on the proceeds of his grandfather's enterprise.

Richard, the inheritor of Wotton, had proved shrewd, cautious and able. 'My father, ...,' writes John,[4]

was of a sanguine complexion mix'd with a dash of Choler ...; his haire inclining to light, which (though exceeding thick) became hoary [at] thirty years of age; it was somewhat curled towards the extremes; his beard, (which he wore a little picked .[pointed] as the mode was), of a brownish colour ... his countenance was cleare, and fresh colour'd, his eyes extraordinary quick and piercing, an ample fore head, in summ a very well composed visage and manly aspect. For the rest he was but low of stature, but very strong.

Ascetic and sparing, this robust little man had 'never in all his life been surpriz'd by excesse'. 'His Wisdome was greate, and judgment most acute; of solid discourse, affable, humble and in nothing affected; of a thriving, neate, silent and methodical genius.' A just and hospitable High Sheriff of his county, he had been a 'studious decliner of Honors and Titles', being 'already in that esteeme with his Country [county] that they could have added little to him besids their burthen'.

With the then immense, and perhaps overestimated, income which Evelyn assigns to him of about £4,000 a year, this country gentleman could afford to be independent, and keep clear of the flamboyant and debt-ridden Jacobean court which, in Ralegh's words, 'glowed like rotten wood'. Richard was representative of the conservative, independent, affluent provincial gentry who were reluctantly driven into the king's party only by the attack on the established church, and who even in 1642 would still hope for a negotiated settlement.

As well as prudently developing his estate, to which he added Gosterwood and Westcott, Richard Evelyn had made a prudent marriage. John's mother was Eleanor, sole daughter and heiress to John Stansfield and his wife, Eleanor Comber, of the Cliff, Challenor, and Southfield near Lewes in Sussex in fine open country near the sea.

John, again in the manner of Aubrey, depicts his mother as vividly as he does his father. She was 'of proper personage, well timber'd, of a browne complexion; her eyes and haire of a lovely black; of constitution more inclyned to a religious Melancholy, or pious sadnesse; of a rare memory, and most exemplary life: for Oeconomiq prudence esteem'd one of the most conspicuous in her Country'.[5]

John clearly had a warmer feeling for both his parents than the conventional and distant respect common at that time, and though as the second son he did not inherit Wotton until he was seventy-nine, they left him well provided for. He was fortunate, too, in being brought up in beautiful country, both in Surrey and in Sussex. He claims that when at Wotton, following the custom of persons of quality, he was 'put to nurse to a neighbours wife, and tennant; of a good comely brown and wholsome complexion, in a most sweete place towards the hills, flanked with woods and refreshed with streames', he 'succked in the affection to this kind of solitude with [his] very milke'. Hence, perhaps, the romantic sense of place of one brought up in the then entirely unspoilt wooded country between 'Darking', as he wrote it, and 'Gilford'.

Wotton was a spacious house, 'large and antient, suitable to those hospitable times' and 'so ... sweetly environ'd with those delicious streames and venerable woods'.[6] In a sheltered valley with hills to the north rising to Polesden Lacey and then descending to Leatherhead, and with hills to the south rising through well-wooded country to Abinger and then to Leith Hill at 965 feet, Wotton had particularly good air – 'I will say nothing of the ayre,' wrote John, 'because the praeeminence is universally given to Surrey', and it was flanked by the other Evelyn properties at Westcott and Abinger. It lies today near the tortuous and still well-wooded road that runs from Dorking through Shere and Gomshall, then branches north-west to Newlands' Corner on Merrow Down or continues to Albury and so to Guildford. The area was a sheltered and well-watered tract which caught the sun, and would encourage John's developing interest in the design of gardens and the cultivation of trees, which would win him fame as 'Sylva' Evelyn. He particularly enjoyed the prospect from 'Lyth hill ... where one may discern 12 or 13 shires, with part of the sea, on a serene day', as well as the comfortable 'contiguity of 5 or 6 [family] Mannors and the Patronage of the livings about it'.

But during his most impressionable years, John was not brought up at Wotton. In 1625, still only four, he was sent away to his grandfather Stansfield's household near Lewes to avoid the plague. It was then raging in London and preventing the coronation of Charles I; 'the Pestilence,' he later recorded, 'was so Epidemical ... and I well remember the strict Watches, and examinations upon the Ways as we pass'd.' And even after John Stansfield's death two years later and after John's grandmother Eleanor had re-married to William Newton, John continued to live with them near Lewes until he was sixteen. Growing up almost within sight of the sea and ships, he may early have become more curious about the Continent than boys brought up in a land-locked county.

## II

John's early education was therefore sketchy, if untrammelled. Initiated with other children into the 'rudiments' by one 'Frier in the Church porch at Wotton', it was not until 1628 that he was 'put to learn the Latin Rudiments and to Write by a Frenchman in Lewes'. And when he showed a talent for drawing, his father strongly disapproved: 'Painting and such things,' he said, 'will do you no good hereafter.' Then, aged nine, John went to a school at Cliffe, but following his grandmother's second marriage, and after the Newton household had moved, he transferred to the free school at Southover close to Lewes. Here, at this local day school, John remained for seven years until, in 1637, he went up to Oxford. His father, he records,[7]

Would very willingly have weaned me from the fondnesse of my too indulgent Grand-mother, intending to have sent me to Eaton; but being neither so provident for my own benefit, unreasonably terrified with the report of the severe discipline there; I was sent back again to Lewes, which perversenesse of mine, I have since a thousand times deplor'd.

He had some cause to do so; Eton, following the reign of a lay Provost, Sir Henry Savile, who had appointed many distinguished Fellows, had since 1624 been ruled by Sir Henry Wotton, the former ambassador to Venice and the Emperor, appointed in part in compensation for unpaid arrears of salary. Wotton was a learned cosmopolitan humanist and poet,[8] and a 'constant cherisher of those youths in that school in whom he found either constant diligence or a genius that prompted them to learning'. Under his influence and that of his own contemporaries, the young Evelyn might have become less of a prig, though perhaps at the expense of his attractive and rambling originality. Even at Lewes, he was becoming aware of the events of a wider world. He could just remember the echoes of the opening of the Thirty Years War and 'the Effects of that Comet of 1618 still working in the prodigious revolutions now beginning in Europ, especialy in Germany, whose sad commotions sprung from the Bohemians defection ... upon which quarrell the Sweds broke in, giving umbrage to the rest of the Princes ...'. In 1629 he had been 'awaken'd in the Morning with the newes of the Duke of Buckingham's being slaine by that wretch Felton, after our disgrace before La Rochelle', and in 1631 heard of the resounding scandal of the arraignment of Mervyn Touchet, second Earl of Castlehaven, of Fonthill in

Wiltshire 'for [his] many shamefull exhorbitances', which cost
that dilapidated peer his head.

In September 1635, another year of plague, John, aged
fourteen, was summoned back to Wotton where his mother was
very ill. Her daughter Elizabeth, wife of Edward Darcy, had died
in childbirth, and John's mother, depressed by the loss of a series
of her own infants, had 'caught a malignant feavor' from which
she was soon 'forc'd to succumb'. 'Having endur'd the sharpest
conflicts of her sicknesse [including Sir Sanders Duncumb's
'famous powder'] with admirable patience', she now 'quietly
expired'. 'Thus,' comments John, 'ended that prudent and pious
Woman in the flowre (almost) of her age, to the unconsolable
affliction of her husband, irreparable losse of her Children and
universal regret of all that knew her.'

Richard now faced his declining years alone, and the Evelyn
brothers, George, John and Richard, became more dependent
on each other. George was already at Trinity College, Oxford,
and after much consultation, it was decided that in 1637 John
should go up to Balliol.

# CHAPTER TWO

# Balliol and London

Evelyn only went up to Balliol in May 1637 as a Fellow Commoner 'rather out of shame of abiding longer *sub ferula* [under the rod] than for any fitnesse, as,'[1] he had written in the *Kalendarium*, 'by sad experience I found, which put me to relearne all I had neglected',[2] and indeed his immediate record of his life there is meagre. In *A New Almanack and Prognostication for the year of our Lord God 1637*,[3] he records in April 'the 3rd day of this month I went from the free schole of Lewes (where M^r Smalt was my Master) for Wotton, in order to my going to Oxford'. In May, 'the 9^th I came to Oxford from Wotton and the next day was entered Fellow Commoner of Balliol Coll.' Then, 'I was matriculated the 19^th. Dr Brayly Vice-Chancellor ... when I first came to the Coll Dr Parkhurst was Master.' Then, on 10 July, 'My Bro' G. Evelyn went from Trinity Coll : Oxon : to Wotton and we were both entred in the Middle Temple, but I remained at Oxford.' There are no other entries save an occasional record of attending Communion and one of returning to Oxford in October of 1637. A few longer entries for September and December are meticulously, thoroughly and tantalizingly blotted out. We know from his voluminous and learned publications that Evelyn must have made up for lost time when he got to Balliol, for he became a considerable scholar and well able to plan massive books; as in the masterly design of *Sylva, a Discourse of Forest Trees*, which brought him fame. But he was a late starter and distracted, like many born writers, by a multiplicity of interests.

Indeed, he bothered very little with the *Almanack*, which is valuable more for its representative embellishments, advice and 'prognostications' that illustrate the popular *idées reçues* of Evelyn's adolescence than for Evelyn's own entries. With 'an Anatomie of Man's Body as the parts thereof are governed by the celestial signs,' a pretentious and nonsensical explanation of 'Astronomie for the Vulgar', and of the 'working of the heavenly spheres', the *Almanack* itself makes gloomy reading. In the 'Prognostications of the four quarters of the year' it plays safe in the pessimistic tone of most weather forecasters; if spring be overmoist, fruit will rot and weeds flourish; if cold and dry, frosts will endanger the fruit; in an over-hot summer, fruit will perish, sickness abound; in a dry one, 'want of grain' is feared, and 'fishes will die in ponds'. Whatever the climate, the editor foresees horrible illnesses. 'Diseases attending Spring: Leprosies, Red spots, Fevers, Tooth ache, Ringwormes, paines in the neck and throate, small pox. Falling sickness [epilepsy] and the King's evil [scrofula].' In summer expect 'spleen, sore eyes, fevers of the blood and jaundice'; in autumn, 'Paines in the back, darknesse of sight, retention of urine, gravel and the stone'.

In surveying the past 'according to the best writers', the *Almanack* is less trammelled by reality. The Creation took place 5599 years ago, Noah's flood 3993, 'Brute' came to Britain 2745 years back, and dates, which do not include the year of the Armada, only become accurate from 1066. But the diarist is encouraged by moralizing verses at the top of each month.

> Rise early now this present month of May
> Frequent the fruitful fields in their array,

and a steady breeze of agricultural lore dispels some of the gloom. In May you should 'sow Barley, set and sow tender herbs and seeds such as sweet marjoram and ... sweet basil', 'stir your land for wheat and rye', and 'set stills to work using May dew'.

If Evelyn may not much have pondered the commonplaces of his almanack, they reflect the popular and pervasive beliefs among which he grew up, and which consciously or unconsciously probably conditioned his mind.


## II


Balliol was not then one of the great colleges. It had been chosen instead of Trinity in part because it was more welcoming to Fellow Commoners, accepted at Trinity only if they were the eldest sons of knights. For in 1610 Balliol, then very poor, had admitted them for the substantial fee of £10, and these *extraneos quoscumque quae appellant communarios* or 'Gent: Communers', were 'obliged to the same exercises as the Communers'.[4] Moreover, after the ineffective Mastership of John Parkhurst – 'a bookworm of neutral opinions whose natural inertia had

enabled him to satisfy without disquietude the requirements of
two successive Primates so widely different in their views as
Abbot and Laud',[5] in 1637 the conservative Anglican Thomas
Lawrence had just been appointed Master. He was already
famous for 'scholastical Divinity', 'exquisite in the excellencies of
the Greek and Latin tongues', and was later to be one of the
king's chaplains and Lady Margaret Professor of Divinity. George
Evelyn had already advised their father to send his brother to
neighbouring Balliol, a move also pressed by Henry Weston,
squire of Ockham near Wotton, the incumbent of whose parish
had a son, George Bradshaw, a Fellow of Balliol, who could
become Evelyn's tutor, and who would say that he found John 'a
very ingeniose young gent', who took kindly to the strict
linguistic discipline of the current classical curriculum.

Unfortunately Bradshaw, perhaps, Evelyn thought, related to
Bradshawe afterwards the regicide, spent more time attacking
the Master than attending to his pupils. 'I ever thought my Tutor
had parts enough; but ... his ambition (and I fear vices) made
him very much suspected of the Colledg'. Indeed, in 1648 he
supplanted the royalist Dr Lawrence as Master, but Evelyn
records that there was 'never any mor negligent of his Pupils
proficiency, proving a plague to the Colledge'.[6]

According to custom, Gentlemen Commoners presented the
college with the equivalent of £10 in plate; Evelyn presented it in
books: 'Mine was in Books to the value of the *plate*, which was all
Coin'd into mony to inable the King to maintain his Forces, and
Court, which was quartered about Oxon: the Plate was Gon but
my Books remaine in the Library.'[7] They were all by 'Authors, it
seems, desired for the students of Divinity'.[8]

As a Gentleman or Fellow Commoner Evelyn obtained a
bedroom to himself; he could dine with the dons,[9] and 'the
reminiscences recorded in his diary breathe a gentle odour of
respectability'.[10] He made friends with James Thicknesse or
Thickins, a scholar on the foundation and 'a very learned young
man' who, expelled from Balliol when a probationer fellow by
Bradshaw's faction, in 1643 would accompany Evelyn to France
and Italy.

Still only seventeen, Evelyn records that on 2 July 1637, having
attended his first communion in chapel, 'the greatest part of the
following Weeke I spent in Visiting the Coleges, Scholes,
Publique Library and Curiositys, which much affect young
Fresh-men as they are called'. In December he was declaiming in
chapel before the Master, Fellows and Scholars according to

custom, and in January 1638 he learned to dance, and that April his father allowed him to 'manage [his] owne Expenses'. In the summer, he was visiting at Lewes and inspecting the fortifications at Portsmouth – 'a greate rarity' in England in that blessed Halcion tyme.[11] With his young brother Richard, he sailed over to the Isle of Wight, and also visited Chichester, 'where having viewed the Citty we lodged that night'. In September, back at Wotton, he was 'grievously afflicted with a quartan ague' (malaria) which 'held him' until December.

In Oxford John had met at least one exotic character. In 1636 Archbishop Laud, one of the greatest Chancellors and second founder of St John's College, had drastically modernized the Statutes of the University in the 'first comprehensive embodiment of its rules', and appointed Levantine scholars to teach Greek and Arabic. Among them was Nathaniel Conopios, formerly chaplain to Kyrillos Lukaris, Patriarch of Constantinople, who had sent him to the West. Harboured in Balliol after the Patriarch's murder, the refugee needed his morning coffee which he made in his own rooms, 'the first that I ever saw drink *Coffé*'. But it was not till 1650, when an enterprising Jew opened the first coffee house, between St Edmund Hall and the Queen's College, that coffee drinking became a 'general entertainment', and when the Civil Wars broke out and his pension from Laud ceased, Conopios, not a Cretan for nothing, thought Constantinople safer than Balliol without a pension, and ended up as Patriarch of Alexandria.

In January 1639 John began to 'looke upon the rudiments of Musick', in which he afterwards 'ariv'd to some formal knowledge' though, diverted by other inclinations, only to 'small perfection of hand'.[12]

In May he took 'a short journey of pleasure' to Bath, Bristol, Cirencester, Malmesbury and Abingdon, and spent the rest of the summer at Wotton. Back in Balliol that December, he was joined by his brother Richard, but in February 1640 both were recalled to Wotton by their father's severe illness. It was the end of John's time at Oxford, for in June he went to London with George to take possession of their 'new Lodgings in the Mid. Temp:', a 'much handsomer Appartment than was then the students chambers of most of the Inns of Court ...'.[13]

That May, George married Mary Caldwell, daughter of Daniel Caldwell of Hordon, Essex, an occasion which caused Richard to settle on him the estates of Wescott and Paddington near Abinger, and to declare that the whole Wotton estate would descend to George, with remainder, if George's male issue failed, to John and then to young Richard. In due course, long after and after many vicissitudes, Wotton would come to John.

### III

When John reluctantly submitted himself to 'th' impolish'd study of the law' in London, he was confronted with a crisis long mounting between Charles I and his parliament, following the king's impolitic attempt to compel the Scots to conform to the Laudian ritual of the Anglican church. After the King's discontented and inefficient army had been scared away from Berwick-on-Tweed, in June 1639 the Scots, under Alexander Leslie, had ended the First Bishops' War by the Pacification of Berwick. Charles had been forced to summon Sir Thomas Wentworth, now Earl of Strafford and Lord Lieutenant of Ireland, to take control but 'the disorders in Scotland continuing', he had been compelled for lack of money to call the first parliament for eleven years.

John was already in London when this 'Short' or 'Addled' Parliament, which sat from 13 April to 5 May 1640, assembled and raised the accumulated grievances of more than a decade. They were exploited in the Commons by the politicians led by Pym and backed by influential magnates, Essex, Bedford, Pembroke and Hertford in the Lords, who, though Pym merely wanted to control and exploit it, wanted to dismantle the very structure of Tudor conciliar government itself.

So John was compelled to observe a political crisis at first hand. '*London*, and especially the Court', he wrote long afterwards,[14] was at this period often in Disorder, and greate Insolencys committed by the abused and too hapy People; and in particular the A-Bish– of Canterbery, whoss Palace at *Lambeth* was furiously assaulted by a rude rabble from Southwark, set on doubtlesse and fomented by the *Puritans* (as then we call'd those we now name *Presbyterians*) ... many scandalous libells and Invectives were now scatter'd about the streets to the Reproch of Government, which increased those distractions which after follow'd.

By the end of June, however, family concerns claimed John. His father was now so ill that, as a last and futile resort, his doctors persuaded him to make the long and tiring journey to Bath to take the waters. This of course merely exhausted him and George and John, riding post haste to Wotton, found him weaker. But he 'held out' until October, 'somewhat revived'; and on the 15th, 'it being Mich: Terme', John returned to the Middle Temple. He was in time to see the apparently popular return of Charles I from Scotland after the Second Bishops' War when, although 'despising the rebels' strength, had 'brought him and his State into great straits', he rode 'in a pompous cavalcade and a kind of ovation with all the marks of a happy accommodation'. But the Scots, sustained by a heavy subsidy under the Treaty of Ripon, had remained in occupation of Northumberland and Durham.

The illusion of royal popularity did not last, for on 3 November 1640, John recorded how Charles was compelled to summon 'that long ungratefull and fatal Parliament; the beginning of our Sorrows, for 20 years after and the ruin of the most happy Monarch …'.

His father had now 'entred into a *Dropsy*', surprisingly, since he had always been 'exemplarly temperate'; John again returned to Wotton, and on the 24 December 1640 his father died. It was a 'melancholy and lugubrious beginning of a new yeare, when on 2d Jan we at night follow'd the mourning Herse to the Church', and John Evelyn at nineteen was 'left to his own conduct, in a conjunction of the greatest hazard that ever the youth of England saw'.


## IV


He now felt thoroughly inadequate; indeed 'of a raw, vaine, uncertaine and very unwary inclination'. His schooldays had been idle, his studies at Oxford desultory, and now his plans for the future were vague. His compulsive curiosity, which would make him an apparently ubiquitous observer of his age, and his fluent vigour as a writer were not yet apparent. Indeed, he would never have much originality, accepting uncritically the religion and values of his class and time, but he was sociable; if they did not affront his prejudices, he liked people, particularly intelligent women and the young. Most importantly, he had the detachment of a born writer, and the income to be just self-sufficient; so that he could on occasion withdraw from society and 'contemplate'. Moreover, his rather gloomy religion with its haunting sense of providence and sin, would give him certainty, and his keen aesthetic appreciation of painting, architecture, trees, gardens and scenery, unfailing pleasure and posthumous fame.

But at nineteen he must have seemed ultra-fastidious and uncertain. According to English custom, the entire Wotton estate had been left to the eldest son, George, who had gone to live there in affluence, and John, as the second son, had been left £4,000 and property at Malling – a substantial legacy, then enough to make him independent, but not rich. Though his father had designed to make him a lawyer, he felt no inclination for that profession, or for the competition of a jargon-chopping still traditionally scholastic Oxford, which he had only casually attended. His near contemporary, John Aubrey, deeply loved the life of Trinity College where, in his romantic way, he wrote 'ingenious youths like rosebuds absorb the morning dew', and where he immortalized the president, Dr Kettle, with his 'terrible gigantique aspect with his sharp gray eies',[15] his schoolboy jokes about how to inscribe a triangle in a quadrangle by taking a pig by the ear and a dog by the tail, and his 'irreconcilability' to long hair. But Evelyn, coming from a wealthier home, felt no corresponding passion for Balliol, nor had he Aubrey's eye for personality or consistent power of phrase; he was an introspective youth, untroubled by ambition, versatile but rather lazy, though hardly, as he afterwards added to his memoir, thinking of 'nothing but the pursute of Vanity, and the confus'd imaginations of Young men'.[16]

In April 1641 Evelyn repaired to London to see the 'famous tryall of the Earle of Strafford', sacrificed by the King, in fear for the lives of the royal family in a London where authority had broken down; but save for recording that Thomas, Earl of Arundel and Surrey, Earl Marshal of England and his neighbour at Albury near Wotton, was 'made High Stuard upon this occasion', Evelyn throws little light on the trial.[17]

With the city mob of apprentices howling 'in loud and hideous voice' for Strafford's execution and rioters breaking into Whitehall Palace, so that the queen had to retreat to her inner rooms, on 9 May Charles I consented to Strafford's execution and on 12 May Strafford was beheaded. Evelyn again was there.[18]

I went again to Lond: with my Bro: and on the 12th following beheld on Tower-hill the fatal Stroake, which sever'd the wisest head in England from the Shoulders of the Earle of Strafford, whose crime coming under the cognizance of no human-Law, a new one was made, not to be a precedent, but his destruction, to such exorbitancy were things arrived.

Strafford had, indeed, been executed only after the old procedure of impeachment had failed, under a political Bill of Attainder based on garbled evidence, transcribed from minutes of the Proceedings in Council taken by the younger Vane from his father's record. It had been brought in by Pym, who had refused the bribe of Chancellorship of the Exchequer in the knowledge that the City would never pay a subsidy while Strafford lived. Evelyn had neatly summed up the legal facts of a judicial murder, which would haunt the king until he met his own similar fate.

# CHAPTER THREE

# Holland and the Spanish Netherlands

'A Young Gent: apt for all Impressions'

In the summer of 1641 Evelyn decided that as 'the political medal was turning', he would 'absent [himself] from this ill face of things at home'. He had reason for his decision: the Long Parliament, which had assembled in the previous autumn, had already dismantled the Tudor-style conciliar government, abandoned the ship money rates and voted the king tunnage and poundage only for one year. In February Charles had justly declared that they had 'taken the government all to pieces', and the Civil War would be fought after the main political question had been decided.

Having repeated his 'oath of Allegeance' at the Customs House, John had no difficulty in casually procuring a pass to proceed abroad, and on 16 July he set out for Gravesend. Held up by weather, he inspected the *Royal Sovereign* at Chatham – 'a monstrous Vessel so call'd ... for burden, defense, and ornament the richest that ever spread cloth before the Wind'; he then embarked on a Dutch frigate bound for Flushing in convoy, guarded by a man of war.

For the Dutch were still at war with Spain. The truce ending in 1621 had not, following the fall of the republican Oudenbarneveldt, been renewed. The war party backed by the Stadtholders of the House of Orange had been doing too well out of the conflict to end it, and in 1628 the Dutch had at last intercepted the homeward bound Spanish treasure fleet; they had also recently annexed Curaçao and even New Amsterdam at the mouth of the Hudson, the best port for the north American fur trade, as well as driving the Portuguese from Pernambuco in Brazil. In the Far East they had long been established in Batavia, driven the English from Amboyna, and reached Bangkok and Ayuthia; in the year before Evelyn's arrival, they had annexed Colombo.

The United Provinces, emancipated from Spain by their own efforts and since 1635 in alliance with the French, were now at the height of their prosperity, the centre of the first north-western sea-borne colonial empire, signifying the shift of oceanic commerce from the Mediterranean to the Atlantic already begun by the Iberian powers.

## II

Having arrived at Flushing with 'a fresh gale and pleasant passage', John Evelyn, still only twenty, was delighted by his first sight of a foreign country. Having viewed the fine house of the Princes of Orange, hereditary Stadtholders of Zealand, its walls 'washed with Neptune continualy', the English party proceeded to Middelburgh, which with the optimism of youth, John thought 'another sweet town', and thence made their way to Veere on the north coast of Walcheren, then a considerable port. From Veere with its well-fortified harbour and headquarters for Scots merchants, still extant, John sailed to Dort (or Dordrecht) the scene of the momentous Synod (1618–19) which had briefly discomforted the extreme Calvinist followers of Gomerus and encouraged the followers of the moderate Arminius, and where John for the first time saw storks building in the chimneys and undisturbed in the streets.

From Dordrecht he 'took waggon' to Rotterdam, which drove so furiously that it actually covered ten miles in an hour. Here John first entered one of the most prosperous Dutch cities, with its Groute Kirke and Bourse and a statue of the 'learned Erasmus'. Amsterdam had now superseded Antwerp as the main centre of international business and, as earlier in Portugal, the riches of the East had poured into the Dutch cities, where wealthy burghers were patronizing Dutch and Flemish artists and architects. Holland, the leading province, had also become the most influential centre of book publishing, since the Catholic censorship had been broken and the contending Protestant sects were too disunited to impose their own. The best gardens and the best maps were now designed by the Dutch, and though it had long been the fashion to admire the Venetian republic, now it was the done thing to admire the Dutch commonwealth. When Evelyn arrived, Dutch painting was also coming to a climax in Rembrandt's masterpieces, as, for example, in the group paintings of the Regent oligarchy of the steelmakers, or the Company of Captain Cocq's so-called 'Night Watch', completed in 1642, while Ruisdael had already created a novel kind of landscape under the shifting Netherlandish cloudscapes.

John, proceeding by canal to Delft, which must then have looked much as later depicted by Vermeer, does not describe the scented polders of July, the flighting duck and the aqueous setting: he preferred curiosities – the colony of lepers who lived in solitary huts on the brink of the water, who had contracted their hideous disease, he was informed, by eating too much fish.

At the Hague he paid his due respects to the widowed Elizabeth, Queen of Bohemia, and to Sir John Finch, the refugee Lord Chief Justice and Lord Keeper, who had 'fled out of England from the fury of the Parliament', having in 1629 tried to adjourn the Commons and been held down in his chair with the words 'Gods wounds! You shall sit here till we be pleased to rise.' John found Utrecht in the throes of an old Dutch custom – a *Kermas* or Fair – a Breughelesque spectacle, with the streets swarming with 'Boores and rudeness'. Characteristically, he quietly made off to Nijmegen on the Rhine.

By early August he had reached the army, his ostensible objective. He found it encamped around the fortress of Gennep on the Waal, recently surrendered by the Spaniards, where that evening, George Goring's English regiment were engaged in 'shooting off the Canon, and [in] other expressions of military Triumphs'. The Dutch had captured Breda in 1637 and in the following year the French had taken Breisach, cutting Spanish communications with Spain. So John found the allied armies laboriously preparing an offensive.

Having joined Captain Apsley's company as a volunteer and 'ridden about the lines of Circumvallation', John was asssigned a 'commodious Tent'; but since the August sun 'pierced the Canvass' he found the heat insufferable and at night complained of the mists and fogs from the river. He was thankful at least to obtain a hut. He then did sentry duty and 'trail'd a pike', until, relieved by a company of French, he inspected the siege trenches, mining galleries and a 'Wheel-bridg' of planks on cartwheels for crossing the moat: he was struck by the 'ramparts of Earth ... broacken and crumbl'd' by the mines.

But he soon got bored with military life. Among the rumbustious English cavaliers he found 'hot service for a young drinker', and 'being prety well satisfied with the confusion of Armies, and sieges', by 12 August he 'took his leave of the Leagure, and Camarades', and embarked upon the Waal in the more congenial company of 'three grave Dutch divines disputing in Latin about the lawfulnesse of Church Musick'. A well-to-do

volunteer could then take or discard as much of war as he
wished: in less than a fortnight John Evelyn had had enough.


### III


Passing the formidable Castle of Loevenstein, whence in 1619 the
learned Grotius had escaped in a trunk of laundry and Arminian
theology, with holes bored for air, John was soon back in
Rotterdam, buying 'landscapes and drolleries' at another *Kermas*.
The demand for pictures in Holland, he wrote, was due to the
want of land, so that a 'common farmer' would lay out two or
three thousand pounds as an investment in the commodity.
Dutch houses were thus full of pictures, and the ordinary people
would vend them at fairs and make very great gains.

John now saw his first elephant: 'a beast of monstrous size yet
… flexible and nimble in the joints', contrary to the venerable
tradition that, being jointless, it could not get up unaided. He
also encountered a pelican: 'white, wall eyd, the legge red and
flatt footed', and tactlessly told its keeper that it was quite
different from the picture of the 'real' fabulous bird – whereat
the old man was naturally 'very wroth'.

But John already cared most about houses and gardens. He
delighted in Ryswyk, the Prince of Orange's country house, with
its delicious walks and lime trees, and the modern paintings
within. He admired the Prinzenhoff at the Hague with its
northern Renaissance 'ornament, close-Walkes, Statues, Marbles,
Grotts, Fountaines and artificiall Musique'.[1] Then, at
Amsterdam, John 'procur'd to be brought to a Synagogue of the
Jewes', not yet officially admitted to England, and so a novelty.
He found that their ceremonies afforded matter for wonder and
enquiry, so he investigated a Jewish cemetery, and with his stick
he callously 'raked out divers leaves' from ancient books buried
with the rabbis. He also visited the incongruously neat 'spin
house', where 'incorrigible and Lewd Women were kept in
Discipline and Labour', as well as the ancient Stadthuis, 'one of
the most costly and magnificent pieces of Architecture in Europ,
especially for the materialls'. He also made friends with some
English Presbyterians, who carefully chalked up the psalms for
their services on a slate, and he observed that the 'Brownists'
sectaries 'kept the best table'.[2] But he was most struck by a
'hospital for lame and decrepid soldiers', it being 'for state, order
and accommodations one of the worthiest things I thinke the

world can shew of that nature'. It is 'most remarkable,' he concluded, 'what provisions are made and maintained ... to protect the poore from misery, and the Country from beggers'.[3] So early began Evelyn's interest in 'welfare', which, after the Restoration, would lead him to become a Commissioner for the care of sick and wounded prisoners in the Second Dutch War.

Meanwhile he admired the setting and the architecture of Amsterdam, where 'every particular Man's Barke, or Vessell' could 'anker before his very doore', yet the streets were 'exactly straite, even and uniforme ... and shaded with the beautifull lime trees, which are set in rowes before every man's house, affording a very ravishing prospect'. He found the most impressive sight the Kaisersgraacht paved with burnt bricks, and shaded by stately and umbrageous trees, the whole area having been reclaimed from the 'maine Sea' and supported by piles at 'immense Charge' with 'everlasting foundations': 'Prodigious it is to consider those multitudes, and innumerable Assemblys of Shipps, and Vessels which continualy ride before this Citty.'[4]

John also loved the elaborately chiming Dutch bells, particularly 'a Chime of Purselan dishes which, fitted to clock worke, rung many changes, and tunes without breaking', and he pored over splendid maps in Hondius's famous shop on the Dam.

Proceeding by canal to Haarlem, he observed that although there were two organs in the great gothic church, they were used only 'to recreate the people before and after their devotions', while the Burgomeisters walked about the church doing business. Then, after being matriculated at Leiden university by a 'Magnificus Proffessur' in Latin for a Rix dollar, John inspected the celebrated Elzivir printing house, 'renowned for the politeness of its characters and editions', as well as 'many curiosities out of China', and the original knife extracted 'from a Dutchmans gutts after the sottish fellow had swallowed it' (handle first) 'when tempting to make himself vomit'. Back at the Hague, John ordered a suit of armour made to measure and a complete horseman's harness.

It was now September and, again at Dordrecht, he attended the reception of Marie de Medici, Dowager of France, mother of Louis XIII and mother-in-law to Charles I, who had long harboured her with increasing embarrassment. Exiled from France by Louis XIII and Richelieu, this exacting royalty, who had offended the English by her hauteur as the widow of Henri IV, was being passed on to the court of her granddaughter

Princess Mary of England, and of her husband, the young
William of Orange. The Earl of Arundel had conducted her to
Holland on her way to Cologne,[5] and John found 'nothing
remarkable in her reception save the universal discontent which
accompany'd that unlucky Woman wherever she went'.


## IV


Having seen much of the Protestant United Provinces, John now
determined to visit the Catholic Spanish Netherlands. In 1598
they had been placed under the rule of the Habsburg
'Archdukes', Albrecht, brother of the emperor Rudolf II, and his
wife and cousin the Infanta Isabella, daughter of Philip II of
Spain, who after 1621 had ruled alone. Under these humane
rulers, who had brought about the truce of 1609–21 with the
Dutch, the Spanish Netherlands had recovered from the ravages
of war and iconoclasm and become the principal centre of
Counter-Reformation culture in northern Europe, where Peter
Paul Rubens had died full of fame in Antwerp the year before
John Evelyn's tour. The rich late medieval Burgundian court
civilization had here been blended with Renaissance humanism,
and other Flemish artists had flourished, not least Jan Breughel
(the younger), appointed by the archdukes their court painter.

By October, travellers ran considerable risks from the climate
as well as from the garrisons guarding the frontier. John had first
obtained an exit permit from the Prince of Orange, then, as
'designing to go into England', a pass from Brussels to traverse
Brabant and Flanders, and he now worked his way south-east
along the northern shore of the Scheldt towards Antwerp. After
his boat had been nearly sunk crossing an estuary and suffered
much peril 'by reason of two contrary tydes', he arrived at
Steenbergen, where he had to 'foote it at least a league in a most
pelting shower of raine', and then share a one-horse 'tumbril' to
Bergen-op-Zoom, a garrison town on the frontier. Then,
marching 'half-leg deepe' to a ferry, the party arrived at the fort
of Lillo, close to Antwerp.

But their troubles were not yet over. Shown John's pass, the
Dutch commander demanded two Rix dollars and, on John's
demurring, snatched the paper and flung it under the table,
bidding him 'try to get to Antwerp without his permission'.
Characteristically John paid up at once, whereat the commander
'surelily' returned his passport; but, taking his victim's measure,

demanded fourteen Dutch shillings for his 'searcher'. John
handed them over, and, before he got clear, it cost '6. schill more
among the souldiers ... and 31 stivers to the Man of Warr ...
blocking up the River'.

So at last John Evelyn arrived in the Spanish Netherlands. He
found the Spanish officials much more polite than the Dutch,
and 'after many cross accidents of these natures twixt these two
jealous States, we at last ariv'd safe at Antwerp about 11 in the
morning'.[6]


# V


After this brush with the gross political facts, John turned to his
main concern – aesthetic appreciation. Antwerp had been ruled
since the death of Isabella in 1633 by the Cardinal Infante Don
Fernando: it was still the showplace of the Counter-Reformation
in the north, and though damaged by war and undermined by
the competition of Amsterdam and the stranglehold of the
Dutch on the Scheldt, it was outwardly splendid. The most
impressive building was the new church erected in 1621 by the
Jesuits – the first great entirely Italianate church that John had
ever seen, built by Pieter Huyssens and dedicated to St Ignatius.[7]
So ostentatious had been the building that the General of the
Jesuit order had relegated the architect to a monastery and
forbidden him to practise his art; but the Infanta Isabella had
reprieved him and commissioned him to build a chapel for
herself. John now greatly admired

that sumptuous and most magnificent Church of the Jesuites, being a
very glorious fabrique without; and within wholy incrusted with
marble inlayd and polish'd with divers representations of histories,
Landscips, Flowers, etc. ... the Quire is a most glorious piece, and the
Pulpet supported by fowre Angels adorn'd with other carvings and rare
Pictures,

including the large altarpiece 'by the hand of Rubens, now newly
deceased'.

John preferred this baroque building to the old gothic
Vroukirke, which he thought had too tall a spire, and he was
much interested in the famous Jesuit school with its 'neat
dormitorys' and its aviary, 'besides the Eagles, Foxes, Monkeys,
etc to divert the Boys withall at their times of remission'; he also
found the Antwerp citadel 'the most matchlesse piece of modern

Fortification in the World ... the Graffs ramparts and Platformes are stupendious.' But what 'ravished' him most were 'the delicious shades, and walkes of stately Trees ... [of] the magnificent and famous Citty'.

Setting out thence by water to Brussels, he was intrigued by the floating dwellings for whole families kept 'so sweete and polite' along the canal; he then visited the pictures by Titian, Rubens, and young and old Breughel in the Cour des Princes and admired a 'rural park' with a heronry, cascades, rocks, grotts and fallow and red deer, all bounded by a 'hedge of water' turned up by a *fontanière*.

He called on the resident English ambassador who, having to send a coach and six down to Lord Arundel, Earl Marshal of England, at Ghent, put it at Evelyn's disposal, and he noticed on the way the little wagons drawn by mastiff dogs in harness, which the Belgians used for 'pedling merchandize'. Ghent seemed a diminished city with fields and desolate pastures within its extensive medieval walls. Here John met Arundel and together they drove to Bruges where the pompous authorities formally conducted the Earl Marshal to his lodgings, but where John seems, appropriately enough, best to have remembered the 'Cheezes, and butter pild up like heapes of Mortar'. When on 9 October they reached Ostende, John inspected the river and harbour by boat, and next day, with a 'jovial Commissary' went by waggon all along the sands to Dunkirk, where the harbour was full of prizes taken by the Spaniards from the Dutch. Then on 11 October 1641 Lord Arundel and John, saluted by thirteen great guns, took a packet-boat frigate to Calais, where they anchored till midnight. They then crossed to Dover in four hours, but, the wind changing and driving them westward, could not make the pier until four in the afternoon of the 12th.

From Dover that night they rode to Canterbury, where, next morning, John found the cathedral 'in greatest splendor, those famous Windoes being intire, since demolish'd by the Phanatiques'. They proceeded by Rochester and Gravesend, avoiding the inns, since the plague was again infecting London, though not the Dutch or Spanish Netherlands. Landing at Arundel stairs, John took leave of the Earl Marshal, and by two in the morning reached his own rooms in the Middle Temple.

So ended John Evelyn's first brief expedition abroad. In Holland he had seen a civilization better organized and more humane than the English, and in the Spanish Netherlands a wealth of Italianate architecture and superb painting; in both areas, also, Protestant and Catholic, elaborate gardens, fountains, avenues and grottoes had stimulated his own eager interest in the arts, gardening and aboriculture, and in the ingenious mechanical contrivances then so much in fashion.

## VI

John's journey to the United Provinces and back by the Spanish Netherlands had opened his eyes to the art and architecture of the Continent in a way that probably made England appear provincial: indeed, in 1652 he would record that he thought the Netherlands the best country in which 'a young gent apt for all impressions' should begin his travels.[8] He would then declare unfashionably that a youth would best begin with the Netherlands, then proceed to Germany and Italy; thence to visit Spain, and only finally visit France, the most rewarding of all countries, particularly considering 'the *grandezza* of the French empire'.

In England, by the autumn of 1641 the tension between king and parliament had become acute. On 31 October John, who had ridden down to Wotton to see his brother, heard of a new crisis in Ireland, where eight days earlier the Catholic Irish had risen in murderous revolt, led in Ulster by dispossessed Catholic landowners. The Irish had massacred about five thousand Protestant settlers, driven twice as many out of the country, and added to the king's difficulties by professing fervent loyalty to the Crown. In a wave of anti-Catholic feeling, the queen and the crypto-Catholics at court were becoming even more detested.

The faction in the Commons led by Pym were determined that the army now necessary to put down the Irish should not be under the king's control. They quickly brought in a *Grand Remonstrance on the State of the Kingdom*, and when on 23 November John returned to London, the Commons were debating it till midnight. It listed the accumulated grievances of years, struck at the king's right to choose his own ministers, and demanded that he should only 'employ such councillors, ambassadors and other ministers as the Parliament may have cause to confide in'. The debate became a brawl from which the *Grand Remonstrance* emerged with the slender majority of eleven – 159 against 148. The majority then made the novel decision to have it printed, thus appealing beyond parliament to the political nation.

The king, in a hurried return from Scotland where he had

been trying to appease his enemies, was now at Theobalds, and
John witnessed his state entry to London, when, accompanied by
the young Prince of Wales, he was received with apparent
enthusiasm, and, with unwonted expansiveness, knighted seven
aldermen at once and created the Lord Mayor a baronet. In the
general festivity, the mainly royalist Inns of Court put on a show,
and in mid-December they elected John 'one of the Comptrollers
of the Middle-Temple-Revellers, as the fashion of the young
students and gentlemen was; the Christmas being kept this Yeare
with great Solemnity'.

But they had misjudged their man: rather unsportingly, John
soon 'got leave to resign [his] Staffe of Office' and retired with his
younger brother to stay with George at Wotton. Though in the
following March of 1642, again in London, he admits to 'dancing
and fooling', John Evelyn was no 'reveller'.

During the spring and summer of 1642 the collapse of public
authority continued, and the terms 'Cavalier' and 'Roundhead'
were coined. But the Evelyns were concerned with their own
business; riding to Northampton to buy saddle horses likely to be
in short supply, observing the 'contemplative monument' to
Lord Chancellor Bacon near Verulam and in July making a
'journey of pleasure' to Lewes.

And when in October 'that bloody difference between the
King and Parliament [had] broken out which ended in the fatal
tragedy so many years after', John merely rode over to
Chichester 'and thence the next day to see the Seige of
Portsmouth'. And when the royalist governor, Colonel George
Goring, had to surrender, John, unwilling to let war interfere
with the amenities of private life, came forward politely, if
perhaps superfluously, to take leave of the governor 'now
embarquing to France'.

At last, after the battle of Edgehill that month, John decided to
join the king, whose prospects looked good and whose army was
threatening London at Brentwood on the Thames, in a crucial
battle to break into London. But John arrived too late: 'I came in
with my horse and Armes,' he writes, 'just at the retreate.' The
king's failure had left Surrey exposed to the parliament, who
controlled London, and John continues that he was 'not
permitted to stay longer than the 15th [November], by reason of
the Armys marching to Glocester, which had left both me and
my Brothers (at Wotton) expos'd to ruine, without any advantage
to his Majestie'.[9] In fact, the king retreated on Reading and
Oxford, but, like most of the gentry, Evelyn wanted to protect

the family property, in his case so dangerously near London. The Evelyns had never been courtiers or office-holders, nor was John drawn to military adventure. A few days of mild campaigning in the Netherlands had been enough; at twenty-two he was already an amiably self-contained character, more at home with pictures and architecture than in battle.

# CHAPTER FOUR

# Evelyn in France

'An Intelligent and Taciturn Observation'

Back at Wotton in the spring of 1643 with the Civil War now raging but 'resolving to possesse my selfe in some quiet if it might be, in a tyme of great jealosy', John, by his brother's permission, built a study and made a fishpond and 'some other solitudes and retirements'; the first occasions, as he afterwards added, 'of improving them to those Water-Workes and Gardens which afterwards succeded them, and became the most famous of England at that tyme'.[1]

As the Civil War intensified, in mid-July he showed a rather tepid loyalty by sending his black horse and furniture, in custody of a friend, to Charles I at Oxford. Then, on 23 July, when parliament was imposing the Presbyterian Covenant as part of their strategic alliance with the Scots which would decide the war, John 'absented' himself to avoid taking it. Finding it 'impossible to avoid doing very unhandsome things' in an area controlled by parliament, and disregarding George's conventional advice to 'think on your own country', he decided to leave England and travel again.

Early in October 1643 he obtained a licence to travel signed by the longsuffering king himself at Oxford, and by 7 November he had taken boat with only one pair of oars in 'an hideous storme' from Tower Warfe to Sittingbourne; then, accompanied by young Thicknesse, his friend from Balliol, he had ridden to Dover. In snow and hail their shallop to Calais mistook the tide, but they made the heavily fortified port and next day, caught in a heavier snow storm, had to spend the night in a village on the way to Boulogne. The French were still at war with Spain, and Montreuil had been burnt by a Spanish raid from the Netherlands, but at Beauvais they saw their first vineyards, not at their best in November, and so proceeded to St Denys and Paris.

John's decision to spend 'the prime of his youth' abroad was made as much to complete his education and through enterprise as from political caution. 'That which first rendered me of this apodemick humour', he would write in the *State of France* (1652) already cited,[2]

proceeded from a certain vaine emulation ... to see the best of education, which everyone so decrying at home, made me conceive was a commodity only to be brought from a far countrie; and I cannot say without a little ambition of knowing, or at least having the priviledge to take something more than others could reasonably pretend to, that had never been outside the sight of their own chimnies' smoke.

Travel, then as now, exacted its price: 'ill entertainments', absence from friends, 'watchings', perils and expense; but for a well-to-do traveller with introductions it then presented more ample social opportunities. John had determined properly to master the languages and manners of the countries he would visit, to frequent the courts, study the arts, and 'observe things mechanically curious and usefull as well as the mysteries of government'. He was not content just to 'Count steeples' or make a tour 'like a goose swims down a river', but tried to practise an 'intelligent and taciturn observation' with a 'prudent regiment of health and affections, especially in point of drink and tobacco, which is our northern national and most sordid of vices'. One should never, he declared, exceed in liquor, but keep sober and watch one's companions who thus often revealed their true selves.

When he first entered France, he was already a wise and reflective youth, and his travel notes, though later written up and swamped by a spate of information culled from fashionable guide books,[3] already reveal a fastidious and quietly determined temperament fortified by a connoisseur's detachment.

The Trésor of St Denis, the burial place of the French kings since Dagobert, was then a medieval revelation. In the Netherlands most of the art and architecture had been modern; John was now dazzled by accumulated French splendour: by a great Carolingian cross with 'a noble oriental Amethist in the middle', and by another 'set with Saphyres, Rubies and greate oriental Pearles', though he remained staunchly Anglican and unmoved when confronted with 'some of the B. Virgin's haire', by the 'Linnen used ... at Christ's nativity', and by 'something stain'd red which the Father would have us believe was the natural blood of our Saviour'. Shown a large agate vase, decorated with a Bacchanalia and a sacrifice to Priapus, he observed with just the sarcastic tone of Andrew Boorde, the early Tudor traveller, that it was a 'very holy thing and fit for a Cloyster'. He admired many superb bejewelled relics; as, for example, a great crown of Charlemagne and a 'cloak-royal' of Anne de Bretagne, books bound in jewelled gold plate, and the effigy of the Queen of Sheba (who had a 'moorish' face). There was also a brass lantern full of crystals 'said to have conducted Judas and his company to apprehend our B: S:'. The tremendous collection sounds similar to that carted away from the shrine of St Thomas at Canterbury by order of Henry VIII – the accumulated and priceless treasure of centuries mixed with the junk of popular piety.

Arriving at Paris for the first time, John put up at the inn most frequented by the English – the well-known Ville de Venize – he then paid a formal visit to Sir Richard Browne, Charles I's resident ambassador. It proved a fateful visit, for the ambassador would become his father-in-law and the means of his finding his own home at Sayes Court near Deptford. During December and over Christmas 1643, John records a thorough tour of Paris, afterwards elaborated from Varenne's *Voyage* and other later seventeenth-century descriptions.

## II

Following the death of Louis XIII earlier in 1643, France was now under the regency of Anne of Austria, mother of the five-year-old Louis XIV. Her principal minister, and reputed lover, was the Italian adventurer, Cardinal Mazarin. Though the government was precarious, Paris was already becoming the cultural capital of Europe; John particularly admired the twelve-arched Pont Neuf built by Henri III and Henri IV connecting the Ile de France with the South Bank, with a separate passage for coaches and two, four feet higher, for pedestrians, all of hewn freestone with a presiding statue of Henri IV. He found the already prodigious 'confluence of People' an agreeable diversion, and Paris 'one of the most gallant Cittys in the World, and best built'. It was 'large in Circuit' and 'infinitly populous, but situat in a botome … which renders some places very durty, and makes it smell as if sulphure were mingled with the mudd'.[4] Like Tom Coryate, a less privileged traveller, who in 1608 had remarked that the streets were 'the most stinking of all I ever saw in my life', and unlike most of his contemporaries, John was disgusted with the smell, as he would be with the smoke-laden pollution of Restoration London; yet he adds of Paris, 'it is pav'd with a kind of freestone, neere a foote square, which renders it more easy to walke on than our pibbles of London'.

At Notre Dame, 'the prime church of France for dignity', John observed the entry of the young Louis XIV with his guard, who entered the nave with drums and fifes playing, and how the king was there 'entertain'd with the Church musique, and so I left him'.

In company with John Wall, originally an Irish friar, but now an irrepressible soldier of fortune and an 'absolute Cavaliere' from the German wars, John visited the Sorbonne, recently rebuilt by Richelieu. Here a professor was dictating a lecture on divinity, whereat 'up starts our Cavalier and begins to dispute with the Doctor', and the students, put off by his Spanish dress, broke into brisk Parisian mockery. But the loquacious Irishman won: he debated so skilfully in Latin that he 'baffled the Professor': derision changed to admiration, and the students, relieved perhaps that the *dictée* was interrupted and respectful in the French way to intellectual brilliance, 'rose up and did him very greate honors'.

John, who had 'taken a Master of the French tongue' since February, now explored the Old Louvre, bought classical books from the king's printing house, and marvelled at the 'prodigious number of Barges and boates of incredible length, full of hay, Corne, Wood, Wine and other Commodities which this Vast City consumes'. The then Italianate Tuileries gardens, laid out by Catherine de Medici, seemed 'rarely contrived for Privacy, shade, company, by Groves, Plantations of tall trees ... Elmes, ... and Mulberys, and that Labyrinth of Cypresse ...' with 'noble hedges of Pome-granads, ... fountains, ... Piscianes', an 'Aviary' and even an 'artificial Echo'.[5] John visited St Germain, 'that stately Country house of the Kings', and St Cloud, where the archbishop of Paris had an elaborate palace and garden with statues and fountains. Here, too, was an inn for 'great persons' with 'Princely furniture and plate', but 'they pay well for it, as I hav don'; yet the cost was not excessive for 'the excellent manner of dressing their meate, and the service'; though, he concludes, rather censoriously, 'here are many debauches and excessive revellings ...'.

At Cardinal Richelieu's villa at Rueil the gardens were even more spectacular, with groves of perennial green and vast walks, and a painting of the 'Arco of Constantine' in oil on a wall 'so rarely perform'd that it is almost impossible to believe it Paynting, ... swallows ... thinking to fly through, have dash'd themselves to pieces' – a remark revealing mid-seventeenth-century connoisseurship.

It was now March 1644 and the Civil War in England was mounting towards the loss of all the north to the king at Marston Moor in July, but John Evelyn was entirely engaged in an insatiable experience of pictures and architecture. Whether or not added later, not a detail is omitted, and medals and flowers are now included, especially the tulips, then so fashionable and expensive.

If now less intolerant of Catholic ritual, John was shocked by the utter bareness of the Protestant service at Charenton: they had no pews – 'as in our Churches', although, trained from childhood, the congregation sang well. In the spring weather he now ventured as far as Fontainebleau, finding the way encompassed by 'hidious rocks' and 'Mountainous heights ... horrid and solitary', which now look less formidable from the motor road. Wolves and bears abounded, and it was even rumoured that a lynx had lately 'devowred' some passengers. Passing these 'solitudes, not without howrly expectation of Rogues who frequently lurke about these denns (for whom we were all well appoynted with our Carabines)', John thought the famous palace inferior to Hampton Court. But, as usual, mainly from Varennes, he laboriously lists all the curiosities, including the carp which 'come familiarly to hand' and the 'incomparable walks'.

That spring, he also went down to Normandy with Sir John Cotton from Cambridgeshire. They passed Pontoise and Magny, where, again, wolves were common, and saw pear and apple orchards and half-timbered houses. From Rouen they rode across the open country to Dieppe, 'situated between two mountains' and 'washed by our English sea', then along a rugged road to Le Havre. Here the Duc de Richelieu, the commander, allowed them to see the fortifications in detail, and John noticed the motto on the cannon: *ultima ratio regum* – 'the final argument of kings'.

## III

Back in Paris, John resolved to spend the summer of 1644 in some remote town on the Loire, and on 19 April he set out for Orléans. Though the *pavé* protected travellers from the dirt and ill ways common in England, he thought it 'somewhat hard on

the poore horses's feete', so that they seldom went beyond a trot;
but if his care for horses seems modern, he ran ancient risks
from brigands, who had recently, shooting from the hedges,
killed four travellers including 'a Captain of Swisses of the
Regiment of Picardy'. Indeed, John thought he had 'great cause
to thank God for his escape' when he arrived safely at Orléans,
where he observed an effigy of 'Jane d'Arc, ... the famous Pucele
... her hayre dischevel'd as the Virago who deliver'd the Towne
from our Countrymen ... the valient Creature being afterwards
burnt at Rouen for a Witch.'[6]

At Orléans the Loire wine proved 'grosse and strong', and
having arrived for the first time far enough south for the full
light and warmth of France, John took a boat to St Dyé where he
hired horses for Chambord, which had intrigued him for the
reported extravagance of its design. But the impact of the superb
chateau seems to have been lost on him: he thought it smaller
than many English great houses and the staircases more
extensive than useful. Even the extraordinary Italianate
chimneys merely seemed 'like so many Towres'.[7]

At Blois, with his passion for 'curiosities', he was happier,
seeing a picture of a stag 'with twenty brow Antlers', and with a
companion he walked out into the woods to see if they could
meet any wolves. In spite of horrendous rumours, they met
none. Proceeding by boat to Amboise, they came to Tours,
where the straight and spacious streets seemed singularly clean
after Paris; at Marmoustier John saw the Holy Ampoule used in
anointing the French kings, and then visited the tomb of
Ronsard near Plessis.

His August routine at Tours of learning French and
sightseeing was now rudely interrupted. He had rashly hired a
Biscayan Spaniard as *valet de chambre*, who, when discharged,
demanded 100 crowns for his return to Spain. John refused, and
the Spaniard cited him to appear in court before the *Lieutenant
civile*. The *Lieutenant*, however, at once took John's side, and
acquitted him against a servant's accusation, apologized that a
stranger should have been so barbarously treated and
accompanied him to the 'very streete dore' of the court. In the
cosmopolitan hierarchy of the day the matter had been settled
between gentlemen. Though the 'Varlet afterwards threatened
to pistol' his former employer, John soon regained his
accustomed serenity.

But by mid-August he was touched by a backwash of Charles
I's defeat. Henriette Maria, Queen of England, had escaped from

Exeter, and after many adventures, boarded a Dutch ship at
Falmouth. Chased by parliamentarian warships, fended off only
by the intervention of the French, her ship had run before a
storm into Chastel, a cove near Brest, where she had found
refuge in a fisherman's hut. Haggard but rehabilitated, she was
now being ceremoniously conducted through Tours to the
French court, and John felt he should at least pay his respects.

He also now visited Richelieu, a model of the latest town
planning called after its founder, and 'built most exactly
uniforme, after a modern handsome designe'. It included an
Academy and a finishing school, with professors 'stipendiated by
the greate Cardinal'; but the project had evidently failed, being
'not well situated either for health or pleasure', and was 'but
thinly inhabited'. The Cardinal's own palace, however, was still
stately and richly furnished; with its groves, meadows and several
excellent walks, a 'real Paradise'.


## IV


John had now determined after nearly five months in Tours, to
move into the more southern parts of France, 'minding now to
shape my Course so as I might Winter in Italy'.[8] Still
accompanied by Thicknesse of Balliol, he made for
Chenonceaux, 'which stands on a bridge' and through an
account heavily supplemented from Sir Theodore de Mayerne
Turquet's *Sommaire de la France* (1591) we can discern that he
proceeded to Bourges – 'high and well placed for defence, and
environed with excellent vines' – where he describes the bones of
a giant in the cathedral, but does not mention the superb stained
glass. From Roanne, he made for Lyons, but, falling in with
some English travellers whom he wished to join, he could spare
too little time for it, and on 30 September the party bargained
with a waterman to transport them to Avignon down the
Rhone.

At Vienne, the first stop, John first encountered truffles,
'which is a certaine earth-nut, found out by an hogg, train'd up
to it, and for which those Creatures are sold at a greate price: It is
in truth an incomparable meate'.[9] After Valence, the Rhone was
so swift that they had to take horses, and entering Avignon, sold
in the mid-fourteenth century by the Angevin-descended queen
Joanna of Naples to the Popes, they had their firearms strictly
impounded by Papal guards. Evelyn thought the walls '(being all

square huge free stone), absolutely the most neate and best in repair that in [his] life [he] ever saw,' and the city full of well-built palaces and sumptuous churches. As he had inspected the tomb of Ronsard, he now duly admired the 'Tomb of Madona Laura, Petrarchs celebrated Mistris'. By the end of September 1644 he was for once noticing the scenery: round Aix-en-Provence, 'all the heaths or commons are cover'd with Rosemary, Lavander ... and the like sweete shrubs for many miles together, which to me was then a very pleasant sight'.[10] And from Aix they had 'a most delicious Journey to Marselles through a Country sweetely declining to the South and Mediterranian Coasts, full of Vine-yards and Olive-yards, Orange trees, Myrtils, Pomegranads and the like sweete Plantations.' The pleasant white villas seemed like heaps of stone dropped out of the clouds among the perennial green. For the first time in his life John had set eyes on a Mediterranean landscape.

They had arrived at Marseilles – 'well wall'd with an excellent port for ships and galleys' – in the evening, and, breaking away from Varenne's information, John directly describes the life of the royal galleys.[11]

We went then to Visite the Gallys being about 25 in number. The Captaine of the Gally royal gave us most courteous entertainment in his Cabine, the Slaves in the interim playing both on loud and soft musique very rarely: Then he shew'd us how he commanded their motions with a nod, and his Wistle, making them row out; which was to me the newest spectacle ... beholding so many hundreds of miserably naked Persons, having their heads shaven clToose, and onely red high bonnets, a payre of Course canvas drawers, their whole backs and leggs starke naked, doubly chayned about their middle, and leggs, in Cupples, and made fast to their seates: and all commanded in a trise, by an Imperious and cruell sea-man: one Turke amongst them he much favour'd, who waited on him in his Cabine, but naked as he was, and in a Chayne lock'd about his leg; but not coupled.

The English party having bestowed something on the galley slaves, the captain sent a band of them (presumably still chained) to the travellers' lodgings to play music during dinner.

The ghastly system was, indeed, tempered by such casual permissions, and though the 'miserable Catyfs' lay huddled horribly in their galleys, yet they 'nearly all were allowed some occupation or other: by which at leasure in Calmes they could get a little money – (and keep their thoughts from despair and mutiny) by saving up over Yeares of Cruel Servitude ... to purchase their liberty.' But their 'rising forwards, and falling back at their Care [was] a miserable spectacle', and 'the noyse of their Chaines with the roaring of the beaten Waters had something strange and fearfull in it'. They are ruled, he wrote, 'and Chastized with a bull's-pizle dry'd upon their backs, and the soles of their feet, … yet for all this they are Chereful and full of vile knavery'. The galley slaves came of all classes and many nationalities; and Marseilles itself was thoroughly orientalized, swarming with slaves jingling their huge chains, while the chief trade was in silks from the East and drugs out of Africa.

In early October 1644 it was still hot, and Evelyn, like Tom Coryate in Italy, who had first described the novel and ingenious device to his countrymen, bought his first umbrella – against the heat. On 9 October, since Turkish pirates made the sea unsafe, the party took to mules and so rode to Cannes, by way of Fréjus. From Cannes, then only a small port, they 'agree'd with a Seaman to transport [them] to Genöa', and having obtained a clean bill of health, without which no Italian town would admit them, they coasted along touching at the *Iles de Lerins* to the vicinity of Antibes, then 'the utmost city of France'. Thence by Nice, which belonged to the Dukes of Savoy, and, 'built all of brick' presented 'a very pleasant aspect towards the sea', they arrived at Monaco, the principality of the Grimaldis who had already placed themselves under French protection, and where, the wind being contrary, the travellers put in at the harbour. But the avaricious master of the boat refused to allow time for sightseeing, and sailed for Menton, then for Ventimiglia, the first city of the republic of Genoa, in Italy.

CHAPTER FIVE

# Evelyn in Italy

Having passed the boundary of Ventimiglia and so of Italy, the travellers coasted along the Riviera di Ponente, with Corsica in view. The 'rivage' of San Remo 'was incomparably furnished with Ever green orange, citron and even date trees'; then at Albenga they were sailing off territory belonging to Philip IV of Spain. Afraid of attack, the French boat 'ply'd both sayles and oars' to get protection from a Genoese galley as far as Savona. Foul weather set in, but the captain took the risk of doubling the Cape of Savona by making out before the wind, which, descending from the mountains, drove the ship far out into a rough sea.

Some passengers confessed themselves to an itinerant Irish bishop, the pilot thought all was lost, and the rest, tired out with pumping and baling, almost gave up hope; but suddenly, it 'pleas'd God to appease the Wind' and slowly they recovered the shore, from which John first smelt the 'peculiar joys of Italy, in the natural perfumes of Orange, Citron and Jassmine flowers for divers leagues to seaward'.

By 16 October 1644, they were anchored under the pharos off the mole of Genoa, though, the sea still running high, they only ventured at evening into the harbour. Strictly examined for a clean bill of health, and registered at the Ducal Palace, they were conducted to an inn kept by one Zachary, an Englishman. Here they dwelt upon their narrow escape; but the inkeeper boasted of such lurid adventures in the West Indies that 'after his story we no more talk'd of our danger, for Zachary put us quite downe'.

Next day, with undiminished zest, John went to view the rarities of Genoa;[1]

never was any artificial sceane more beautiful to the eye of the beholder ... so full for the bignesse of well designed and stately Palaces; as may be easily concluded by that rare booke in a large folio, which the greate Virtuoso and Painter Paule Rubens has publish'd.

Crossing the harbour, John 'could not but observe the suddaine

and devlish passion of a sea-man who plying us, was intercepted
by another fellow, that interpolated his boate before him and
tooke us in'. Weeping with rage, the infuriated Italian almost 'bit
off his finger by the joynt, shewing it to his antagonist, as an
assurance to him of some bloudy revenge', and indeed, John
concluded, that though it was a 'gally matter' to carry a knife
with an unblunted point, Genoa was more 'stayn'd with such
horrid acts of revenge and murthers than any one place in
Europ, or haply the World besides where there is a political
government; which renders it very unsafe for strangers'.

Like the Dutch, having only a small territory to develop, the
Genoese merchants spent their wealth on grand houses and rich
furniture. In the Palazzo Doria, for example, were 'whole tables
and beadsteads of massy silver, besides many of them set with
Achates, Onyxes, Cornelians, Lazulis, Pearle, Turquizes, and
other precious stones: The Pictures and Statues innumerable'.
Gardens were full of[2]

Orange-trees Citrons and Pomegranads, Fountaines, Grotts and
Statues, amongst which one of Jupiter of a Colossal magnitude, under
which is the Sepulcre of a beloved dog, for which one of this family
receiv'd of the King of Spain 500 crownes a yeare during the life of that
faithfull animal,

a tradition of relentless realism long carried on the vast Campo
Santo behind the town which now includes life-like effigies of
nineteenth-century worthies in full contemporary dress.

The ornate churches were as splendid as the palaces, one with
an altar having 'four sumptuous Columns of Porphyrie and a
prodigious Emrald'; the mole a stupendous feat of engineering,
the pharos or 'Lanterne of incredible height', while the new
walls, extending impressively around the city, were made with
'herculean' industry and perched on the edge of artificial
precipices. And the city itself was spared the noise and jostle of
coaches, for since the streets were so narrow, as in the old city
they still are, only sedans and litters were allowed. The style and
atmosphere of this waning rival of Venice was Spanish and
stately.

It was now 19 October 1644, and the party set out by *felucca* for
Livorno; but after a night spent at Porto Venere for fear of a
rising sea, they landed at Lerici; and where today the motorist
rushes through tunnels or between hedges of clumped
oleanders, Evelyn took post-horses through hilly olive groves
past Sarzana and the marble quarries of Massa-Carrara down to
Viareggio. At Pisa the next morning he chanced to meet an old

friend, Thomas Henshaw, an Oxford man who had joined
Charles I at York, but, taken prisoner by the parliamentarians in
London, had been allowed to retire to Holland. He had then
become a major in the French army and had arrived at Pisa from
Spain. He now joined Evelyn in travelling in Italy for a year, and
after the Restoration became one of the earliest Fellows of the
reconstituted Royal Society as well as king's undersecretary of the
French tongue.[3] John Evelyn, in addition to Thicknesse, now had
another congenial travelling companion.

As an eager traveller, John had to describe the campanile or
'leaning tower of Pisa',

– strangely remarkable for this, that the beholder would expect every
moment when it should fall; being built exceedingly declining by a rare
adress of the imortal Architect: and realy I take it to be one of the most
singular pieces of workmanship in the World; how it is supported from
immediately falling would puzzle a good Geometrician.

He believed that it had been built by a German and that the tilt
had been deliberate: in fact it had been begun by the Italian
Bonnano Pisano (1174) and the tilt was due to its unintended
settling to one side during a construction incomplete until the
*quattrocento*.

The Duomo, with its suggestion of the East, he considered
superb; beautiful with six columns of great antiquity, and he
admired the great bronze doors (which he describes as 'brass') by
Pisano, still in place. His only comment on the splendid baptistry
is that the cupola is so artificial that the voice or word uttered
under it seems to break out of a cloud, and that its font,
supported by four lions, is of 'inestimable value for the
preciousness of the material'. He had no feeling for its
importance as a neo-classical Sicilian-designed precursor of
Renaissance style.

The Campo Santo, 'cloistered about with marble Arches',
interested him mainly for its 'Carcofagus earth', which
consumed dead bodies in forty hours. Though few cities in Italy
had more stately buildings, he concludes that Pisa, since coming
under the Dukes of Tuscany, had become 'thinn of Inhabitants',
with spacious fields and gardens within its walls.

But Fernando III of Tuscany had made Leghorn a great port,
strongly fortified and joined by a sixteen-mile canal to Pisa. To
obtain a bill of exchange, John went down there through a new
park full of cork trees and myrtles. It was a centre for English
merchants and shipping as well as a long-established slave
market for Turks and Moors and other 'natives in prodigious

numbers and confusion'. John even found a tent where 'many sottish persons would in drunken bravado try their fortune ... staking their liberty against a few Crownes', and when, as usual, they lost, they were put to the galleys.

On 22 October, armed with his bills of exchange, John proceeded by coach to Florence, a two-day journey by way of Empoli. At Florence, apart from immensely elaborate descriptions of the contents of palaces and churches drawn from fashionable guide books,[4] John makes the obvious observations: of the Arno, broad but 'very shallow', gliding under 'sumptuous' bridges, the Ponte S. Trinita, the Ponte Vecchio with its goldsmiths' shops; he observed the Palazzo Strozzi and the clumsy Pitti palace, 'of late infinitely beautified by Cosimo, with Statues, Urns, Pictures ... Grotto and Water-workes and with a garden full of all Variety'. Here lived the duke himself, with his Swiss guards, 'after the frugal Italian way', even 'Selling what he can spare of his Wines, at the Cellar under his very house', and, oddly, with wicker bottles dangling over 'the very chiefe entrance into the Palace; serving for a Vintners bush'.

John found the grim Palazzo Vecchio and the statue of David by Michelangelo more to his taste, and a 'repository of admirable Antiquities': while in the Loggia dei Lanzi he admired Donatello's statue of Judith and Holofernes. Having followed the usual celebrated round of churches, John inspected the Grand Duke's stables and their 'incomparable Horses of all Countries', as well as his zoo, which included 'Wolves, Catts, Bares, Tygers and Lions'. 'I tooke great pleasure,' he records,[5]

to see what an incredible height one of the Lyons would leape, for which I caused to be hung downe a joynt of mutton: They are loose in a deepe, Walld-Court, and therefore to be seen with much more delight than at the Tower of Lond, in their grates.

From this lively touch, John reverts to the 'black and white polish'd Marbles', the statues, the alabaster fonts, the mosaics in the Greek manner, and describes in detail the church of San Lorenzo with the famous Medici statues and tombs. He duly admired Santa Maria Novella, where Politian and Pico della Mirandola lay buried, and so moved on to the factories for making silk damask and velvet; the streets of Florence he thought very clean, fair and well built, but – and it seems incredible today – 'thinly inhabited'. The great days of the cultural and economic climax were long over.

After a week in Florence, John and his companions took horse for Siena. At Poggio Bunci (Poggibonsi), still a junction for

devious roads, the people made 'perfumed tobacco' or 'snuff'
and took it freely, a custom not adopted in England for another
forty years. At Siena, in contrast to Florence, they found
'incomparable air'; provisions were cheap, the inhabitants
courteous and 'Italian purely spoken'. It presented an
'incomparable prospect' with its defensive brick towers, the
brick so rarely made as to seem 'with a kind of natural politure',
like porphyry. The piazza, was like 'an escallope shell', and there
were many public fountains as well as a university 'where the
High Germans ... addict themselves to Civil Law'. As for the
Duomo, it was 'of black and white marble ... of inexpressible
beauty ... with a pavement exceeding all description'.

It was now 2 November, and the English were anxious to be in
Rome for the celebrations for Gian Battista Pamphili, elected in
mid-September as Pope Innocent X. So they rode out of Siena to
sleep at San Querico d'Orcia. Here they fell in with amiable
Cardinal Donghi, who had arrived in state with his own bed and
furniture, but refused to allow them to vacate the best room in
the inn for him, saying that he had once been in England. At
Radicofani they ascended high through the clouds, which 'look'd
like rocks', till they emerged into a most serene heaven, as if
above all human conversation 'with a sea of thick Clowds rolling
under' them and only the tops of a few hills visible: 'one of the
most pleasant, new and altogether surprising objects,' John
recorded, 'that in my life I had ever beheld'. He took the
prospect with his black lead pen.

By 4 November they were descending towards the Lago di
Bolsena, with its island convent of 'melancholy' Capuchins and
its surrounding Etruscan hills; and so rode to Falernum, source
of the famous wine, where lay buried a 'Dutch bishop' under the
epitaph '*Propter Est, Est, dominus meus mortuus est*'.[6] Passing Viterbo,
they were soon down on the Campagna or 'Playnes of Rome'.

Here, John, still twenty-three, felt 'strangely elevated', a mild
excitement checked by a 'dismal showre of raine which fell on us
just as we were contemplating that prowd Mistriss of the World';
and when at last, at five in the evening, he entered the city by the
Vatican Gate, he was wet to the skin.

The anticlimax continued, as 'perplex't for a convenient
lodging', they wandered up and down on horse back, until
conducted to the house of a Frenchman, situated on the Pincio
above the Piazza d'Espagna, evidently not far from the site of the
present Hassler Hotel. Here John took a rather expensive room
for twenty crowns a month (about five guineas), at once had a

good fire lit, dried himself out and went to bed.

## II

Once arrived, his social contacts were easy. The very next morning, resolved not to waste a moment, he called on the superior of the English College at Douai, long a famous Seminary for the Catholic English, and this Benedictine Father proved a person of singular learning, religion and humanity. Evelyn also called upon Abbot Patrick Cary, a younger brother of Lucius Carey, second Lord Falkland who, after creating a circle of learned men at Great Tew near Oxford, had deliberately perished the year before at the first battle of Newbury, apparently in despair at the state of England. Patrick, who had been brought up in France by direction of his mother, a Catholic convert and daughter of the wealthy Sir Lawrence Tanfield of Burford, had been provided, at the request of Queen Henriette Maria, with the headships of an abbey and a priory by Pope Urban VIII. Evelyn found him 'a pretty witty young priest', and added 'one who afterwards came over to our church':[7] Indeed, he was a minor poet who wrote *Trivial poems and Triolets* (1651).

Evelyn also encountered the Jesuit Father Courtney, briefly head of the English College in Rome, and Viscount Somerset, younger brother of the Marquess of Worcester. These eminent residents soon instructed the visitors 'how to behave in Towne, what directions, Masters and bookes to take in search and view of the Antiquities, Churches, Collections, etc.', and accordingly Evelyn concludes, 'the next day, being November 6t, I began to be very pragmatical'[8] – briskly active.

First he saw the Palazzo Farnese – 'a most magnificent square structure' – still externally intact, and built 'when Architecture was but newly recovered from the Gotic barbarity'; here he admired the Caracci Gallery where, with his docility to current connoisseurship, he wrote 'it would require more judgement than, I confesse, I had, to determine whether the figures were flat or emboss'd'; he admired a profusion of antique statues in white marble, the vast fountains and the entrance brought from the Baths of Titus. Next day they visited the Forum, still then *Campo Vaccino*, and ascended to the Capitol 'by a very broad ascent of degrees'. Here, John recorded,[9]

stands [as it does today] that incomparable Horse, bearing the Emp: Marcus Aurelius of Corinthian mettal, as big as the life, placed on a

Pedistal of marble … and esteemed one of the noblest pieces of worke now extant.

The catalogue, based mainly on Pflaumern, Raymond and P. Totti, *Ritratto di Roma Antica* (1627) and *Ritratto di Roma Moderna* (1638), extends over the wealth of architecture and art then available in a city far smaller but less crowded than it is now, and to investigate and compare Evelyn's elaborate record would need an exhaustive and specialized study. Suffice it to say that the travellers paid their respects to the Tarpeian rock, from which criminals in antiquity had been flung, but Evelyn merely observed 'the goodly prospect towards the Tybur'; they saw the Palatine and Aventine and the Circus Maximus, wholly converted into gardens and 'a heap of ugly ruins'.

The contemporary Romans were now busy preparing for the grand procession of Innocent X to St John de Lateran: even the Jews were putting up an arch in gratitude for papal protection. Evelyn particularly admired the Palazzo Barberini designed by Bernini, the pope's architect:[10]

as superbe, and princely an object, as any moderne building in Europ … furnished (with) whatsoever Art can call rare and singular, and a Library full of worthy Collections … but above all, for its unknowne material, and antiquity, an Ægyptian Osyris.

The baroque church of the Jesuits by Vignola which contained the remains both of their founder and of Cardinal Bellarmine, deeply impressed the travellers, who were civilly entertained by the Dutch professor of mathematics who showed them the refectory and gardens, and finally a 'hall hung round with the pictures of such of their Order as had been executed for their pragmatical and busy adventures'.

They returned to the Pincio in time to view the villa Medici with its 'incomparable prospect'; here every morning the occupants usually rode the great horse and gave Evelyn, watching from his own room, much diversion. He also attended an evening service of rare music at the Chiesa Nuova of S. Maria, where in the Oratory of St Philip Neri, by candlelight, a child of about nine pronounced an oration.[11]

with so much grace as I never was better pleased in my life, then to heare Italian so well spoken, and so intelligently: This course, it seemes, they frequently use them to, to bring their scholars to an habit of speaking distinctly, and forming their action and assurance, which none so much want, as ours in England.

The motets were sung under a lofty cupola by a eunuch,

accompanied by 'Theorbas, Harpsicors and Viols' – a ravishing 'entertainement'.

John continued to revel in the splendours of Rome – in spacious parks full of fountains, cypress walks beset with statues, statues of 'Oriental Alabaster' – 'entire views' and 'glorious sights for state and magnificence'. 'I walked up,' he records, 'to Dioclesians Bathes, whose ruines testify to the vastnesse of its original foundation. ... This monstrous pile was built', he alleged, 'by the Sweate of the Primitive Christians'. More recently, in the church of Santa Maria della Vittoria, Pope Gregory XV had hung up the standards taken at the battle of the White Hill near Prague, where in 1621 the Protestant King of Bohemia had been routed, and the current wars in Germany had begun under the papal motto *Exterpentur* – let them be exterminated'. The triumphal arch of Titus, with its images of the Jewish seven-branched candlestick, the tables of the law and of crowned and laureated figures bearing the Roman fasces, intrigued Evelyn so much that he caused his painter Carlo 'to copy it exactly out'; and he himself transcribed the inscriptions on the nearby arch of Constantine.

The Villa Borghese, completed only in its original form eleven years before, was already an art gallery, and its garden 'an Elysium of delight ... abounding with all sorts of most delicious fruit, and Exotic simples', fountains and rivulets; there was also a *Vivarium* with 'Estriges, Peacoks, Swanns, Cranes etc. and divers strange Beasts'.

But the architectural climax, then and now, was St Peter's, 'that most stupendious and incomparable Basilicam'.[12] Its immense piazza then afforded an uncrowded prospect and already a big fountain broke upon a 'round embosse of Marble into millions of pearles, which fell into the subjacent basin; making an horrible [awesome] noise: I esteem this,' he concluded, 'one of the goodliest fountaines that ever I saw.' Inside the vast dome at the summit of the cupola, Evelyn was human enough to engrave his name among those of other travellers.

The church of St John of the Lateran did not compare with St Peter's, being 'of Gotique Ordonance', but there was a wonderful concourse of people at the Scala Sancta nearby: they were ascending the twenty-eight stairs on their knees, using 'some lip devotion' at every step, and under a grate you could see red specks of blood, supposed to have been shed by our Blessed Saviour. Other sacred relics then in the Lateran are elaborately listed, including 'a sumptuous Cross besett with precious stones containing some of the very wood of the Holy Cross itselfe', the heads of St Peter, and St Paul, and a magnificent monument in porphyry of St Helena, the mother of Constantine. Amid these august relics, a statue of Henri IV of France had been relegated to a 'darke hole' – 'perhaps,' John comments, 'they did not believe him a through [thorough] proselyte'. He could hardly compete with the towel with which Christ dried his disciples' feet, the reed, sponge and some of the blood and water from His side, the rods of Aaron and Moses, 'and many other such bagatells.'

Concluding that this venerable church in truth 'had a certain majesty in it', they descended to the remains of Nero's Golden House, 'nothing but an heape of vast and confused Ruines, to shew what time, and the vicissitudes of human things doe change from the most glorious and magnificent, to the most deformed and confused'.


## III


It was now 23 November, the day of the 'greatest ceremony of all the state Ecclesiastical', the *Cavalcado* of his Sanctity Pope Innocentius X. First came the Swiss guard and an Avant Guard of mounted lancers, then the cardinal's mace bearers and train bearers, and the Pope's 'domestical officers'. They were followed by five 'noble Neapolitan Horses, white as Snow, cover'd with embroider'd trappings' and led by grooms in rich liveries, the feudal service paid by the king of Spain for Naples and Sicily; then came bevies of papal officials, cardinals' hats on staffs, and the Master of the Sacred Palace, all on mules and wearing 'flat episcopal hatts'. They followed after the Roman nobility and courtiers with their pages, on horseback, and were themselves followed by the Governor of Rome, guarded by more Swiss.

The formidable-looking Pope himself then appeared,[13] on a richly embroidered open chair of crimson velvet, borne by two 'stately' mules, holding up his two fingers to bless the kneeling crowds and those who packed the windows. He was supported by the cardinals and archbishops in red or green flat hats with tassels, all on 'gallant mules' richly trapped in velvet. Finally came the trumpets of the rearguard, two pages of arms in helmets with 'mighty feathers', carrying lances, and finally the great pontifical standard of the church.

The crowds were enormous and the night ended with fireworks, particularly elaborate before the Spanish and French embassies: the streets were full of bonfires, cannon roaring, music playing, fountains of running wine. The Roman populace had enjoyed a bloodless, splendid and papal circus.

The ancient Pamphili pope came of a Roman family; he had made his career as papal nuncio in Naples and cardinal legate in Spain. He would reign until 1655, and, ineffectively, support the waning Spanish power while allowing his kinswoman, Olimpia Maidachini, to make more than the usual inroads on the papal revenues.

By early December Evelyn had naturally become 'pretty weary of my continuall walkings'; but by Christmas Eve he was again hurrying from church to church in admiration of the pageantry, and by mid-January 1645 he was describing Michelangelo's 'Judgement' in the Sistine Chapel – 'a vast designe and miraculous fantsy, considering the multitude of Nakeds, and variety of posture'. He was shown the pope's tiara, and 'divers' bejewelled and crimson covered 'Pantofles that are kissed upon his foote', always a peculiar curiosity to Anglicans. The pictures by Julio Romano, Raphael and other great masters in the Vatican were called The Paynters' Academy, 'for you shall never come unto them but you find some young man or other designing from them, a civility which in Italy they do not refuse them where any rare pieces of the old and best Masters are extant'.

## IV

At the end of January, Evelyn, Sir John Manwood, a former Governor of Dover Castle, Thomas Henshaw and a Dutch gentleman who spoke perfect English and passed for an Englishman, 'two Cortizans in Mans Apparell' who 'rid astride, booted, Sworded and Spur'd' (one was 'marvelous pretty') and a Milanese squire, their gallant, hired lusty mules and set out along the new Appian way for Naples. Passing many ancient sepulchres – for 'it was [the Roman] manner to bury much by famous highroads where they also placed their statues', they rode beneath the hill of Frascati to Velletri where they drank excellent wine, but next day among the Pontine Marshes Evelyn suffered a festering of the hand and complained of his 'base unlucky stiffnecked carrion mule ... the most wretched beast'. On the way to Terracina they collected a guard against the local banditti and Evelyn turned aside to explore the Cave of Circe with its roaring 'horrid' waves on the Circean promontory.

Arrived at Fondi, they soon entered Neapolitan territory, still by the Via Appia, here again beset with sepulchres and antiquities and full of sweet shrubs among the hedges. In the January sunshine, they were given oranges and lemons for nothing. The Plaines of Campania or *Terra di Lavoro* Evelyn thought the 'most fertile place that ever sun shone upon'. Between Capua and Naples they found the broad road swarming with more travellers than any road round London, and noticed vines festooned among the fruit trees, as well as rice fields and sugar cane. Here, having been very merry with the two courtezans and the *Capitano*, their gallant, the English at noon entered Naples in the dominions of the King of Spain.

The Spaniards had been ruling Naples since Gonzalvo de Córdoba by his final and victorious campaign of 1501–4 with a brilliantly reorganized army, had defeated the French at Cerignola, and the kingdom had reverted to Fernando II as King of Aragon. Since then part of the empire of Charles V and Philip II, like Sicily and Sardinia, Naples, had been ruled by Spanish viceroys. The responsibilities and vast expense of empire, which in spite of mounting infusions of gold and silver from Central and South America, had bankrupted the government of Philip II, in fact had weakened the Spanish state, and from being the most powerful in Europe it had now become under Philip IV (1621–60) and the over-ambitious Olivares even more ineffective. In 1635, Olivares, now Conde Duque de San Lucar, had become involved at immense cost in the war against France; in 1638 the Spaniards had lost Breisach and their communications between Milan and Brussels, and in 1639 been defeated by the Dutch in the sea battle of the Downs. The Catalans and the Portuguese, exasperated by taxation, had both revolted, the former backed by the French, and in January 1643, two years before Evelyn's arrival in Naples, the Conde Duque had been compelled to retire to his estates. Spain had since been ruled in effect by Don Luis de Haro, whose policy was cautious and pacific, and the Spaniards were already negotiating at Munster to conclude a peace with the Dutch.

The delapidation of Spanish power had suited the Neapolitans, who had profited from its casual inefficiency, and relations between the Neapolitan establishment and their Spanish government were still fairly cordial.

Evelyn and his party put up at the Three Kings inn, a place of excessively plentiful and 'maraculously cheape fare', which provided eighteen or twenty dishes of the 'most exquisite meate and fruites'. Next day they drove round the city in a coach and took in the entire prospect from the high castle of St Elmo, laid out 'in the shape of a Theatre on the Sea brinke, with all the circumjacent Ilands as far as Capra, famous for the debauch'd recesses [retirement] of Tiberius'.[14] From this fortress, garrisoned by Spaniards, they descended to the Castello Nuovo, with its four thick towers by the sea, and then 'tooke the Ayr upon the Mole' built out into the harbour, where they met many of the nobility on horseback and in their coaches taking 'the fresco from the sea as the manner is'. John then indefatigably visited the magnificent cathedral and many churches, and on the following day again

consider'd the goodly Prospect towards the Sea, and Citty, the one full of Gallys, and ships, the Other of stately Palaces ... Mount Vesuvius smoaking, ... Capra, Ischia ... and the rest, doubtlesse one of the most divertisant and considerable Vistas in the World.

At the riding school of the Spanish Viceroy, he saw 'the noblest horses I had ever beheld, one of his sonns riding the Menage with that addresse and dexterity as I had never seene any thing approch it'.[15] Even more to his taste, he visited a 'repository of incomparable rarities, which included a male and femal Camelion, an 'extraordinary greate Crocodile', a Salamander, and mandrake roots 'of both Sexes'.

By 6 February it was Carnival, and they went by coach to see the 'diversions or rather maddnesse' of it, the local prostitutes, of whom there were reported 30,000 taxed and 'registered sinners', flinging eggs of sweet water at them. Indeed, John records, the place was so pestered with 'these Cattel' that it needed no small mortification to preserve oneself from their enchantments, and some of his companions afterwards 'purchased their repentance at a dear rate'. Meanwhile they rode out on mules to observe Vesuvius, then crawled up the proclivity on hands and feet, not without untoward slips, till they attained the very brim of the 'double top'. John lay on his belly to look down into the 'stupendious pit, ... through the foggy exalations and impetuous noise and roaring, ... one of the most horrid spectacles in the World'. Only fifteen years before there had been a major eruption.

John and his party thoroughly explored the whole volcanic district, its caves and its Graeco-Roman antiquities, including sailing by *felucca* to Baiae and its ruins – 'heretofore infinitely addicted to Lust and wantonnesse. Here were those famous pooles of Lampreys that would come to hand when called by name.' Such places and the sites of many ancient villas 'renowned for the sweete retirements of the most opulent, and Voluptuous Romans ... and the stupendious rarities ... of these blissful abodes', visited before the party returned to Naples, made John consider that 'the very winter here is summer', 'as in midst of February we had Melons, Cheries, Abricots'.

Besides enjoying the climate, he found the Neapolitans a cheerful people. Though the upper classes 'greatly affected the Spanish gravity', they delighted in good horses, and had invented sedan chairs, since, he added later, introduced into England. And if the women were excessively libidinous, the country people were jovial and musical, the very husbandmen almost universally playing on the guitar, 'will go to the field commonly with their fiddle'.

Indeed, John considered Naples the *non ultra* or climax of his travels; but he now felt 'sufficiently sated with rolling up and downe' and resolved, if he ever got home again, to be no more a wandering traveller – an *individuum vagans*, having been assured that there was 'little more to be seene in the (civil) World after Italy, France, Flanders and the Low-Country but plaine and prodigious Barbarisme'.[16]

# CHAPTER SIX

# Venice and Switzerland

In Naples early in 1645 John began to think of home, where, in May of the previous year, George's wife had died at Wotton; in June his sister Jane had complained that they were 'so wasted with intolerable taxes' it seemed impossible they could long subsist, and 'envied' John's 'happiness at having the world so much at large for pleasure'. Following the late Roman poet Claudian, he even broke into some rather clumsy verse,[1]

> Happy the man who lives content
> With his own Home and Continent:

concluding that he

> Scorns Us who Travell Lands and Seas
> Thinkes there's no Countries like to his:
> If then at Home such Joys be had,
> Oh, how un-wise are We, how mad!

So inefficient was the protecting Spanish power that, with Turkish pirates hovering off the coast, John and his companions feared to return to Rome by sea, and, proceeding by Albano, on 13 February, arrived in the city. This time they saw what they could of the Castle of St Angelo, inspected the awesome Pantheon, and bought some bric-à-brac in the market in the Piazza Navona. In the Dominican church of S. Maria near the Capitol, they witnessed the baptism of both a converted Turk and a Jew, by a bishop *in pontificalibus*. The Turk turned out to be sincere and lived afterwards in Rome, but the Jew was a 'Counterfeit'. At S. Croce in Jerusalem they were shown a wealth of relics, including two thorns of Christ's crown, 'St. Thomas' doubting finger ... Some of Judas' pieces of Silver and innumerable more if one had faith to believe it'. Returning tired out to their lodgings, they were next day confronted with the Roman carnival 'where all the world is as mad at Rome, as at other places'. There were three races 'of the Barbarie horses', riderless, but stimulated by hanging spurs; of Asses, and of naked men – old, young and boys – and the streets were swarming with 'whores, buffoones and ... rabble'.

John now visited the catacombs of Domitilla, 'a *Roma Subterranea*': we 'crep't on our bellies into a little hole ... which deliver'd us into a large entrie that lead into severall streetes or allies, a good depth in the bowells of the Earth, a strange and fearefull passage for divers miles'.[2] They came into 'pretty square roomes, some adorned with ancient painting, very ordinary'; but 'that which renders the passages dreadful is the *Skeletons* and bodies, placed on the sides ...'. After two or three miles of this 'subterranean Meander', they returned, almost blinded by the March sunlight and choked with dust, to their waiting coach. It had been rumoured that 'a French bishop, and his retinue, adventuring it seemes too farr in these denns, their lights going out, were never heard of more'.

More lively entertainment followed; as when at Prince Gallicano's, there was old-fashioned tilting at barriers, then at the formal entrée of the ambassador of Florence, or in an expedition by coach up to Frascati, not least delectable, Evelyn considered, for its 'Theaters of Water' and the incomparable walks and shady groves at the Villa Aldobrandini. They also visited the Villa d'Este at Tivoli (built 1560–71), 'very ample and stately'; the terraced gardens then, as now, a delightful spectacle. 'The Grotts are richly pav'd with ... Shells, Corall etc.: Towards *Roma* triumphans leads a long and spacious walk, full of Fountaines ...'. They 'feasted their curiosity with these artificial Miracles', and observed in the distance 'the *Hadrian* Villa', then 'onely an heape of ruines', today elaborately restored.

John, with surprising ease, had hitherto obtained money from an England torn by Civil War; but now, although since entering Italy he had spent only 616 *ducati di banco* (about £138) he found himself in Rome 'disappointed of Moneis long expected,' and decided to return by Livorno where he could raise credit, and arrange for the transport of his collections by sea. But he felt it again incumbent on him to mark leaving 'the once and yet glorious Citty' with some heavy verse. After describing in the Pastoral Mode the life he had left, he commemorates the sights:

> That *Steede* which so the *Capitol* dos grace
> Wants nought save motion. Yet dos without it pace
> For he's so full of Mettal, one would sweare
> T'were an enchanted *Horse* erected there:
> Th'enveloup'd *Laocoon*, a Serpent twines
> And threids his Children, whilst the Father Pines

Thro' anguish, and believ't, I did mistake
Myself and fled, it is so like a snake.'

Gamely John keeps up this doggerel to its exhausted conclusion:

Glory of Citties, for thy *Ruines* are
More glorious than be other *Citties* far:
With speaking stones, and breaking *Statues* set
Justly art term'd the *Worlds sole Cabinet*
Of all the *Universe* none dares contend
*With* thee *Ô ROME, nor will thy Praises End.*

John Evelyn had many gifts, but poetry was not one of them.


## II


Leaving Rome by coach on 18 May, they arrived by the 21st at Siena, where the Cathedral's striped black and white marble showed up with particular lustre after rain, and then they proceeded again to Pisa and so to Livorno. Here Evelyn took up 90 crowns (about £75) with a supplementary letter of credit for Venice, essential after the failure of his arrangement in Rome. Thus fortified, he penetrated to the 'neate' and independent city of Lucca, with its marble cathedral, venerated for the 'Sacret Volto' or Holy Face, which, like many visitors after him, he apparently failed to see. So he bought some gloves and embroidered stomachers (waistcoats) instead and observed that the place abounded in excellent olives.

During his second visit to Florence he apparently visited all the curiosities omitted during the first; masterpieces by Michelangelo, Raphael, Titian and Paolo Veronese, the tombs of Pietro and Iovanni dei Medici by Michelangelo, the library designed by him and the ascent to it – all 'incomparable'.

But now, crossing the high Apennines, they arrived at Bologna, a prosperous papal city, with its brick-built twelfth-century Torre d'Asinello, 156 feet high, and its magnificent arcades and university. Here John was greatly impressed by a Persian in the full 'fashion of their Country' ... 'a young handsom person of the most stately mîne I had ever observ'd'. He also encountered some 'pigmie Spaniels', whose deformed noses had been broken when they were puppies, and sampled a variety of incomparable wines, preferable, he considered, to the sausages, parmigiano, and caviare of which the streets were redolent. The cattle, he observed, in the rich surrounding country wore housings of linen, to protect them from the flies.

From Bologna they travelled north by canals and fens and, surrounded by fireflies, took coach and arrived at Ferrara, the burial place of Ariosto. Thence, after thirty miles by boat down the Po, they arrived at Malamocca, then the main port of Venice, and after presenting clean bills of health, took lodgings near the Rialto, in one of the best quarters of the town.

John, who for once admits himself 'extremely beaten' by the journey, now ventured into a Turkish *bagnio*, an unwonted luxury which promptly resulted in a violent cold, for he had rushed out from it to see the sights. Having travelled so fast, he had arrived, as intended, for Ascension day, when the Doge, embarked upon the *Bucentoro*, was rowed into the gulf to cast a gold ring and cup into the sea, a climax acclaimed by the great guns of the arsenal. Evelyn describes the '*Gundolas*' – 'very long and narrow, having necks and tailes of steel somewhat spreading at the beake like a fishes tail and kept so exceedingly polish'd as to give a wonderful lustre'. The gondoliers 'effect[ed] to leane them so on one side, that one who is not accustom'd to it would be afraid of oversetting' and in the jostling crowd of vessels on the Grand Canal seemed ready to sink one another during the celebration.

In the Piazza San Marco John observed the already famous clock, on which the three kings, the Infant Christ, the Virgin and the star, emerged at noon, while an 'Automat' struck the quarters. In spite of his dislike of 'Gothic', John much admired the splendid mosaics over the entrance to St Mark's, and the precious marbles of its floors, the sumptuously encrusted walls and the incomparable mosaics of the roof, and records detailed inventories of the treasures of the interior and of the reliquaries. He penetrated to the Ducal Palace, its great chamber decorated with pictures of the battle of Lepanto, and to the armoury, still a most interesting relic of Venetian glory. Emerging on to the 'sea side', he admired the two columns bearing the statues of St Mark's lion and of St Theodore, and took in the broad prospect of the island of San Giorgio and the shipping, before ascending the old campanile.

The 'proud dames' of Venice, who then wore very high-heeled shoes and an extraordinary complication of coiffeur and dress which John painstakingly describes, were to be seen 'stalking, half as high more, as the rest of the World',[3] while the aloof Venetian aristocracy contrasted with the Asians and Levantines who swarmed in the Piazza and streets – Turks, Armenians, Jews, Persians, Moors, Greeks and Slavs.

With his near-contemporary, Lord Bruce, afterwards first Earl of Ailesbury, Evelyn went to the opera where Monteverdi's *Coronation of Poppaea* had been first performed in 1642, and enjoyed its 'excellent recitative music' and 'variety of sceanes – one of the most magnificent and expenseful diversions the wit of Men can invent.' Under the stimulus of Venice, John now even decided to embark for Jerusalem, Egypt and Turkey; he even laid in provisions and medicines and 'snow to cool our drink', but, the Turks having just attacked Crete, the ship was commandeered by the Venetians to provision their fleet only two or three days before she was due to sail. So a large further instalment of the diary was never written, and by June 1645, having spared the reader the usual facetious account in the manner of Tom Coryate of the whores of Venice, John briefly left the republic for the fair of St Antony of Padua.

He travelled by horse-drawn barge by the Brenta canal through well-irrigated Venetian estates; and he was glad of the shade of the arches at Padua in the summer heat, admired the equestrian statue of the Condotierre Gattamalata by Donatello, wrongly attributed Alessandro Leopardi's cathedral to Palladio, and, having spent a day 'rambling', returned to Venice.

He next visited the celebrated arsenal, with smiths' forges in full blast, and carpenters hard at work on oars, masts, and furniture for the galleys and *galeazzas de guerra*. Here lay the *Bucentoro*, her ample deck contrived to conceal the galley slaves, and an immense store of arms and armour. But the University of Padua then contained the most famous school of medicine in Europe, and by the end of July John had obtained a pompous Latin Paduan Certificate of Matriculation. Here he again met the Earl of Arundel, who invited him to visit the gardens of Mantua, but John returned to Venice and inspected the already famous glass factory at Murano, where he enjoyed the excellent oysters, 'like our Colchester' – 'the first, as I remember, that in my life I ever could eat; for I had naturaly an aversion to them'.[4] Next day, none the worse, he dined with the captain on the boat in which he had planned to voyage to the Levant – on 'a good dinner, of English pouderd beefe, and other good meate, with store of Wine and greate Gunns (flagons of ale) as the manner is'.

Informed in early August that he had been elected to be *Syndicus Artistarum* at Padua, John characteristically and promptly evaded the expensive and time-wasting honour – to the annoyance of the local English who had obtained him the highly honorific award. But he settled down at Padua to study medicine with occasional excursions to Venice, in spite of the 'barbarous liberty' of the students, who, when they 'went to their strumpets' made the streets dangerous at night.

It was now October, and John developed a dangerously acute sore throat, cured by the radical seventeenth-century treatment by '*Old Salvatico*', that famous Paduan physician, who cupped and scarified his back in four places, so that he gasped so much that he got back his breath and was well in a fortnight.

Having wintered in Padua, early in 1646, when the Civil War in England had ended in the king's defeat, he attended the Carnival in Venice. 'It was impossible,' he recorded, 'to recount the universal madnesse of this place during this time of licence', and three days afterwards he finally left for Padua, for the famous month-long lecture on anatomy illustrated by dissections. He was fascinated – bought charts of the veins and nerves, of liver and lungs, of the gastric veins – indeed, he brought back to England, 'the first of that kind [that] had been ever seene in our Country and, for ought I know, in the world'.

Nor did Evelyn shirk visiting the hospitals where doctors were attending the poor, though he was shocked at the Italian freedom in 'letting in young gentlemen travellers to see their operations upon the femal sex, who even in the midst of their tortures' were 'not very modest, and when they began to be well, plainly lew'd'.

For a change, he enjoyed some excellent English potted venison with an English agent for the Levant Company, and attended a Jewish wedding in the Ghetto.

Before starting on his return journey over the Alps by the Spanish territory of Milan, Evelyn breakfasted with Lord Arundel, who wept over the misfortunes of his family in the Civil War, the contrariness of his relations and the miseries of England, but gave him a list of curiosities to acquire on his behalf. They never met again, for in 1646 Arundel would die; in comparative poverty and still at Padua.


## III


Travelling to Vicenza through country 'flat as a bowling greene' and planted in an orderly way with fruit trees entwined with vines, Evelyn reached Verona, and marvelled at the amphitheatre, 'the most intire now extant in the World of Ancient remaines. The Vastnesse of the marble stones is stupendious.' He thought the environs of Verona preferable to anywhere else he had seen in Italy, and compared the westward downs to those about Winchester towards Dorset. It was now early May, and by the Lago di Garda, recommended by Arundel as the most pleasant area in Italy, John found '*Oranges, Citrons, Olives Figs* and other tempting fruits', and the trout by Sirmione were abundant. He proceeded to Brescia, where he bought a fine carbine – 'every shop abounding in *Guns*, Swords', and with 'Armourers etc.', most of whom had come out of Germany.

Outside Spanish-ruled Milan, some of the English travellers thought of throwing away their Protestant books for fear of the notorious Inquisition, but for a small fee the lenient customs officers allowed them into the city without enquiry. Here John greatly admired the snow-white statues on the enormous cathedral, 'unfortunate in nothing save the Gotick design'. Tempted by the splendour of the governor's palace, he even ventured into it alone, to be chased out as a suspected spy, before visiting the celebrated '*Cena domini* of Leonard: da Vinci' an 'incomparable piece', already 'exceedingly impaired'. The great citadel of Milan was garrisoned entirely by Spaniards, as essential for their communications with the north and the Austrian Habsburgs.

Following an afternoon at the opera, the English were now sumptuously entertained by a retired Scots mercenary colonel, who showed them his collection of captured weapons and presented one of the travellers, a Captain Wray – 'a good drinking gent', with a pair of pistols and Evelyn with a Turkish bridle 'Curiously embossed' and 'taken from a Basshaw that he had slaine'. Then, a little spirited with wine, the colonel mounted an ungovernable horse which crushed him against the wall and left him speechless and vomiting blood. This disaster made the English quickly hire a coach to the foot of the Alps to escape the Inquisition; a wise if callous move, since the colonel died.

At Lake Maggiore it was raining, and they proceeded by boat to Arona, where the Spanish governor let them pass, and they first observed 'the horrid prospect of the *Alps*, cover'd with Pine Trees, and Firrs, and above them Snow'.

Their hardships now began. At an inn at the foot of the mountains John had to lie on a bed of beech leaves which so pricked his skin that he could not sleep, then mount an ass with loops of rope for stirrups, which, bridled with the 'Turkish present', brought him to Duomo (Domodossola), now the modern frontier. Having shown a Spanish pass, prudently acquired in Venice, the party, in mid-May 1646, began to ascend the mountain to the Simplon.


## IV

They had exchanged their donkeys for mules and hired a guide, for the Simplon was then the most dangerous of the passes. The track led through 'horrid ... Craggs' and pine forests, inhabited only by bears, wolves and wild goats; over narrow bridges of felled fir trees above roaring cataracts, and along precarious ledges cut out of the rock. They traversed narrow passes between 'fallen mountains', and the sparse inhabitants, disfigured by monstrous goitres, spoke a barbarous 'mixture of corupt high *German*, *French*, and Italian'. Indeed, the Swiss seemed of monstrous stature, 'extremely fierce and rude, yet very honest and trustie', and their houses seemed built strangely low for such tall people.

One of the English company, suspected by Evelyn of being a parliamentarian, was the swashbuckling Captain Wray, whose Water Spaniel ('a huge filthy Curr, that had follow'd him out of England'), now hunted some goats into a stream,[5] to the fury of their owners. Meanwhile the travellers, having arrived at the saddle of the pass, had to make do with cheese and milk and 'wretched' wine, and sleep in 'Cupboards' reached by ladders. Then next morning, as they were mounting their mules, a huge young fellow demanded payment for a goat allegedly killed by the spaniel, and when, impatient of the cold, the English started to ride off, a mob of peasants surrounded them, beat them off their saddles, seized their carbines and thrust them all into a hut. Six 'grimm Swisse' then entered, and sitting on the table, demanded a *pistol* [16s. 7d.] for the goat, and a fine of ten more for trying to ride away and 'going about to shoot them' – 'as indeed the Captaine had been about to do'. Fearing for their lives, the party, including Evelyn, felt it 'safer to rid [them]selves out of their hands than expostulate it among such brutes', and 'layd downe the money'.

After this 'cold entertainment', they rode on through the snow, following 'masts' marking the track, until, this time, the captain's horse which carried their baggage made trouble. It slid down a precipice, and the 'Choleric Cavalier', its master, was just going to send a 'brace of bullets into the poor beast', to prevent the Swiss guide rescuing it and decamping with the baggage. But

John and his other companions by shouting and pelting the animal with snowballs, so excited it that it fell further down, and near a path they would soon pass. Rescued from the snow and the captain, the horse recovered, and the travellers staggered on past mountain torrents and huge precipices until, late that evening, they got down to Brigue far below, where they found most of the houses ornamented by the heads of wolves, foxes and bears.

Next day, changing their guide and their mules, they proceeded down the valley of the upper Rhone, which seemed excessively hot, while the 'goodly river glided by them', irrigating the country. At Sion they were entertained by another 'true old blade', once a colonel in France, who displayed his hunting trophies, books and pictures, and at once wrote them a letter to the governor, resident at St Maurice near Lac Leman, asking him to avenge the affront inflicted by the goatherds of the Simplon: 'a more debonaire brave Gentleman I never saw, nor could possibly expect to find in this rude Country and among the blunt Swisse'. Like the Scots colonel in Milan, this old soldier, having done well out of the wars, now needed some travelled company.

The ordinary Swiss, on the other hand, seemed very 'clownish', and oddly dressed, mainly in thick blue cloth, without distinction between the gentry and the common people: but there were no beggars, and 'though exacting in what they parted with', the people seemed honest and reliable. They all wore swords and the country seemed 'well disciplined', indeed, 'impregnable, which made the Romans have so ill success against them, one lusty Swiss at their narrow passages sufficient to repell a Legion'. Though their military methods were now obsolescent, they still went abroad for years as mercenaries; already John wrote,

I looke upon this Country to be the safest spot in all Europ, neither Envyed nor Envying nor are any of them rich, nor poore; but live in great Simplicity ... and though of the 14 Cantons halfe be *Roman Catholics* the rest Reformed, yet they mutualy agree.

Having entered Savoy, John now began to develop smallpox, presumably, given the time for incubation, contracted in Milan. Stricken with a blinding headache at Le Bouveret, he carried on by boat over Lac Leman, still well enough to enjoy serene late May weather, smooth water, and temperate air, until he arrived at Geneva, where, after visiting various learned men, he collapsed, 'imagining that [his] very eyes had droped out'. He was

attended by Dr du Chat, physician to the late king Gustavus
Adolphus, of Sweden, who purged and bled him and applied
leeches 'and God knows what', until, to the physician's surprise,
the smallpox appeared. The doctor fortunately refrained from
bleeding John again, and kept him warm in bed for sixteen days,
attended by a 'vigilant Swiss Matron' whose goitre gave him
nightmares. No one thought of isolating him: he was visited by
several acquaintances, and after five weeks he recovered. Luckily
the illness had not developed on the Simplon.

Convalescent, John stayed a night at lodgings in the hills
outside Geneva for better air, but having 'no company there but
his pipe', had himself rowed on the lake to see the cherry
orchards, then in full blossom, and inspected some fisheries
containing enormous trout. Next day, following Genevan
custom, he attended a sermon, and then observed the well-
fortified city, its houses 'deformed but sheltered by the projecting
wooden roofs.' Booksellers abounded, but of badly printed
books, and watchmakers of very good watches: provisions were
good and cheap. Since the Genevan territory was so small, the
city was on continual alert, but could rely on the other Swiss for
help in a siege. Moreover, this 'precise people permitt their
youth to exercise arms and shoot with guns'. The church
government was severely Presbyterian, if not so rigid as that of
the Scots or the English sectaries, but 'Adultery [was] death'.

Captain Wray now fell so mightily in love with a German girl
that he was reluctant to proceed into France: but now, in July
1646 the heat coming on, and having spent 45 pistols (about £35)
on his lodging during his illness and 5 pistols on the doctor, who
gratefully gave him an elaborate instruction in Latin for the
conduct of his health, Evelyn and his party left Geneva for Lyons
by Seyssel, then by boat down the Rhone. Having ridden from
Lyons to Roanne, they then 'indulged themselves with the best
that all *France* affords' and lay that night in Damask beds and
'were treated like Emperours'.

## V

Now at last in France, where John felt thoroughly at ease, they
agreed with a fisherman to row them down the Loire to Orléans.
The passengers took turns at the oars, walked through the
meadows and shot birds, played cards and composed verses,
Edmund Waller, the poet, joined the company, and a pleasant

journey was marred only when Evelyn's spaniel, acquired in
Rome, was stolen – 'a great displeasure because the curr had
many useful qualities'. At Orléans they left their 'mad Captain'
(Wray) behind them, and Evelyn arrived at Paris after so many
'disasters and tedious peregrinations', thankful that he had now
'gotten so neere home'.

# CHAPTER SEVEN

# Marriage: England and Paris: *The State of France*

At Paris Evelyn at last took a rest, 'the only time in my whole life I spent most idly', but 'soon recovered his better resolutions', learnt high Dutch (German) and Spanish and refreshed his dancing. So he passed the winter of 1646–7, becoming close friends with Richard Browne, still the royalist English ambassador to the Court of France, and falling in love with his only daughter, aged thirteen. He was now twenty-six.

By June 1647 the marriage had been arranged. The Brownes had held high rank in the rudimentary Elizabethan and Jacobean civil service, and the ambassador had been Clerk of the Council to Charles I before, in 1641, he was appointed to France. His wife was Elizabeth Prettyman of Gloucestershire, and her uncle was in occupation of Sayes Court, their property at Deptford. The marriage would bring lasting happiness at Sayes Court and Wotton, and a well-conducted home. Determined that it should be celebrated by the Anglican ritual, John obtained the services of Dr Earles, one of the Prince of Wales's chaplains and afterwards bishop of Salisbury. The marriage took place on 27 June in the Anglican chapel of the ambassador, at the peak of the summer on the feast of Corpus Christi, when the streets were gay with tapestries and strewn with flowers.

With meticulous care John also composed *Instructions Oeconomiques* which he presented to his young wife, 'to be kept under lock and key'. It was dedicated in gold ink, 'To the Present Mistress of My Youth, the hopeful companion of my riper Yeares and the Future Nurse of my Age, Mstrs Mary Evelyn, my dear wife'.[1]

Moved by the affection of a husband so much older and more learned than herself, Mary Evelyn took this rather overwhelming tribute in good part; an older and more experienced girl might have found it altogether too serious. For John dilates on 'the experience of so many happy unions which offset those uncomely not to say uncivill accidents which soe frequently

64

disturb the Peace of many families'. He distinguishes between the 'two degrees of Wedlock, Spousalls and marriage', and remarks that Hesiod would have the woman sixteen and the man thirty, while Plato and Aristotle prefer eighteen and thirty-five; he cites the happy marriage of Caius Cecilia and Tarquinius Priscus, and concludes that 'the perfect friendship cannot be between more than two'. He also dilates upon the 'Society Paternal' and praises country life, so much appreciated by the Romans: while Cyrus, King of Persia took delight in planting trees and the great philosopher Seneca daily 'made fishponds with his own hands'. Turning to 'conjugal offices', he advises that 'both should mutually pass by the infirmities of each', and denies that a husband ought to 'correct his wife's exorbitancy by stripes'. Wives should never be sluttish or improper, but thrifty, industrious and charitable; while combining their sweetness with modesty and convenient authority over the children. All these exacting standards Mary Evelyn would maintain.

Though Evelyn wrote that at first he had no more idea of making her his wife than of 'diving for pearls on Salisbury Plain', the match proved a great success: fastidious, difficult but kindly, he was probably better suited for a young girl whom he could guide and educate than for a worldly and spirited woman of his own age, while her father, the royalist ambassador, though heavily in debt, had high social standing. As ambassador he had helped Evelyn recover goods stolen by a French valet, and they had humanely combined to avert the death penalty incurred by the thief. Evelyn, comparatively wealthy, made a desirable son-in-law in need and the girl's mother had favoured the match. It was not quite the financially advantageous marriage which might well have been arranged over John's head by his father, had he survived, but it was made by his own initiative out of affection for a girl of 'early steadiness' who, 'at the age of playing with babies would be at her book', into a congenial family of good standing.

## II

By September 1647, after nearly four years abroad, John needed to settle his affairs in England; on 4 October, leaving his young wife with her mother after having declared and sealed his Will, and travelling by Rouen, Dieppe and St Valery, on the 11th he got safe to Dover, for which he 'heartily put up ... Thanks to God'. Hastening to London, he found horses awaiting him from Wotton, and next day rode down there to greet his brother. He made a point of kissing the hand of Charles I at Hampton Court, 'he being now in the power of [the army] those execrable Villains who not long after murder'd him'. He records the king's unruffled and still confident demeanour, which, as he wrote to his father-in-law, 'made him ride out this storm with so much assurance'.

Later in October he reconnoitred Sayes Court, Deptford, the Brownes' property, then in charge of William Prettyman, his wife's maternal uncle. It was an old timbered manor house of eighteen rooms, set in an estate worth £453 a year. Thence, by way of the Middle Temple and Wotton, where George had now married Mary Ottley, his second wife, John visited his younger brother Richard at neighbouring Baynards. John had bought some miniatures and a fine chimneypiece with water colours by Breughel from Sir Clepesby Crew, formerly MP for Downton, Wiltshire, and was interested in the chancy market in land following the sales and confiscations of the Civil War. By May 1648 he had sold his interest in South Malling in Sussex for £3,000 and bought an estate at Hurcott in Worcestershire from George for £3,300.

The Second Civil War now broke out, and before attacking Maidstone the royalists made their first rendezvous near Sayes Court; though John continued sitting for his picture by 'that excellent painter' Robert Walker, and found time to kill a buck. But he observed the royalist rebels' chances closely and sent a discouraging report to the ambassador in Paris about their incompetent leaders and their quarrels, 'the Royal party engaging themselves in all places so preposterously, that it is now conceived it will be no difficulty to weed them out'.[2] In August, meanwhile, Richard made an affluent marriage to the co-heiress of George Mynne of Woodcote Park near Epsom. By September John was showing them Sayes Court and Greenwich, and spent the autumn between Sayes Court, Woodcote and Lewes, where he visited his family property at Cliff.

In spite of the bitter Second Civil War, these well-to-do crypto-royalist gentry remained unmolested, but early in December 1648, when the king had been taken from the Isle of Wight to the gloom of Hurst Castle on the Solent, John wrote to his father-in-law in Paris signing '*Aplanos*',[3]

It is (as imagined) the general sense and inclination of the forces (now sufficiently at liesure) to think on mischief, chastise the citty and cudgell the Parliament for daring to treat with the King who standeth so ill in their *bonnes graces*.

'The grandees here,' he had already written, 'will push it to the uttermost and make a bloody catastrophe, if the Scots be but resolute, for they are so affrighted at what they have done that they can neither look back nor advance ... they will certainly run where their treasure is'.[4] Indeed, on the eve of Pride's Purge of the Commons, John was expecting a *coup*: 'You will shortly hear of Cromwell's vision, and how on Friday night last he being stricken blind for ... four hours, during which he held a Conference with God, persuading him to adjust with the Holy Agitators, he next day put it in execution.'

On 6 December Pride's Purge would remove the last vestige of constitutional authority from the parliament, and John was selling Hurcott for £3,400, netting £100. He was now, he wrote to his father-in-law, 'quite off from purchasing till times were better and the lands now coming on us afresh' more 'supportable': he then recorded how by Pride's Purge the parliament had been 'surpriz'd by the rebell Army', and 'the members dispers'd, and great confusion everywhere in expectation of what would be next',[5] and on 19 December he wrote in utter discouragement,[6]

I wish you could advise me how I may prevent my absolute ruin as to some part of my fortune, which I would willingly dispose in some more peaceful and sober corner of the earth. Sir, I am altogether confus'd and sad for the misery that is upon us.

He had already been horrified at hearing a debate of the Army Council under Ireton, between 'young, raw ill spoken officers', who were discussing Lilburn's *Agreement of the People*; he had heard 'horrid villanies' and rightly feared anarchy if such people gained power. He also heard the 'rebell Peters' preaching 'to incite the Rebell powers in the painted Chamber to destroy his Majestie', and saw 'the Arch Trayter Bradshawe, who not long after condemn'd him'.

During January 1649, as a mild winter turned bitter cold, royalists and crypto-royalists were helpless while the judicial murder of Charles I was carried through; on 30 January John recorded

The Villanie of the Rebells proceeding now so far as to Trie, Condemn, and *Murder* our excellent King, the 30 of this moneth struck me with such horror that I kept the day of his *Martyrdom* a fast, and could not be present, at that execrable wickednesse.

George, with stronger nerves, had witnessed the tragedy, and given John all the circumstances of the occasion. But two days later, his artistic enthusiasm unimpaired, John was inspecting a collection of pictures already dispersed from the king's collections.


## III


During the crisis of January 1649, John had, in fact, risked striking a blow for the king. On 21 January he had published a strongly royalist preface to his translation of *De la Liberté et Servitude* by a well-known and tedious political theorist, François de la Mothe le Vayer.[7] When the English army commanders and their political allies were about to behead their sovereign, a translation of a monarchical French political theorist fell rather flat, but John, in his preface, had indeed taken a small risk. Liberty, he had pointed out, was not merely an 'uncontrolled ball' exhibited to the people and then thrown into the hands of a few private persons, nor was it a mere Platonic chimera. It can be and has been realized. There is naturally in life no absolute perfection, but not for five thousand years has there been a 'more equal and excellent form of government than that under which we have lived during the reign of our Gracious Sovereign'. So why should we, 'in those halcyon days the happiest of subjects, now make ourselves the "most miserable of Slaves" '. 'God is one; it is better to obey One than many.'[8]

The preface, signed *Phileleutheros*, was garnished with Latin verses by the veteran Scots divine Alexander Ross, who would afterwards write *Leviathan Drawn Out with a Hook*; or *Animadversions upon Mr Hobbes his Leviathan*.[9] Evelyn's own translation was dedicated as 'the first time of my approach upon the theatre', to his brother George.

He had, in fact, chanced upon the treatise itself in Paris and translated it for practice in the winter of 1646–7. It was a pedantic defence of the absolute monarchy of young Louis XIV, 'the Just', and dedicated to Mazarin. 'Liberty,' it begins, 'is desired by all creatures', and Philostratus asserts that even the elephant, the most obedient of all animals to mankind, 'cannot forebear in the night time to deplore his servitude'; that humane 'Chineses' out of sheer devotion purchase fish, simply to set them free, and that even the Fallen Angels desired liberty, not equality with God. It follows that man of all creatures ought to be the freest. In fact he is not.[10]

Liberty has, indeed, been won from slavery in most Christian lands, but not always of spirit, and most people remain slaves to ambition, avarice, gluttony and lust. The ideas of Plato are Utopian, and the Stoics Diogenes and Seneca desired the impossible. There never can be any absolute freedom. Since, therefore, political subjection is inevitable, we all ought quietly to acquiesce in the life that providence has determined, particularly in the good government of Louis the Just, best of all princes.

In the raucous English pamphleteering of the time the longing for liberty of the elephant could hardly count for much, and both translation and preface were soon sunk without trace; but Evelyn afterwards claimed in pencil on the fly leaf of his own copy of this, his first publication, 'I was like to be call'd in question by the Rebels for this book, being publish'd a few days before his Majestie's decollation.' In his *Diary* he even records that he was 'severely threaten'd'.[11]

## IV

Although the official inventory of the king's goods and pictures was only ratified on 4 July 1649, when an Act was passed for them to be sold, John was already writing in February that the republican government were selling some of them: for 'now they had plunder'd sold and dissipated a world of rare Paintings of the Kings and his Loyale Subjects'. He had already seen at the Exchange 'some rare things in miniature of Breugls' plundered from Sir John Palmer, father of the first Earl of Castlemaine; Dutch and French dealers were already at work, and Jan van Belkamp, an under-copyer of the king's pictures, had shown John a copy of 'his Majesties Venus Sleeping, and the Satyre, by Correggio'; he was also shown a head of Sir Thomas More by Holbein and pictures of Queen Elizabeth, Henry VIII and Francis I – that of Henry VIII by Holbein and 'rare indeed'. Already the 'art world' was anticipating the dispersal of the great royal collection.

But though now provisionally established in part of Sayes Court, John wanted to return to Paris, where the disturbances of the first Fronde threatened to cut off his wife and her parents from England. William Prettyman, returning by devious ways, had been robbed by Dunkirk pirates and lost some of Evelyn's own property, including a treasured portrait of his wife. Now the Grand Condé was blockading rebellious Paris on behalf of the Queen Regent and Louis XIV.

There was not much to keep Evelyn in England. Under the republican regime Anglican services were put down or furtively conducted. 'I heard Common Prayer,' he records, 'at St Peters Paules Warf Lond:', and archbishop Ussher of Armagh had to preach in the chapel of Lincoln's Inn. But by April 1649 John felt it safe to make an inventory of 'moveables' hitherto 'dispersed for feare of Plundering'.[12] In May he also bought in one of his mother-in-law's properties, the manor of Warley Magna between Brentford and Hornchurch in Essex; it cost £2,500 and he later settled it on his wife, hoping to keep the property in the family. But he could not avoid the public outrages of the government. They were such that some royalist hopes even revived. Friction developed between the grandees of the army and the Levellers led by John Lilburne, now deservedly in prison; 'The levelling distemper', Evelyn informed Sir Richard, had 'epidemically spread'; it was even rumoured that the Levellers might support a restoration of Charles II – arguing that if they had to be 'slaves' they had 'better be slaves to him that hath the right', not to fellow subjects, and that, if free, 'they could in a month make a great mutation' and 'call great ones to account'. They might even 'incline to a monarchy strictly regulated'. But, John reflected, 'how facile a thing it [was] to deceive the credulous Cavalier. In his hope he hugs himself, sits still and expects.'[13]

On 30 May 1649 the 'Parliament Act', abolishing the monarchy was formally proclaimed by the Lord Mayor and Aldermen of London, when, as John put it, 'was un-King-ship proclaim'd and His Majestie's Statues throwne downe at St Paule's portico and Exchange'. Then, on 13 June, they celebrated the pompous funeral of Isaac Dorislaus, the Dutch jurist from Alkmaar who had prosecuted Charles I in the 'Court of Justice' at Westminster, and been clubbed to death in Holland by royalist exiles when negotiating an alliance between the English Republic and the Dutch – 'the villain who managed the Triall against his sacred Majestie slaine at the Hague'.

To keep up his spirits, John 'went to Putney by Water in a Barge with divers ladies' to a dinner given by the royalist Colonel Sir John Owen formerly governor of Ruaban castle who in March had been reprieved from execution after leading a rising for Charles I, and where one Carew 'playd incomparably on the Welsh harp'.

In Paris the troubles of the first Fronde had now subsided, and having held his Manor Court at Warley, on 17 June John got a pass from the 'Rebel' Bradshawe, President of the Council of State and, collecting Richard from Woodcote, rode to Wotton. The three brothers then 'went all to be merry at Guildford', and by 12 July, having collected bills of exchange in London, John took oars for Gravesend and, riding through the night for Dover, next evening boarded a barque for France. It was guarded by a pinnace of eight guns, and a threatening pirate sheered off, so after a night of seasickness, John arrived at dawn at Calais.

Though he lost another spaniel, 'taken up, I suppose, by the Souldiers', the war continuing between France and Spain after the main Peace of Westphalia had been concluded, and the passengers in the coach having to 'walk with our Guns ready, in all suspected places', John arrived safely at Paris.

Here he was warmly welcomed at a dinner party which included the highest royalist officials – Lord Cottington, the High Treasurer, Lord Clarendon, the Lord Chancellor, Sir Edward Nicholas and Sir George Cartaret, governor of Jersey. John had not seen his wife for more than a year and a half, so they were very 'cheerful' and 'the rest of the Weeke taken up by visites from, and to my friends'.


V


While in England Evelyn had to lurk about to find Anglican services celebrated; in Paris the close little community of eminent refugees made a point of observing the religion for which, they held, Charles I had died a martyr, and welcomed Evelyn as a man of substance who supported their cause; indeed this intimacy, now habitual, would make him welcome after the Restoration at the court of Charles II. It seems strange that Bradshaw had allowed him to leave England to join a defiantly royalist ambassador in Paris; but the richer English gentry, if outwardly conformist, were seldom molested by the republican authorities, now anxious to conciliate the social establishment and so legitimize their own power.

Already thoroughly cosmopolitan, John Evelyn in 1649 was happier in royalist circles in Paris than under the shadow of an English Republic at home, and glad to have the Anglican chapel at the embassy to hand, 'where my Wife received with me the H. Sacrament the first time'. On 18 August he went to St Germain to kiss the hand of Charles II, travelling in the same coach with Henry Wilmot, first Earl of Rochester, victor in 1643 of Roundway Down, and with the young king's mistress, Lucy Walter, 'a browne, beautifull, bold, but insipid creature', prospective mother of James Scott, afterwards Duke of Monmouth, born the following spring in Rotterdam. Evelyn also paid his respects to Louis XIV and the Dowager Queen of France, and, when again at St Germain, to kiss the hand of the Queen Mother of England, saw 'divers great Monsieurs that came to visit his Majestie, including the Grand Condé'. It was now 'even nois'd about' that Evelyn was knighted, 'a dignity I often declin'd'. Doubtless more to his mind, he inspected a small chateau designed by Mansart for the Marquis de Maisons:

the Gardens very magnificent, with extraordinary long Walkes set with Elmes, and a noble Prospect on the *Sienne* towards Paris, but above all, what pleased me, the Artificial Harbour cut out of the River. The house is well furnish'd, and it may compare with any Villa about Rome.

From Ireland there now came an ominous rumble of Drogheda being taken by the (republican) rebels and all being put to the sword, 'which made us very sad, forerunning the losse of all *Ireland*'; but John enjoyed a lecture by Dr Davison, Prefect of the Physical Garden and Professor Botanicus, and attended the funeral of one Mr Downes, a sober English gent, at Charenton, where he was 'buried in a Cabbage-Garden'.

In November he attended with his father-in-law, now a baronet, on his audience at the French Court, where as ambassador he delivered new credentials from Charles II. Louis XIV and the regent received them with marked graciousness in the Palais Cardinal, built by Richelieu, and John was much taken with the gallery adorned with portraits of 'all the most illustrious persons, and signal actions in *France*'; but the young king, for once taking a spontaneous pleasure, became 'buisie in seeing a Bull-baiting', so John left him to it. Though 'it had been a very sickly and mortal autumn', he thankfully 'concluded this yeare in health'.

## VI

In 1647 John had already written a singularly able and perceptive account of the *State of France* (London, 1652) of which the introductory advice to 'young gents apt for all impressions' of travel has already been cited.[14] What, he asks, in France's situation and government has raised it to such 'national lustre'? And he analyses the French monarchy, 'absolute', he considered, 'since Lewis XI', its military, administrative and fiscal resources, in their strength and weakness. He then portrays French society as it appeared to an Englishman, an account which shows how constant many French characteristics have long remained.

The royal power having emerged from the wars with the English, the monarch, he observes, is still heavily and constantly guarded: by the ornamental King's Company of Gentlemen, by the hundred Scots archers – the 'Guard de la Manch', now much diluted by recruiting from the French – by the Swiss Guard of that grim nation in sixteen companies, and by the horse musketeers from the prime youth of the nobility. Louis XIII had been so particular or 'physiologically punctual' in their election that it was reported 'he would admit no musketeers with red hair'. Surrounded by this variety of royal guards, 'the Great Monarch is environed with men of iron wherever he goes', and sustained by an intensely martial tradition.

The revenues are derived from various 'douanes', and from the salt taxes which together produce 'monstrous treasure', and all are organized by '*bureaux*' (from 'stuff of that name') under a Superintendant of Finance; but the nobility and clergy enjoy an exemption from taxes which ours in England have 'never so much tasted of'.[15] Policy is executed through a Council of State, at the summit by a cabinet or 'upstairs' Council, below, by one subordinate, decisions being ratified by parliament 'in name only', and though there are regional parliaments as well as a central one, they are concerned with legal matters, not high policy. The military and naval establishments are also directly under the Crown.

Yet, Evelyn observes, in spite of this apparently absolute power, since the death of Richelieu 'the Government of France does rather totter than stand',[16] and it is subject to women and favourites. The great nobles in their wealth and pride contrast with a populace he considers 'naturally slavish', and spend the revenues of their vast estates on luxurious ostentation in Paris; they are urban-minded and compete in building Parisian palaces, while the local *noblesse* of Normandy, Bretagne, Provence and Gascony are provincial and litigious. All the *noblesse* of whatever standing scorn even the professions and 'no gent in France will bind his sons to any trade or mechanique art whatsoever other than the military life'. Hence a social chasm unknown in England.

On the other hand, the French Catholics seem an indifferent [tolerant] sort of Christian; not so precise and bigoted as those in Spain or Italy; and the Protestants, though now with little power, do not harbour so many schismatic sects as do their English equivalents.

As to their armed forces, the French have an excellent strategic position, but have not sufficiently developed their navy, since at sea Francis I had relied too much on that 'stout miscreant', the Turk. Their strength is on land, and greatest in cavalry – 'what incomparable souldiers this country hath in all ages bred!' They hold that any youth of quality should have been in battle by eighteen, and make a cult of military 'gymnastics' and of the management of the horse. Moreover, by their prolific multiplying the French provide 'abundant victuals for the belly of that cruel beast call'd Warr'. They also have excellent artillery, and strong forts on their frontiers. Their weakness is that they are too impulsive, indeed, as Machiavelli observed, 'those who would vanquish the French should be sure to withstand and break their first brusk and onset'.

They are also 'egregious talkers', and as 'trim wits' as the Italians, though one should beware of their physicians who think bleeding their patients 'the panacea for all diseases' and so enervate the body more than the disease. One should distrust these French 'leaches'.

French children are misleadingly attractive: 'angels' in the cradle, 'devils in the saddle', and though the women of quality may be exquisite beauties, most French women's looks do not last. Their well-born youths do not seem so literate as the Dutch or the English, and are less inquisitive about travel; nor are they so debauched as the English about drink, tobacco and gaming. They all love good bread – 'nor will a true Monsieur be brought at any rate to taste a glass of wine *sans premier manger*'. But if 'the best eat like Princes, the Commons eat worse than dogs'.

They are very polite and far from 'the constrained address of our sullen nation, who never think themselves acquainted till they treat each other with Jack and Tom', but they are so quick in the uptake that they 'imagine to comprehend all upon an instant' and are thus apt to be dogmatic and superficial. They have a natural dread and hate of the English, and their antipathy to the Spaniard is deadly. Underneath their civility they have 'little charity when they see no evident interest'. They are a short people and, save in the north and east, mostly dark; their passions, of course, are 'mercurial'.

Relating them again to their politics, Evelyn concludes that they are the 'only nation in Europe to idolize their sovereign', to whom they have freer access than other peoples; but they are fickle, and 'if their Choler is stirred there never wants some Raviliac – or cut throat'.[17]

During his stay in France, John Evelyn had not missed much.

CHAPTER EIGHT

# Paris: Sayes Court

In January 1650 Paris was again threatened by the second bout of the Fronde when the Grand Condé turned against the Regency and failed: but after his return Evelyn was mainly concerned with concerts, masquerades and riding competitions, and with inspecting Francis I's palace which he had called 'Madrid' to save his oath to Charles V, 'equivocating that he would not go out of Madrid without leave'. John also watched an operation for a stone taken out 'bigger than a turky's Egg. The manner thus: The sick creature [aged forty] was strip'd to his shirt, and bound armes and thighs to an high Chaire, 2 men holding his shoulders fast down: then the Chirurgian with a crooked Instrument prob'd til he hit on the stone' and 'made Incision thro' the *Scrotum* about an Inch in length'. Having 'put in his forefingers to get the stone as neere the orifice of the wounde as he could, then with another instrument like a Crane's neck', he pulled it out, 'with incredible torture ... especially at his after raking so unmercifully up and downe the bladder with a 3d Instrument: The effusion of blood is greate.'[1] Not surprisingly, the danger was of fever and gangrene.

The next patient, a boy of eight or nine, stood the operation cheerfully, 'expressing great joy, when he saw the stone was drawn'. John does not record whether either patient survived; merely thanks God 'he had not ben subject to this Infirmitie', as the reader may well do for not having to face a seventeenth-century operation.

Paris then also presented other risks. When John, his wife and Lady Browne, along with the Second Earl of Chesterfield and Lord Ossory, made an expedition to 'Vamber' near Paris, Ossory had trespassed into a garden and struck a man on the head who had tried to turn him out. The party, defending themselves with swords, were then chased by an 'armed concourse of the baser sort' into a 'turret'. All the English suffered minor casualties, until the assailants, realizing that they were not merely Parisian

76

bourgeois but 'persons of quality', began to waver: meanwhile one of the party, having escaped to Paris, had brought the bailiff of St Germain with his guard 'to rescue us; which he did'. The affair was patched up; under pressure from the Court, the owner of the garden was made to apologize to the Resident Ambassador, and the ringleader punished. Ossory would afterwards affirm that in all his conflicts on land and sea, he had never been in such danger and 'used to call it the *Bataill de Vambre* and remember it with a greate deal of Mirth as an Adventure *en Cavaliere*.'[2]

## II

In June John was sitting to the portrait engraver Robert Nanteuil, who made him the most attractive of any of the portraits of him, as well as drawing his wife and her parents. But by the end of the month he had briefly to return to England on business. Setting out in a well-armed company of seventeen 'Portugezes, Swisse and French', he got to Calais in three days, intact save that his face peeled from the sun.

In London, 'having a mind to see what doings was among the rebells', now in full possession of Whitehall, he found one of their clergy 'at exercise' in the chapel 'after their way', and another of that persuasion preaching at St James's. Since May 1649 England had been officially a 'Commonwealth' or 'Free State'; but Charles II had now appeared in Scotland, so round Epsom and Wotton the country was 'much molested by Souldiers who tooke away Gentlemen's horses for the Service of the State as then call'd'.[3]

But at Wotton normal life continued: at the end of July John was hardy enough to bathe one evening in the pond, 'after I had not for many years ben in cold Water'. He visited Richard at Woodcote, and his sister, Jane Glanville, who now had a son.

Then on 12 August 1650 he again set out for France. 'Surpriz'd at Canterbury by the Souldiers', and 'having onely an antiquated passe', he managed 'with some fortunate dexterity' to get clear of them. But 'not without extraordinary hazard, having before counterfaited one with successe', 'it being so difficult to procure one of the Rebells without entering into oathes, which I never would do'. At Dover, however, 'Mony to the Searcher and officers was as authentique as the hand and Seale of *Bradshaw* himself', and 'I had not so much as my Trunk open'd.'[4]

The sea was more malignant; leaving Dover at six p.m., they were not off Calais until five the next morning, and, making for the harbour in a long boat, they were nearly sunk by huge seas: sea-sick and 'neer the middle up in Water', John was lucky to get to Calais and go at once to bed, for once 'sufficiently discompos'd'.


## III


The French war with Spain continuing, after the Peace of Münster had settled Germany, the Spanish troops from the Netherlands had now pushed further into France, and the countryside was worse disordered. So taking up with a company of horse and foot of the regiment of Picardy, John and his servant made their way under their protection to Boulogne, 'though 'twas a miserable spectacle to see how these tatter'd souldiers pillag'd the poore people of their Sheepe, poultry, Corne, Catell ... but they had such ill pay, that they were ready themselves to sterve.' Even at St Denis the people were 'running with their goods ... to Paris ... so miserably expos'd was even this part of France at this time'.

During Cromwell's campaign in Scotland, the English royalists had been further persecuted, and Paris, indeed all France, was full of loyal fugitives. The ambassador's Anglican chapel, with its regular royalist sermons, was one of their rallying points. But John found time to take his wife and friends to the Chateau Maisons, with its incomparable prospect on the river and towards the forest, so to 'take it alltogether', he had hardly seen 'anything in Italy to exceede it'. He returned to Dean Cosin preaching on the psalms, and 'shewing upon what occasions Cursing was lawful', though, on the Duke of York's own chaplain, John had to write 'This Gent: has not the talent for preaching.'

He particularly enjoyed the Palais d'Orléans with its gilded roof and parquet floor: 'I have seldom seene a looking glasse of so large a size.' He also got into fast if distinguished company – dining with 'my lord Stanhop where we drank too liberally', and shooting for a wager of five louis d'or (17s. each) with Sir Thomas Osborne, afterwards Earl of Danby. The English Consul at Aleppo also told him of the Bedouin Arabs cutting the throats of their own corrupted daughters themselves, and how artful they all were at concealing desert wells. They dwelt in long weather-proof black tents of wool-like felt and their safety was in their excellent horses.

Early in February 1651, as the second crisis of the Fronde mounted, Cardinal Mazarin was banished from France to the Electorate of Cologne. He would not return to permanent power until 1653, and two years after that, he would conclude peace with the English republic. Meanwhile the course of archaic French justice rolled on, using torture to procure confession. In March John visited the Chastlett prison, where they bound a supposed malefactor's wrists with a small cable fastened to an iron ring four feet from the floor, then the feet with another looser one, attached to another ring opposite. They then slid one 'horse' of wood under the second rope which horribly stretched the victim's legs, then another. But knowing that confession meant execution, the 'malefactor' refused to confess. Whereat the executioner with a horn 'such as they drench horses with' stuck the end into his mouth and poured in two buckets full of water, 'which so prodigiously swell'd him, face, Eyes ready to start, brest and all his limbs as would have pittied and almost affrited one to see it.' For all this, the supposed culprit denied the charge. He had to be taken down, warmed and revived. The lieutenant in charge said he had always expected that this 'leane dry black young man' would 'conquer the Torture', and escape hanging. He would go to the galleys. With a humanity rare at the time, John found this spectacle too uncomfortable to stay and watch another.

In September, turning to a less uncomfortable side of life, he called on Mr Hobbes, 'the famous *Philosopher* of Malmesbury, with whom [he] had long acquaintance', and they both watched the cavalcade of the thirteen-year-old Louis XIV passing to parlement where he first took the kingly government upon him, 'as now out of *Minority*'. Presumably with approval, Hobbes watched this display of princely power, with the 'Swisse in black Velvet *toques* led by 2 gallant Cavalieres habited in scarlet colour'd Satin after their Country fashion, which is very fantastick', then the Heralds and Marshals of the nobility, and the King's Escuyer, alone, carrying the king's sword in a scarf which 'he held-up in a blew sheath studded with flor de lyss'; then the king's footmen and pages. Louis himself, 'like a young Apollo, in a sute so covered with rich embrodry that one could perceive nothing of the stuff under it', rode hat in hand 'saluting the Ladys and Acclamators'. Indeed he seemed a 'Prince of a grave, yet sweete countenance'.

Back in the Anglican chapel, Dr Steward preached on 'the blessedness resulting from the right use of persecution'; but on the 22 September 1651 came the delayed news of the defeat of Charles II at 'the fatal battle of Worcester, which exceedingly mortified our expectations'.

John now decided that since Charles II's campaign had failed, there was no hope of a Restoration in the foreseeable future, and, like Hobbes, he determined to return to England and make the best of the republic.

Having discussed chemistry with the famous Sir Kenelm Digby and concluded that he was an 'errant mountebank', and leaving the Anglican chaplain to preach, following His Majestie's personal deliverance after Worcester, on patience under affliction, and a congratulatory sermon on the Powder Conspiracy, John made up his accounts, sent away his goods by Rouen, and late in January 1652, set out by coach to Calais in an extraordinarily hard frost through deep snow in country plundered by soldiers and infested by wolves. He then, for fear of pirates, had to wait until several large vessels could depart together, until at last he arrived at Dover in darkness on the evening of 6 February, by English reckoning still 28 January.

Exhausted, he rested three days at Sayes Court, then went to London, saw the 'Magnificent Funeral of that arch Rebell Ireton', and returned to see about 'settlements', no more intending to go out of England, but to[5]

endeavor a settled life, either in this place, or some other, there being now so little appearance of any change for the better, all being intirely in the rebells hands, and this particular habitation, and the Estate contiguous to it (belonging to my F in law, actualy in his Majestie's service) very much suffering, for want of some friend, to rescue it out of the power of the Usurpers;

and so

to preserve our Interest, and to take some care of my other Concernes, by the advise, and favour of my Friends, I was advis'd to reside in it, and compound with the Souldiers; being besides, authorized by his Majestie so to do … I had also addresses and Cyfers to correspond with his Majestie and Ministers abroad,

Evelyn thus endeavoured to make the best of both private interest and public duty.

## IV

He was now thirty-one, and tired of a nomadic life; 'having now run about the World, most part out of my owne country neere 10 yeares'. Like his contemporary, Aubrey, he was thoroughly English; even romantic about the old English way of life. He wanted to strike roots in a conservative society, still redolent, as he later wrote, of 'the days of our fathers, simple plain men as they were who courted and chose their wives for their modesty'; where girls could care for 'cupboards of ancient useful plate, chests of damask for the table and store of fine Holland sheets fragrant of Rose and Lavender for the Bed', and 'youths could sing old Simon, Chevy Chase, and dance Brave Arthur, and drawe a bow that made a proud Monsieur tremble at the whizze of a grey goose feather'.[6] After ten years abroad, this may even have still been the sort of England in which John hoped to settle down, to raise a family and to leave an enhanced inheritance to his heir.

Meanwhile he went down to Wotton, where he helped George and his second wife, Mary Offley, to set his garden in order, long neglected during the Civil Wars, and they 'levelled that noble area where now the garden and fountains are'. By 1 March 1652 George, ever a man of peace, showed his brother a copy of Cromwell's Act of Oblivion to all who would submit to the government, and by mid-March John was writing to his wife in Paris concerning 'my resolution of settling'. Next day after a course of devastating physic, he was let no less than nine ounces of blood, to prevent, he believed, his usual spring afflictions of swelling in the throat and piles. But he was now more sceptical about astronomy than medicine: by the end of the month all England had been so terrified by an eclipse of the sun that 'hardly any would worke, none stir out of their houses; so ridiculously,' he wrote, 'were they abused by knavish and ignorant star-gazers'.[7]

Back in Sayes Court in May, John learnt that his wife Mary was with child, and called on his old school-fellow, Colonel Morley, 'now one of their Council of State', to obtain a pass for Mary's return with her goods to England. This was 'courteously granted' – in an early example of the English 'old boy' network – and letters granted as well to the officials at Rye to show her every civility.

John then went down to Rye himself, where, playing bowls on the green, he 'discover'd a vessel' which, when it arrived that

evening, proved to be his wife's. It had taken three days in the
crossing and, mistaken for a fishing boat, apparently passed
through the whole hostile Dutch fleet, now, in the First Dutch
War, defying the English Commonwealth.

John, Mary and Lady Browne made for Tunbridge Wells,
where John left them to ride himself on to Sayes Court to
prepare it for their reception. But, riding alone in hot weather
near Bromley, he was set upon by two cut-throats who, striking
with long staves at his horse and seizing the reins, threw him
down and snatched his sword. They dragged him into a thicket
and stole two rings, one of emerald and diamonds, the other of
onyx with his coat of arms, as well as two ruby and diamond
shoe buckles. Always reasonable, John pointed out that the onyx
would be unsaleable; but in vain; the 'lusty foot padders' tied
him up and made off. Grievously tormented by flies and ants,
John managed to wriggle free and regain his horse and the
highway, then rode at once to a local 'Great Justiciary', Colonel
Sir Thomas Blunt, near Blackheath, who immediately sent out a
hue and cry. Next morning in London, John immediately had
five hundred tickets printed and distributed at Goldsmiths Hall
describing the lost jewellery. Thanks to the amateurishness of the
'foot padders' and John's own prompt action after escape,
within two days the jewels were retrieved, and John thanked God
for his deliverance. Such were the risks of seventeenth-century
travel near Bromley, particularly for anyone wearing diamond
and ruby shoebuckles.

John later magnanimously refused to appear in court against
one of the robbers, 'not willing to hang the fellow', who was
reprieved. Afterwards, accused of another crime but refusing to
plead, he was 'press'd to death' – a fate worse than hanging.

At the end of July, John went to London for advice about
purchasing his father-in-law's interest in Sayes Court. In 1649 the
house and manor had been seized by the Commonwealth
government, and in 1650 the house sold to a William
Somersfield; Evelyn now planned to buy him out, having been
promised by Charles II the fee farm of the estate in perpetuity if
it ever reverted to the Crown.

John now had greater need of a settled home: on 24 August
1652 Mary gave birth to their first son, soon christened Richard
after both his grandfathers. But a month later Lady Browne died
of scarlet fever at Woodcote, to be buried by special permission
with 'decent' (Anglican) rites at Deptford, and 'thus ended an
excellent and virtuous lady'.

That Christmas, 'to that horrid pass were they come', there were no sermons anywhere and no Anglican church congregations permitted to meet; but Sayes Court was now, in effect, Evelyn's property and on 21 January 1653 he recorded 'I went to Lond: and sealed some of the Writings of my Purchase of Sayes Court.'

## V

He had already begun to[8]

set out the *Ovall Garden* ... which was before a rude *Ortchard*, and all the rest one intire fild of 100 *Ackers*, without any hedge: excepting the hither holly-hedge joyning to the bank of the mount walk: and this was the beginning of all the succeeding *Gardens*, *Walks*, *Groves*, Enclosures and Plantations there,

which afterwards attained such celebrity as 'exquisite, being most bocaresque, and as it were an exemplar of his book on Forest Trees'. He also records thankfully that at Deptford 'now and then' an honest orthodox man got into the pulpit, and that even the present incumbent, 'though some what Independent, ordinarily preached sound doctrine and was a peaceable man', which was 'an extraordinary felicity in this age'.

On 1 February 1653 'Old Alex Rosse' presented Evelyn with his Book against Mr Hobbes's *Leviathan*: on the 19th, Evelyn recorded in a famous phrase 'planted the *Ortchard* at *Says Court*, *New Moone*, *wind West*'. Then, at last, on 22 February 'was perfected the *sealing*, *livery* and *sesin* of my Purchase of Says Court': It had cost £3,500, £300 more than he had bargained for, and he celebrated the occasion by a dinner party. But early in March he nearly died of 'five fits of a feverish Ague'; then, convalescent and taking the air in Hyde Park in his coach, he had to pay a 'shill: and horse 6d. by the sordid fellow who had purchas'd [the park] from the State, as they were cald'.

By June he was well enough to visit the neighbouring house of Sir Henry Newton, built by his father, secretary to the late Prince Henry the eldest son of James I, and

consider the Prospect, which (after *Constantinople*) is doubtless for Citty, river, Ships Meadows, hill, Woods and all other distinguishable amenities, the most noble the whole World has to shew: so as had the house running water, it were a princely seate.

By August John even risked beginning a course of 'yearely

washing my head with Warme Water, mingl'd with a decoction
of Sweete herbs, and immediately, with cold Spring water, which
much refresh'd me, and succeeded very well with me divers
yeares'.[9] He also took Mary for the first time to Wotton to divert
her after her mother's death, over which she was still
melancholy.

But it was hard to avoid the prevalent religious conflict. That
autumn at Deptford Evelyn was disgusted when a fanatical
'mechanic' preached in 'our Church' on the lurid text from 2
Samuel 23.20, '*and Banaiah ... went downe also and slew a lion in the
midst of a pit, in the time of Snow*', and concluded that all dangers
should be risked when 'the Saints were call'd to destroy
temporal Governments, with such truculent (anabaptistical)
stuff.' Only in the privacy of his library could some sequestered
Anglican clergyman celebrate the rites on which John relied and
preach the sort of sermon that he approved.

Not that Cromwell scorned impressive public ritual. On 8
February, Ash Wednesday, 1654 'In Contradiction to all
Costome and decency, the Usurper *Cromwell* feasted at the L
Majors, riding in Triumph through the Citty';[10] but property,
the most essential consideration, was now relatively secure: on
the 13th Richard, Evelyn's younger brother, could repay him
£1,000, and next day Evelyn, in high spirits, visited a tame lion –
'I thrust my hand into his mouth, and felt his tongue rough like a
Catts'. In March 1654 he even ordered a new coach, and in May
he bound his lackey Thomas Heath apprentice to a carpenter,
giving him, with his usual generosity, £5 and new clothes; the
youth, he afterwards recorded, would thrive and prosper.

And social amenities continued, though 'Cromwell and his
partizans having shut and seized on Spring Gardens', the
Mulberry Garden was the only 'place of refreshment for persons
of the best quality': John was twice entertained there and his
hosts were grossly overcharged. So, under the 'rebel' regime the
pleasures of fashionable life continued.

Evelyn's representative obstinacy in carrying on an
accustomed way of life under the Protectorate shows at least the
resilience of the English social establishment, and how they
scorned the upstart rebels; if deeply worried at the abolition of
the Anglican ritual, they were not, save for a few provincial
gentry, as in the risings of Penruddock in Wiltshire and Booth in
Cheshire, romantically loyal enough to the Crown to risk their
lives and property: they would have been prepared, in the
English way, to compromise and muddle through. It was not the

conservatism of discreet royalists like Evelyn, but the breakdown of the military regime following the death of Oliver, when the strife of military grandees threatened property and order, that forced royalists and crypto-royalists alike to discover that the only solution was the one they had despaired of, and incredulously to welcome an entirely unexpected Restoration of the monarchy which assimilated many former rebels into the establishment.

# CHAPTER NINE

# A Tour in England

Brought up in France, Mary Evelyn hardly knew England, and at the end of May 1654 John, having secured a family home at Sayes Court, took his young wife on a round of visits. When they arrived at Windsor in their new coach they found the view from the terrace towards Eton, 'with the Park, the meandring Thames and the swete Meadows', a delightful Prospect, and then apparently proceeded to Newbury, and that 'exceedingly beautiful seat of my Lord Pembroke's on the ascent of an hill, flank'd with woods and reguarding the river'. At Marlborough, the town 'having lately ben fired', had just been rebuilt, and at Lord Seamore's house,[1] on the site of the present College, they ascended the Mound. Apart from listening to any available sermons, the Evelyns were 'feasted and made good cheere' by many friends and relations welcoming Mary, and early in June they arrived in Bath. John bathed in the 'Crosse bathe' – 'only almost for the gentry' – 'trifled and bath'd and intervisited', and proceeded to Bristol – 'a city wholly Merchantile, as standing near the famous *Severne*, commodiously for *Ireland* and the Western World'. Then returning by Hungerford (already 'famous for its Troutes'), Evelyn drove back to Deptford, then down to Oxford to which Mary had proceeded direct. Here John was made much of by the dons, dined with Seth Ward, the Professor of Mathematics, in Wadham, and supped in Balliol 'where they made me extraordinarily wellcome'. Warden Wilkins also gave him 'a magnificent Entertainment in Waddum Hall', and he heard a concert in All Souls, where he visited 'that miracle of a Youth, Mr Christopher Wren'. Bodley's librarian showed both Evelyns a wealth of rare manuscripts, including an eight-hundred-year-old manuscript of the Venerable Bede's history, and in the anatomy school, the skin of a 'Juccal', and 'a rarely coloured Jacatroo [cockatoo?]' or 'prodigious large *Parot*'. At Magdalen, that stronghold of tradition, they found the library and chapel 'still in Pontifical order', with the double organ – an abomination to the Puritans – still intact, and even the organist playing it. What was more, Warden Wilkins showed them his '*Transparent Apiaries* ... very ornamental', and presented Evelyn with an empty one which he established at Sayes Court, which Charles II would 'come on purpose to see and contemplate'. It would also, naturally, appeal to Pepys. Wilkins displayed many artificial mathematical and magical curiosities as well; for example a 'Way-Wiser' for measuring distance travelled, and a thermometer, and Christopher Wren presented John with a 'piece of *White Marble* he had stained with a lively red very deepe'.

Then, 'satisfied with the Civilities of Oxford', the Evelyns drove by Faringdon (burnt during the siege of 1646) to Broadhinton in Wilts, and by 20 July were at Salisbury Cathedral – 'the compleatest piece of *Gothic*-Worke in Europe, taken in all its uniformitie'; then they visited Wilton House, in which 'the most observable are the Dining-roome in the modern built part toward the Garden, ... and divers rare Pictures'. 'But after all,' Evelyn wrote perceptively, 'that which to me renders the Seate delightfull, is its being so neere the downes and noble plaines about the Country and contiguous to it'.[2] At the Hare Warren on the Plain they coursed a hare for 'two miles in sight' towards Salisbury, and then explored the city itself. John found that the canals, though watered by a quick current, were negligently kept, though 'with small charge they could be ... rendred infinitely agreable'.

So they drove up the beautiful upper Avon valley to Great Durnford,[3] 'in a Vally under the Plaine', 'most sweetly water'd' and 'abounding' then as now, 'in Trowts', which were speared by night 'as they came wondring at a light set in the sterne'.[4] With pigeons, rabbits and fowl in plenty, the Evelyns had an excellent meal at an hour's warning, and 'passed on over that goodly plaine ... which I think for evennesse, extent, Verdure, innumerable flocks, to be one of the most delightfull prospects in nature', until they arrived at Stonehenge. John callously tested one of the great stones with a hammer, but 'found it so exceeding hard that all my strength ... could not breake a fragment'. No one had yet published any full study of Stonehenge, but Evelyn, as many after him, wondered how the stones had been brought there, though he realized that some were sarsen stones common near Marlborough: he thought that the bronze age barrows were 'places of burial after bloudy fights', and on departure for 'the Devizes' observed that

Stonehenge, then more intact, 'appears like a Castle at a distance'.[5]

From Devizes the Evelyns drove to Cricklade and over the Cotswolds to Gloucester – 'the Minster a noble fabric with the *Severne* gliding so sweetely by it'. It was now the beginning of August 1654, and they made their way through thick cider orchards to Worcester, where the cathedral had been 'extremely ruin'd by the late Warrs', and so across to Warwick where the castle appeared 'one of the most surprizing seates one should meete with', and so into Leicestershire, and open, rich, but unpleasantly featureless country, to Mary's uncle's house at Horninghold near Uppingham.

Accustomed to the south, John Evelyn thought nothing of this part of England 'where most of the rural parishes are but of mud, and the people living as wretchedly as in the most impoverish'd parts of *France*, which they much resemble, being idle and sluttish ... the Gentry great drinkers'. Leicester he thought 'despicably built, the Chimnies flues like so many smiths forges'.

They proceeded further, past Welbeck and Pontefract (in ruins since the Second Civil War) until they got to York:[6]

the 2d Citty of *England*, fairely Waled, of a Circular forme, Waterd by the brave river *Ouse*, bearing Vessels of Considerable burdens ... but most remarkeable and worthy seeing, is St *Peters* Cathedrall, which alone of all the greate Churches in England, has been best preserv'd from the fury of the sacrilegious by Composition with the Rebells, when they tooke the Citty.

Today when the approach to all considerable cities is blighted by mechanized traffic and its appurtenances, it is hard to realize how impressive they must then have appeared, and though Evelyn's coach would now seem hard going, he at least had time to appreciate an unpolluted countryside.

By Hull and Lincoln where the soldiers had 'lately knocked off all or most of the Brasses which were on the gravestones ... not sparing the monuments of the dead, so helish an avarice [not just fanaticism] possess'd them' – the Evelyns drove to Peterborough and, by 1 September, to Cambridge. Here they saw Trinity College, 'esteemed the fairest Quadrangle of any University in Europ', but as Evelyn oddly considered, far inferior to that of Christ Church, Oxford, though the fountain was 'graceful', the library pretty well stored, and Neville's Court cloistered and well built.

The chapel of King's he found 'altogether answerable to

expectations', especially the roof and the magnificent windows. From the roof they could see Ely and Royston, but Cambridge itself was situated in 'a low dirty unpleasant place, the streets ill paved, the aire thick, as infested by the fenns'. They proceeded by Audley End and Saffron Walden to London, and by 3 September to Sayes Court, after a laborious tour of 700 miles, 'for the variety an agreable refreshment'.

## II

Back at home, the Evelyns settled into a characteristic routine of family visiting, mild entertaining and a pertinacious analysis of sermons. On Advent Sunday (3 December 1654) John recorded 'there being no Office at the Church but extempore prayers after the *Presbyterian Way* ... and most of the Preachers Usurpers, I seldom went to *Church* upon solemn *Feasts*': instead he went to London to hear 'sequestered divines' read the Common Prayer, or procured one to officiate at Sayes Court. Christmas Day, too, he was 'constrained to celebrate ... at home'; but he thought it a special providence that next day they were not in church, for young Richard, aged two, swallowed a jagged piece of mutton bone, and his nurse swooned, losing 'any power to say what the Child ail'd, or call for any help.' At prayer below, the Evelyns heard an 'unusual groaning', rushed upstairs and found their child black in the face and choking: Evelyn held him upside down and on a sudden effort the little boy managed to cast out a sharp and angular fragment; 'Ô my Gracious God,' wrote his father, 'out of what a tender feare, and sad heart, into what Joy did Thy goodnesse now revive us!'[7]

On 14 January 1655 Mary bore another son, in fact the only one to survive childhood. He was christened John at Sayes Court by the Anglican rite. And Evelyn's own piety was now confirmed by friendship with the famous Dr Jeremy Taylor (1613–67), afterwards bishop of Down and Connor, and already author of the *Rules and Exercises of Holy Living* (1650) and the *Rules and Exercises of Holy Dying* (1651), both works which would have a vast circulation in England and North America.[8] At the end of May 1655, John recorded, 'I made a visit to Dr *Taylor* to conferr with him about some spiritual matters; using him henceforth as my Ghostly Father etc.' Commiserating with Taylor on his first imprisonment by Cromwell, in February 1653, Evelyn had written,

It were imprudent ... to inquire into the character of any good man's
suffering in these Tymes. 'Tis true valor to dare to be undon ... these
days when the Soules of men are betrayed, while such as you and such
excellent assistance as they afford us, are render'd criminal and suffer.

But Taylor, he added, had 'preach'd as effectively in the Chaines
as in the Chaire, in the prison as in the pulpitt'.

In March Evelyn wrote deploring the[9]

sad cataclysm and declension of piety to which we are reduced. Certain
it is that we are brought to sad condition. For my part I have learned
from your excellent assistances to humble myself and adore the
inscrutable paths of the Most High God, and Truths are still the same
though the foundations of the World be shaken. Julianus Redivivus
[presumably the apostate Cromwell] can shut the Schooles indeed and
the Temples, but he cannot hinder our private intercourses and
devotions. Deare Sir, we are now preparing to take our last farewell (as
they threaten) of God's Service in this City or any where else in public.

Taylor's reciprocal influence was not entirely happy, for he
tried to undermine even Evelyn's natural pleasure in the
possession of Sayes Court and its garden. After a visit there in
April 1656 Taylor wrote:

Sir, I came to see you and your Lady and am highly pleased that I did so,
and found all your circumstances to be an heape and union of blessings.
I am pleased indeed at the order and cleanliness of all your outward
thinges ... yet my delites were really in seeing you severe and
unconcerned in these things.

Evelyn, touched in an already morbid conscience, duly replied
that his 'poor villa and possessions' were 'indeed gay things', but
that as a sinner he was oppressed by fear of the Judgment:
'Whilst that accompt is in suspense, who can truly enjoy any
thing in this life? My condition is too well: and I do so often
wonder at it ... and fear it.' He apologizes for living in a rather
worldly manner 'neere a great city', and declares that he had the
'misfortune to pitch here more out of necessity, for the benefit of
others than for the least inclination of my own' – a remark that
hardly rings true.

Indeed, Taylor's influence increased Evelyn's streak of
religious melancholy, which as the years wore on saddened his
natural enjoyment of life, so that he could write to his more easy-
going brother George, condoling on the death of one of his
children, 'Children are such blossoms as every trifling wind
deflowres', and hint that by taking them away God showed
disapproval of the 'warmth of nature' that had begotten them,
and even ask 'Are you offended that it has pleased Him to snatch

your pretty babes from the infinite contingencies of so perverse
an age in which there is so little temptation to live?'[10]

## III

But Evelyn was now in full possession of Sayes Court, uncle
Prettyman having ceased to share it: 'in my own house,' he
writes, 'I began housekeeping'.

That spring of 1655 he went over the *Naseby*, afterwards *HMS
Royal Charles*, 'the great ship newly built by the Usurper *Oliver*,
carrying 96 brasse guns, and of 1,000 Tonn', with '*Oliver* on
horseback trampling 6 nations under foote' in the prow, while
'Fame held a laurel over his insulting head'.[11] In March,
unperturbed by the gallant royalist Penruddock Rebellion down
in Wiltshire, John, the crypto-royalist Londoner, dined with the
Sheriff 'with extraordinary cheere and Musique'. The
fashionable concern was now with good works abroad, with the
persecuted Vaudois ('remanents' John believed, inaccurately, of
'the antient Abbigenses'): the government ordered a day of
'national humiliation' and 'collections', and Milton wrote
'Avenge, O Lord, thy Slaughtered Saints'.

In August Richard Evelyn lost the son who might have been
the heir to the substantial property of Woodcote, and John had
to sell his newly acquired property in Essex, designed for his wife.
Taxation was of course now far heavier than anything imposed
by Charles I; and in September John sold the estate at Warley
Magna for £2,600, finding 'the *Taxes* so intolerable that they eate
up the Rents etc: surcharged as that Country had ben above all
others during our unnatural War'. He was lucky to make
another £100 on his original investment.

## IV

In 1659, exasperated by the decline of manners during the
interregnum, Evelyn attacked the boorishness of the Republican
English in *A Character of England*, supposedly written by a visiting
Frenchman.[12] The insular traits are still recognizable: the
'suspicious and forbidding countenances' at Dover and the
'profound difference by so short a transit', if not now the 'boys
hooting after the coach "French Dogs, a Mounser, a Mounser"',

the gross familiarity of the innkeeper at Rochester who sat down 'belching and puffing' in the faces of his guests, or the 'carmen' in London attacking newfangled coaches as 'hell carts'.

The countryside, on the other hand, the visitor found verdant, sweet and fertile, and London 'nobly situated', though 'but a wooden, northern and inartificial congestion' of houses and narrow streets. For anyone fashionably blind to the beauties of medieval architecture, there seemed only two good buildings in London, the new portico added to St Paul's by Charles I, and the banqueting hall, now 'sordidly obscured and built about'; as for Old St Pauls – 'how loathesome a Golgotha!' And the rest of the churches were utterly dilapidated, England being the 'Sole spot in this world where churches are made Jakes and Stables, markets and tippling houses', while 'the religion of England' was now 'in preaching and sitting still on Sundays'. The ubiquitous sermons were not even good – for the 'canting preachers' had encouraged 'every pert mechanick to out preach them'. In reaction to the strict Scots Presbyterians, the English had even abandoned the discipline that distinguished the 'Reformed' churches in France, the spiritual pride of mechanics and corporations had connived at heresy and schism so that the Presbyterians were 'torn to pieces' by Sectarians and craftsmen – 'Pretenders to the Spirit (dubbed Saints)'.

This confusion was worse confounded in London by the smoke and coughing, so that in one church the visitor could not see the minister nor hear him 'for the people's barking'. And in the far-too-many ale houses, the populace, 'universally besotted by tobacco', swilled a 'muddy kind of beverage', while in the taverns men drank Spanish wine and 'sophisticated liquors' in 'bestial bacchanalias' enlivened by organs taken out of churches.

The 'Frenchman' found the English, who drank to everyone at the table in turn, drunken bores, and cites their saying 'drunk as a lord'. Moreover, the custom of men staying at table to drink separately from the women made for further incivility, worsened by the sons of great men being largely brought up by servants.

The only things that the writer admired were the judges, the bowling greens, the verdant countryside and the 'delicious downes', and he admits that the English had fine dogs, horses, and fallow deer; though they all rode and drove much too fast.

Such was the spirited indictment, still not irrelevant, which Evelyn drew up against his countrymen at the end of the Republican decade when 'the Spirit had blown as it listed'. Though he countered it by a perfunctory and anonymous pamphlet, *Gallus castratus*, the writing is so spirited as to be plainly sincere.

He now made the acquaintance of a Czech refugee, the 'learned Mr Hartlib, a public spirited and ingenious person', full of inspiring continental examples, which had somehow gone wrong. 'Here,' he wrote, 'I present you with the model of the Christian Society already begun in Germany, but the bloody Bohemian Wars did destroy so noble and Christian a design, as likewise a Protestant nunnery in Silesia'. Then, 'Campanilla in his tract *de subjugandis Belgis* is said to assert that by the force of schooling and education whole Nations may be subdued.' Children's senses and tempers should certainly be filled with all manner of natural and artificial objects as 'the truest precognition of the after studies, which have been hitherto utterly neglected.' 'By a discourse,' the eager refugee continued, 'of the famous German critic Gilhardus Lubinus, which I have presented you with, see what a lover I am of such foundations,' and so on.

## V

The Christmas of 1657 was a bad time for Evelyn, and the New Year tragic, with the death of his promising and beloved son, Richard. After a Christmas Day sermon in Exeter chapel, in London, the Anglican congregation were surrounded by soldiers, and Evelyn himself confined to a room in the house. That afternoon Colonels Whally and Goffe arrived to examine the prisoners, and demanded of Evelyn why, contrary to the Ordinance, he dared to observe 'the superstitious time of the Nativity', to 'be at the Common Prayer' which was 'but the Masse in English', and 'to pray for Cha: Steward'. Evelyn replied that he had merely prayed for all Christian Kings, whereat they answered that his prayer must have included the hostile King of Spain who was a Papist. They had made a mistake in arguing with him. Evelyn soon managed to make these 'men of high flight' think themselves so superior as to pity his 'ignorance' and dismiss him; so he 'got home late the next day, blessed be God'.

After this unpleasant brush with authority, Evelyn by the end of January 1658 suffered a major bereavement. His 'deere Child *Dick*', died of a quatern ague, aggravated by too many blankets piled on him in a 'close' room overheated by an excessively hot fire, and so, in an interval when his parents were downstairs, in

Evelyn's opinion 'suffocated by the Woman and maide that tended him'. He was also 'liver grown' and had complained of pain in his side, but he had been a brilliantly precocious and intelligent child, full of lively curiosity; 'all life, all prettinesse', good-tempered, unselfish and continually cheerful. Here, concluded Evelyn, after a long eulogy, 'ends the joy of my life, and for which I go ever mourning to the grave'.

Then, in mid-February, in 'the severest Winter that man alive had knowne in England, when the *Crowes* feete were frozen to their prey' and 'Ilands of Ice inclosed both fish and foule frozen, and some persons in their boats', Evelyn's infant son George died also.

Though 1658 had begun so badly, in public affairs it would end with hope. In April 1657 Evelyn had recorded that the Protector Oliver, 'now affecting *Kingship*, is petition'd to take the title on him by all his new-made sycophant Lords etc, but dares not for feare of the *Phanatics*, not thoroughly purged out of the rebell army'. But the régime imposed by the sword of Oliver Cromwell on Great Britain was at last heading for collapse. The Protector had long been ailing, and his heir, Richard Cromwell, would briefly preside over an anticlimax in which he earned the nickname 'Tumbledown Dick'. The grandees of the army were manoeuvering, like the generals in the Roman empire, to profit by confusion, when on 23 November 1658, nothing loath, John went to London to see the 'superb Funerall' of the Usurper.[13]

He was carried from *Somerset-House* in a velvet bed of state drawn by six horses houss'd with the same: The Pall held-up by his new Lords: Oliver lying in Effigie in royal robes, and Crown'd with a Crown, scepter and *Mund*, like a King ... it was the joyfullest funerall that ever I saw, for their were none that Cried, but dogs, which the souldiers hooted away with a barbarous noise; drinking, and taking *Tabacco* in the streetes as they went.

CHAPTER TEN

# The Restoration

In May 1659 Evelyn again recorded 'the nation now in extreame Confusion and unsettled, between the Armies and the Sectaries': by the 25th Richard Cromwell had abdicated as Protector, and Evelyn was reduced to summarizing sermons on 'the paucity of true believers', 'the benefit of filial chastisement', and 'our vicar concerning the marks of sin pardon'd and effects of Confession'. Young John had fever, then ague; but in October Evelyn was taking lodgings 'at the 3 feathers in Russel Streete Covent Garden for all the winter', and in October still lamenting that 'We had now no Government in the Nation, all in Confusion: no Magistrate [supreme authority] either own'd or pretended, but the souldiers and they not agreed. God Almighty have mercy, on, and settle us!'[1]

Evelyn himself was even stirred to action. On 7 November he records 'was published my bold *Apologie* for the *King*, in the time of danger, when it was capital to speake or write in favour of him. It was twice printed, so universally it took'; and in December he was treating privately with Colonel Morley '(now Lieutenant of the Tower & in greate trust and power) concerning delivering it to the King, and the bringing of him in, to the greate hazard of my life'; but 'the Colonel had been my Schole-fellow and I knew would not betray me'.[2]

On 22 January 1660, Evelyn again

went this afternoon to visit Colonel Morley, ... After dinner I discoursd the Colonel, but he was very jealous [apprehensive] and would not believe *Monk* [now on his way from Scotland] came in to do the King any service. I told him he might do it without him, and have all the honour, but he was still doubtfull and would resolve on nothing yet – so I tooke leave, and went home.

The Colonel had clearly grasped the brute facts of military power.

Evelyn's *Apologie for the Royal Party written in a letter to a Person of the late Council of State* by 'a lover of Peace and of his Country' with a

95

touch at the Pretended 'Plea to the Army' (1659),[3] is designed to
convert the recipient from political error. It urges him to cast
back over the[4]

event of things; first to consider the Scots, who, at the instigation of
Richelieu, had first' disturbed the tranquility of England, and what they
have gotten by deceiving their brethren, selling their King, betraying
his Son, and by all their perfidie; but a Slavery more than Egyptian.

Save for the Scots, Evelyn demanded, who had gained any
thing by all the 'ignorant and furious zeal, this pretence of a
universal perfection in Religion and the Secular, after all the
blood and treachery, rapine and injustice'? In fact the power for
which rebels had contended at the expense of so much sin and
damnation had been seized by the army, 'by those very
instruments which they had raised to serve their insatiable
avarice'.

Now chastened for their implacable persecution of an
excellent prince, the rebels had suffered 'Slavery under such a
tyrant, as not being controlled to butcher even some upon the
scaffold, sold divers for Slaves, and others exiled into cruell
banishment', until it 'pleased God to put his hook into the
nostrils of that proud Leviathan and send him [Cromwell] to his
place'. And now the despicable rump of a parliament with which
that mountebank had formerly served himself, has itself changed
the scene, and see how soon their trifles and puppets of policy are
blown away!

Consider also to what you have reduced this once flourishing
kingdom, by taxes, excise sequestrations and customs; not to
mention the destruction of capital in plate, 'even to the very
thimbles and bodkins and other booties' – all dissipated. And
observe the proliferation of schisms and heresies: Jews and
Socinians, Quakers, Anabaptists, Independents and professed
Atheists – all of them spawned under your rebel government.

Take heed too, of God's judgments. Most rebel leaders have
already come to bad ends: as Essex, their commander, Warwick,
their Admiral, Manchester, dismissed by Cromwell, John
Hampden, shot in battle, the atheistical Dutch Dorislaus
murdered in Holland, and 'Ramsburrow', who died mad – such
already have been the fates ordained by providence for some of
the king's most notorious enemies.

Evelyn now presents an optimistic version of the character of
Charles II; no Catholic of course, and a prince ready to pardon
and 'accept repentance'. Mortified by so many afflictions,
disciplined by so much experience, surely this young prince is the

most excellently qualified to govern a people who have 'successlessly tried out so many governments of old, impious, and crafty foxes'.

The *Apologie* concludes by predicting utter confusion if the current chaos continues. England is utterly impoverished and consumed by war; 'you have wasted our Treasure, destroyed the woods, and spoyled the trade', so that 'foreigners are amazed at our madness'. Wrecked by a brutal civil war, we are increasingly vulnerable to our enemies; we must immediately 'propitiate God by an unfeigned repentance'.

According to Evelyn, by 11 February 1660 'Generall Monke', as he spelt him, had shown his hand:[5]

Perceiving how infamous and wretched a pack of knaves would have still usurped the Supreame power, ... [he] Marches to White hall, dissipates that nest of robbers, and convenes the old Parliament, the *rump-parliament* ... being dissolved; and for joy whereof, were many thousands of rumps, roasted publiquely in the Streetes at the Bonfires this night, with ringing of bells, and universal jubilee: this was the first good omen.

According to Aubrey:

They made little Gibbets and roasted Rumpes of mutton: nay, I sawe some very good Rumpes of Beefe. Healths to the King, Charles II, were drank in the streets by the Bonfires, even on their knees, and the humour ran by the next night to Salisbury, where there was like Joy; so to Chalke where they made a great Bonfire on the Top of the hill; from hence to Blandford and Shaftesbury, and so to Land's End, and perhaps it was so all over England. (Aubrey's *Brief Lives*, ed. O. Lawson Dick, London, 1972, p. 368)

In fact, Monck had not himself 'convened' parliament, but astutely demanded the issue of writs by 17 February, so that a parliament should be summoned in the usual way.

But during these most critical weeks, from 13 February to 5 April, John was out of action, seriously ill with a 'kind of double *Tertian*, the cruell effects of the *Spleene* and other distempers' and 'in truth brought very low'. But though bed-ridden, he wrote another urgent pamphlet refuting a brisk attack on Charles II, entitled *Newes from Brussels. The Late News or Message from Brussels unmasked, and his Majesty Vindicated*, which was highly topical.[6]

The pamphlet which provoked it had been a brutal and clever forgery, designed to reveal Charles II as a vindictive, debauched and sinister figure, whom Evelyn now 'vindicated from the Base Calumny and Scandal therein fixed on him'. The *News from Brussels* had purported to be a letter from 'a neer attendant on his

Majesties' person', addressed to an English royalist. 'Honest
Jack,' it began, and it showed up the alleged double dealing of
Charles II and the exiled royalists;

a blue ribbon and a starr we know will unbecome a rebell's shoulder,
but fishes bite at baits. He is an asse that angles and hides not his hookes
... Remember that blessed line I marked in Machiavel that he's an oafe
that thinks an oath ... can tame a Prince beyond his pleasure. Who
doubts that C. Borgia did his business by lulling Vitelloz asleep, than to
have hazarded all. 'Tis a romance that revenge can sleep but like a dog,
to wake at will. Can'st fancy that our master can forget he had a father?
... A Roundhead is a Roundhead, black and white Devils are alike to us.

To this hard-hitting propaganda, Evelyn, already feverish,
could oppose only a rather hysterical reply. It was 'forged and
fictitious stuff,' he wrote, written with 'a lascivious black and
sooty quill ... filthy foam of a black and hellish mouth, arising
from a viperish and venemous heart'. Then in the pamphlet's
own piscatorial idiom, 'Sir, your nets are seen and your fallacies
fail you; the hooks you mention are laid too visibly, the fish you
catch ... will not bite at all.' So 'give over your angling this way
and appear no more in public at the side of the pool that you be
not tumbled in over head and eares'.

Charles, far from being a vindictive crook, is in fact 'one that it
would put the whole Christian World upon some difficulty to
find his parallel: an Illustrious Prince, and with his brothers the
Renown and Glory of our Nation'. Further, and more to the
point, neither he nor his followers are trying to make good their
own losses from other people's estates.

For once, Evelyn had lost his temper, and the *Late News from
Brussels ... unmasked* is less convincing than the *Apologie*. Both had,
however, at some risk, achieved the first objective of political
warfare – to catch and probably to enhance an already prevalent
tide of popular opinion.

Having struck his second blow in political warfare, Evelyn
retired to Wotton, 'to my sweete and native aire', and by the end
of April he was well enough to ride.

On 6 May 1660, the day that Charles II was proclaimed in
London, Evelyn returned to Sayes Court, his wife meeting him at
Woodcote; but he was still only convalescent, and had to refuse
to join Lord Berkeley's delegation going over to Breda to invite
the king to return and assume the government.

It was now Colonel Morley's turn to beg a favour; 'Came to
see me *Colonel Morley* about procuring his pardon, and now too
late saw his horrible error and neglect of the Counsel I gave him,

by which,' Evelyn firmly but unrealistically believed, 'he had certainly don the greate work with the same ease as Monk did it. Who was then in Scotland and Morly in a post to have don what he pleased'. So Evelyn 'addressed him to my L: Mordaunt:* for his favour, which he obtained at the cost of 1,000 pounds, as I heard.: Ô the sottish omission of this gent.'

## II

On 29 May Evelyn was well enough to witness the triumphant return of Charles II to his capital.

This day came in his Majestie *Charles* the 2d to London after a sad and long Exile, and Calamatous Suffering both of the King and Church: being 17 years. This was also his Birthday, and with a Triumph of above 20,000 horse and foote. ... The wayes straw'd with flowers, the bells ringing. ... The Mayor, Aldermen, all the Companies in their liveries, Chaines of Gold, banners; Lords and nobles, Cloth of Silver, gold and vellvet everybody clad in, the windos and balconies all set with Ladys, Trumpets, Musick, and myriads of people flocking the streetes ... as far as *Rochester*, so as they were 7 houres in passing the Citty ... I stood in the strand, and beheld it, and blessed God.

'And all this,' he continues,[7]

'without one drop of bloud, and by that very army, which rebell'd against him. But it was the Lord's doing ... for such a Restauration was nevei seene ... in any history, ... since the returne of the Babylonian Captivity, nor so joyfull a day, and so bright, ever seene ... in this nation: this hapning when to expect or effect it, was past all human policy.

But Evelyn soon found the 'infinite concourse of people' at Court

intollerable as well as unexpresable, the greedinesse of all sorts, men, women and children to see his Majesty and kisse his hands, in so much as he had scarce leasure to Eate for some dayes, coming as they did from all parts of the Nation.

Charles, of course, 'would have none kept out, but gave free

* John, Baron Mordaunt of Reigate and Viscount Mordaunt of Avalon, Somerset (1627–75), second son of the First Earl of Peterborough, had fought for the king in the Second Civil War, and in 1658 planned a rising in Sussex, for which he had escaped the penalty for high treason by only one vote. Undaunted, he had planned another rising in 1659, it failed and he fled to Calais. Charles II made him Constable of Windsor Castle. His eldest son, Charles, Third Earl of Peterborough, became the famous admiral who relieved Barcelona during the Marlborough wars.

access to all sorts of people'. So the fastidious Evelyn addressed himself to the Duke of York, who arranged for him to see the king when only a very few noblemen were with him, and so to kiss hands and be 'graciously receiv'd'.

John was also now able to welcome his father-in-law, who had returned from Paris after an exile of nineteen years, through all of which he had kept up the Anglican services in his chapel. John also tried, unsuccessfully, to get the embassy at Constantinople for Henshaw, his former travelling companion in Italy. When on 25 June he attended the presentation of an address to Charles II from the gentry of Sussex, to which he was a signatory, the king 'owned him particularly', and called him an 'old Aquaintance'. Early in July he saw Charles through heavy rain go to 'the greate Citty feast' with 'as much pompe and splendor as any Earthly prince could do', and on 6 July the indefatigable monarch first began to touch for the king's evil, sitting in state in the Banqueting House. He did not shrink from stroking the faces of the sick with both hands or from himself hanging a gold angel round each of their necks, before the Lord Chamberlain brought him a much needed basin, ewer and towel.

Then at the end of July Evelyn's old acquaintance, Bramhall, now archbishop of Armagh, appeared with a clutch of Irish divines to be promoted bishops, 'most of the *Bishops* in all the 3 kingdoms, being now almost worne out and the sees vacant'. In August, Evelyn declined the commission to raise a troop of horse in Kent, feeling he could 'by no meanes embrace the trouble'; he preferred visiting Mr Boyle to 'see his pneumatic engins performe divers Experiments', and even watching '*Monkyes* and Apes daunce, and do other feates of activity on the high rope, to admiration'.

Then, in September, a magnificent embassy arrived from Spain, received in exceeding state by the king, and the Princess Royal, the king's sister, arrived from Holland. But London was evidently a sink of infection: that month the king's brother, the Duke of Gloucester died, and soon the Princess Royal herself. Smallpox had claimed both.

Lord Chancellor Edward Hyde, Earl of Clarendon, was now at the height of his power, so much that the Queen Mother, who wished to break the misalliance the Duke of York had contracted that September with his daughter, Anne, abandoned her purpose apparently in return for the Chancellor's promising to settle her debts. But in October a whiff from the past struck Evelyn when he encountered the 'quarters' of the executed regicides 'mangled and cutt and reaking as they were brought from the gallows in basketts on the hurdle: Ô miraculous providence of God!'

On 30 January 1661, the anniversary of the death of Charles I, Evelyn also records a day of fasting and humiliation decreed by parliament to expiate the 'gilt of the execrable Murder', an occasion further celebrated when the 'Carkasses of that arch-rebell Cromwell', Bradshaw ... and Ireton, were hanged on the gallows at Tyburn all day and then buried 'under that fatal and ignominious Monument, in a deepe pitt', and their heads stuck on top of Westminster Hall.

## III

In contrast to these gestures of revenge, the Royal Society was now reconstituted, and Evelyn was nominated by the king as one of its council, and 'by suffrage of the rest of the Members' a fellow. He calls it 'The Philosophical Society, now meeting at Gresham Coll: where was an assembly of divers learned gent:'. This nomination and election would lead to some of his most useful public service.

In mid-January he attended the first meeting; it was concerned with demonstrating that the atmosphere has weight, and with new methods of engraving. Prince Rupert (a considerable artist), now Evelyn declares, 'first shewed me how to Grave in *Mezzo Tinto.*'[8] Again, in March he writes 'This afternoone his highnesse *Prince Rupert* shewed me with his own hands the new way of Graving call'd *Mezzo Tinto*, which afterwards I by his permission publish'd in my *Historie of Chalcographie*, which set so many artists on Worke'. This exhaustive and comprehensive treatise, *Sculptura* or the *History and Art of Chalcography and Engraving in Copper*, 'to which is annexed a new manner of Engraving or *Mezzo Tinto* communicated by his Highness the Prince Rupert to the author of this treatise', was published at the request of the Royal Society in 1662.[9]

It is a work of immense scope, opening with 'of Sculpture, how derived and distinguished', and 'of the original of Sculpture', then continuing with 'of the Reputation and Progress of Sculpture amongst the Greeks and the Romans down to the Middle Ages'. It then investigates the 'Invention and Progress of Chalcography' (Engraving on Copper), proceeds to a chapter 'of

Drawing and Design', and concludes with one on 'the New Way of Engraving'.

Only the more dedicated art historians will linger on Evelyn's investigation of antediluvian sculpture, or of the entangled evidence from the history of the Hebrew patriarchs, for Evelyn, like everyone else, was in thrall to the Old Testament. Nor is there, for most readers, anything but tedium in the account of the rise and fall of sculpture in antiquity. Evelyn was entirely docile to the 'best opinions' of his time and could see little but distortion and monkish superstition in the art of the Middle Ages.

But contemporaries were much impressed: and modern readers, if resigning these elaborately pedantic pages to the professionals, must respect the staying power which impelled Evelyn – who was not even writing for money – to complete the *Sculptura* on a topical and useful note.

Before photography, the reproduction and multiplication of works of art was very difficult. The oldest method had been by woodcut, whereby the background of a design had been cut away, leaving it to be inked and screwed down on the paper by a press like a wine press. This technique had been developed by Dürer at the end of the fifteenth century and then by Holbein. Another way was by *Intaglio*, or engraving by incisions on a metal plate, first developed by goldsmiths' engravings on copper and by armourers who had coated steel with wax, drawn through the wax and corroded the result with salt and vinegar or acid. By the seventeenth century Callot and Hollar had developed engraving to a fine art, and Rembrandt (d. 1669) had produced superb etchings. *Mezzo Tinto*, whether or not a discovery of Prince Rupert's, was a kind of drypoint etching, whereby the ink retained in the furrows or 'burrs' made by steel or diamond etching could be regulated by breaking them down, thus producing a wide range of deep black, half tones, or pure white. This technique gave a new range to the art of reproduction, then so much in demand, and justified Evelyn's claim that by popularizing it he had 'set so many artists on worke ...'

Rupert apparently, had invented a rudimentary 'rocker' or rasp which makes the tiny holes clumped on copper, that, inked give a dark impression, but when scraped a lighter tone – the distinctive technique of mezzotint which, unlike any other engraving, proceeds from dark to light.[10]

## IV

On 20 April 1661 the long awaited coronation of Charles II took place. It had been preceded by the ancient ceremonial bathing of the Knights of the Bath in the Painted Chamber. Evelyn remarks 'I might have received this honour, but declined it' – a curious renunciation of a then signal distinction, only conferred on very great occasions. Yet John loved ceremony and describes the coronation in great detail, and how 'the Earles kept on their coronets as cousins to the King', and how the Knights of the Bath 'in crimson robes exceeding rich', were 'the noblest shew of the whole Cavalcade (His Majestie excepted)'. The king, who well sustained the elaborate ceremony for which new regalia had been made, wore a 'Waistcoate so opened in divers places as the A: Bishop might commodiously annoint him,' and could then be 'closed and buttond up ... by the Deane', while the full Anglican ritual was laid on to celebrate the triumphant Restoration – not least of the established church.

Next day John had his great moment when he presented the king with his *Panegyric* in the Privy Chamber after dinner.[11] Lord Mordaunt had tactfully warned him to be brief, writing 'I have spoke with his Majesty, he expects your oration as soon as he has dined. He asked me if it were in Latin, which I resolved; he said he hoped it would not be very long. This I thought fit to intimate to you.' There were limits, clearly, to the Monarch's endurance, though John had tactfully kept the 'oration' to a mere fourteen pages.

## V

Now securely settled at Sayes Court, with close contacts with royalty made originally during the interregnum in Paris, and a valued member of the Royal Society – which never admitted Hobbes, a character of far greater genius but of lower rank, reputed subversive and an 'atheist' – John Evelyn was now in the full tide of writing and reputation. The dilettante youth had become an immensely industrious author, capable of organizing a masterpiece of forestry, and laying down the fashionable lore about architecture; and it was in 1660–4 that he began to write the existing manuscript of the *Kalendarium*, laying the foundations of the main source of the *Diaries* that won him his greatest fame, bringing his account up to 1645. In addition, he was engaged upon the vast *Elysium Britannicum* on gardening, most of which had been written by 1659, but which proved too much for his powers of controlling material and was never published in his lifetime. Add to all this his growing public responsibilities, official and social, and Evelyn now appears at the peak of his energies and career: like the king, he had 'come into his own'.

# CHAPTER ELEVEN

# The Royal Society: *Fumifugium*: *Tyrannus*

On 8 May 1661, Evelyn recorded that Charles II, wearing his imperial crown, rode in state to open the new 'Long' parliament of the Restoration; it replaced the dissolved Convention Parliament and would last until January 1679. The king also now announced his intention to marry Catherine of Braganza, Infanta of Portugal.

On the 13th Evelyn visited Westminster School, which under the redoubtable Dr Busby had survived intact the dangers of the Civil Wars, and

saw such Exercises at the Election of *Scholars* ... to be sent to the Universitie, both in *Lat: Gr:* and *Heb: Arabic* etc in Theames and extemporary Verses, as wonderfully astonish'd me, in such young striplings, with that readinesse, and witt, some of them not above 12 or 13 years of age: and pity it is, that what they attaine here so ripely, they either do not retaine, or improve more considerably, when they come to be men; ... and no lesse is to be blamed their odd pronouncing of *Latine*, so that out of *England* no nation were able to understand or endure it.

Evelyn, with his continental experience, was not a representative critic; the 'odd' English pronunciation continued until well into the twentieth century.

## II

At the Philosophical Society the experiments with Mr Boyle's *Pneumatique* engine went on: 'We put in a *Snake* but could not kill it, by exhausting the aire, onely made it extreamly sick, but the chick died in Convulsions out right, in a short space' – an authentic portent of modern times. And on 3 May Evelyn was going to see 'the wonderfull Engine for weaving silk stockings, said to have ben the Invention of an *Oxford* Scholler 40 yeares since'. According to Aubrey, the inventor of the stocking frame had been William Lee, a Cambridge man, who never got it accepted in England because it was against the interest of the hand-knitters. Sir Christopher Wren, he writes, had proposed such a loom to the silk-stocking weavers of London, but when they had said they could not afford £400 and that it would 'spoil their trade', he broke 'the modell of the engine all in pieces, before their faces', and the original ingenious inventor had long before died in poverty in Paris. Such was the fate of a pioneer of seventeenth-century technology; his kind would have to wait until the Industrial Revolution.

But scientific experiments continued; this time (15 May) 'on *Vipers*, and their biting of *Dogs* and *Catts* to make tryall' of an Indian stone 'as a pretended cure', and appropriately, that Sunday, there was a sermon, directed, of course, at humans, on 'patience in affliction'. More happily, on 22 May, 'the *Scotch-Covenant* [was] burnt by the common hangman in divers places of Lond: Ô prodigious Change!'

The Philosophical or Royal Society were still interested in poisons, and tried more '*Vipers* and poysond arrows to Dogs etc.: but they succeeded not', nor did even putting a viper or *Aspic* to bite a mouse. But at last Evelyn secured a government appointment for his friend Henshaw, as Secretary for the French tongue, for life.

In mid-August of 1661, John visited his wife at Tunbridge Wells, where she was 'taking those medicinal waters'. Here 'among the solitudes', he admired 'the extravagant turnings, insinuations, and growth of certaine birch trees among the rocks', and back in London in September, he presented his *Fumifugium or the inconveniencie of the aer and smoak of London dissipated together with some remedies humbly proposed by J.E. Esq., to his Sacred Majestie and to the Parliament now assembled* (London, 1661). It was dedicated to Charles II, who was 'pleased that it should be published by his special command, being much pleas'd with it'. This sensible pamphlet is indeed one of the most useful of the versatile and indefatigable Evelyn's publications.

'It was one day,' he begins,

as I was Walking in your Majesties Palace in Whitehall ... that a presumptuous Smoake issuing from one or two tunnels neer Northumberland House and not far from Scotland Yard, did so invade the Court that all the Rooms, galleries and places about it, were filld and infested with it.

This nuisance, threatening the Monarch's health, had added indignation to a long-conceived project against such pernicious

Accidents. 'Your Majesty,' Evelyn continues, 'who is a lover of noble Buildings, Gardens, Pictures, and all Royal Magnificences, must needs desire to be freed from this pernicious annoyance'; moreover, the Princess Royal, Duchess of Orléans, late being in London, had complained in Evelyn's hearing of 'this Smoake'. Indeed, the evil is '*epidemicall*, endangering as well the health of Your Subjects, as it sullies the Glory of this your Imperial Seat'.

'Sir,' concludes the epistle dedicatory,

I propose in this Short Discourse an expedient how this pernicious *Nuisance* maybe reformed, and offer another also, by which the Aer may not only be freed from the present inconveniency; but (that remov'd) to render not only Your Majesties Palace but the whole City likewise, one of the sweetest most delicious habitations in the world; and this with little or no expense.

It could be done by 'improving Plantations', so that, like 'the Sent of the orange flowers from the rivage of Genoa', our native plants with 'redolent and agreeable emissions' would both ravish our senses and 'meliorate the Aer about London'.

To the general reader the author is more trenchant; stressing that English public works are much inferior to those of neighbouring countries, and that it is scandalous that this great and ancient city, which 'commands the Proud ocean to the Indies, and reaches to the farthest Antipodes, should wrap her stately head in Clouds of Smoake and Sulphur, so full of stink and darkness'. He deplores the 'mishapen and extravagant houses, narrow and ill paved streets; the deformity of warfes for wood and coal and of boards along the goodly river'. And he reverts to the high hopes then current of 'Our August Charles' and his parliament which 'studies only the publick good'.

After this promising opening, Evelyn cannot resist an elaborately pedantic discourse on the effects of the geographical diversity of air, and on what Hippocrates had written about it, and how 'lucid and noble air' clarifies the blood, while 'dark and gross air' stops transpiration and even disturbs rational faculties, so that the poisoning of the air was ever esteemed 'no less fatall than the poysoning of Water' or meat itself, and 'forborn even among barbarians'. Vitruvius would sedulously examine the air in places where he designed to build, and though the founders of our goodly metropolis lived long before him, they doubtless selected the site of London for health and pleasure as well as profit; for London, as Evelyn points out, at length, is finely situated, on well-watered gravel soil, fit for an 'opulent City'. Yet the whole place is poisoned by 'that Hellish and dismal Cloud of

*SEACOAL*, ... perpetually imminent over her head'. The culprits are the Brewers, dyers, Lime burners, salt and soap burners, more than all the domestic chimnies put together. The disgusting smoke contaminates everything, buildings, furniture, plate, pictures and hangings; it ruins the gardens, kills the bees, and spoils the taste of fruit. When Newcastle had been blockaded during the war, the consumption of sea coal fell off and London gardens had again flourished through the 'penury of Coales'.

More specifically, Evelyn attacks 'a Brew House contiguous to Whitehall and Westminster, and the Lime Kiln or two' on the Bankside near the *Falcon*; both at their worst in a south wind, with stench and halitus, and particularly one near 'Fox hall' in Lambeth: 'to what funest and deadly accidents this smoke exposes the numerous inhabitants!'[1] – 'who do not, like Miners or Iron Workers, live in such conditions by choice'. Even 'old Par' who lived to be a hundred and fifty was finally overcome by the air of London;[2] and how frequently we hear men say of some deceased 'Friend – "*He went up to London, and took a great cold*, etc. *which he could never afterwards claw off again.*" ' One cannot even hang up a gammon of bacon in the London smoke – it only gets 'mummified'.

Turning to remedies, Evelyn advocates burning wood instead of coal, planting copses and importing wood from the north by sea; but his main remedy is to remove '*Nuisances* from the City – Brewers, Diers, Soap boilers, lime burners. I propose therefore that by an Act of this present Parliament this infernal Nuisance be removed[3] five or six miles out of London, at least beyond Greenwich' and out of the prevalent south westerly winds.

### III

Now in higher favour than ever, on 1 October 1661 Evelyn[4]

sailed this morning with his *Majestie* (on) one of his *Yaachts* (or Pleasure boates), Vessells newly known amongst us, til the Dutch (E. India Comp) presented that curious piece [of 92 tons] to the King, and very excellent sailing Vessels.

For a wager of £100 between the new pleasure boat and one of the Duke of York's, they were to race to and from Greenwich to Gravesend and back. 'The King lost it going, wind Contrary, but sav'd stakes returning. There were divers noble Persons and Lords on board, his Majestie sometimes steering himselfe'.

Charles discussed Evelyn's *Fumifugium* – 'my Book inveing against the nuisance of the Smoke of Lond:'; the King proposed remedies, even commanded him to prepare a Bill against the next session of parliament, being, as he said, 'resolved to have something don on it'. And this instruction actually had its sequel, when three months later in January 1662 the Queen's Attorney sent Evelyn the draft of 'an Act, against the nuisance of the Smoke of Lond, to be reformed by removing severall Trades, which are the cause of it, and indanger the health of the K: and his people etc. which was to have ben offered to Parliament, as his Majesty commanded!.[5] But of course the vested interests concerned managed to frustrate this admirable royal initiative.

Meanwhile, on board the yacht, turning to a subject entirely irrelevant to Evelyn, the monarch, in default of a regular civil service official, then commanded him to 'draw up the *Matter* of *Fact* happning at the bloudy Encounter' when the French and Spanish ambassadors had contended for precedency at the reception of the ambassador of Sweden. The king wanted to establish his impartiality in the affair and 'take off' the reports of the spectators' rudeness. Evelyn lost no time in the task, and after being summoned to the king's cabinet and having added a few more clauses by the king's instruction, was commanded to have the final version dispatched to the Earl of St Albans, now English ambassador in Paris. Charles added a touch of intimacy by calling back John to show him some '*Ivorie Statues* and other curiosities'; and next morning, singling him out from a 'great crowde of noblemen standing neere the fire', directed him to 'soften a period or two' in the report, since the French ambassador had since 'palliated' the matter and was now 'very tame'. He even had to bring the 'softened' version to the royal bedchamber, and it was only two days later that he could send all the papers to Sir Henry Bennet (later Lord Arlington) and 'slip home'. But after even this brief experience as an honorary private secretary at the highest level, John felt 'indisposs'd and harass'd, with going about, and sitting up to write, etc'.[6] Even for the king, he detested any routine constraint.

In November the Royal Society were still at their experiments, this time anatomizing a 'camelion', and John was 'so idle as to go and see a play call'd *Love and Honor*'. It was an old play by Davenant, for, so soon after the Restoration, even old plays were still a novelty; but when John saw *Hamlet*, he observed 'but now the old playe began to disgust this refined age; since his Majestie being so long abroad'.

IV

John was now in high favour: Charles II 'discoursing with [him] concerning Bees', and showing himself 'exceedingly skillfull' about shipping; and in December he records 'I saw otter hunting with his Majestie and killed one'. He also published a 'Gentle Satyr': *Tyrannus or the Mode in a discourse of Sumptuary Lawes.*[7] He had evidently found the flood of French fashions brought in by the Restoration Court excessive. But he 'wondered how a nation so well conceited of themselves as the English should generally submit themselves to the mode' of the French, 'of whom they speack with so little kindness'. While admitting that the 'Monsieurs have universally gotten the Ascendancy over other parts of Europe' through conquest, and though he liked the French, he would 'be glad to pay his respects to them in any thing rather than their Clothes'.

For clothes are important. When the Romans abandoned the toga, their decline began; and, Evelyn continues, 'I am of opinion that the Swiss had not now been a nation but for keeping to their prodigious Breeches.' But the English had become the slaves of French fashion, and

it was a fine silken thing which I espied t'other day [in] Westminster Hall that had so much ribbon on him as would have plundered six shops and set up twenty country Pedlars. All the body was drest like a May Pole or Tom a Bedlam's cap. A Fregate newly rigged kept not half such a clatter in a storme as this Puppett's streamers did ... what have we to do with such forreign Butterflies?

Evelyn did not mind change, but 'for God's sake let the Change be our Own'. We 'needed no French inventions for the stage or for the back', and he looked for the day 'when All the world shall receive their Standard from Our Most Illustrious Prince and from his Grandees'.

He proceeded at length to recommend specific dress for each order of society; such laws would maintain the social hierarchy and make home industries prosper while the present waste of gold on embroidery would be diminished. Evelyn thus harked back to early Tudor and medieval sumptuary laws obviously impracticable by the mid-seventeenth century; and when in 1666, under stress of the war with France, Charles II in fact took to pseudo-Persian fashions instead of French ones, Evelyn would flatter himself that the monarch had taken his unpractical advice to heart.

*1* John Evelyn as a young man, by Van der Borcht

*2* John Evelyn, engraving by Robert Nanteuil, 1650

*3* Mary Evelyn, engraving by Robert Nanteuil, 1650

4  Sir Richard Browne, Evelyn's father-in-law,
engraving by Robert Nanteuil, 1650

5  Lady Browne, engraving by Robert Nanteuil, 1650

*6* Charles II, engraving by W. Sherwin

7  Mrs Godolphin, by Mathew Dixon

8  John Evelyn, by G. Kneller, 1689

## V

In January 1662 Evelyn was again 'called into his Majestie's' closet, where Samuel Cooper, 'that rare limner' and miniaturist, was crayoning the king's face and head to make the stamps for the new, milled, money. John held the candle, since the artist preferred candlelight 'for the better finding out of the shadows' – a memorable occasion.

With the Restoration Evelyn had, indeed, become part of the great world of the court and diplomacy, while his interests in elementary science had increased, if rather at the expense of his earlier concern with pictures and architecture.

In May 1662 Catherine of Braganza had arrived at Portsmouth and was brought to Hampton Court. John describes her Portuguese ladies in their 'monstrous fardingals ... their complexion *olivaster*, and sufficiently unagreable ... Her Majesty wore her foretop long and turned aside very strangely'. But he evidently made the best of her. She seemed 'yet of the handsomest Countenance of all the rest, and tho' low of stature pretily shaped, languishing and excellent Eyes, her teeth wronging her mouth by stiking a little too far out: for the rest sweete and lovely enough.'[8] Unfortunately the Portuguese Music consisted of '*Pipes*, *harps*, and very ill voices'. But the queen brought over from Portugal Indian cabinets and large lacquer trunks such as had never yet been seen in England.

That year John was following up his pamphlet against smoke, and sitting on a Commission about reforming the buildings and streets. 'We ordered the paving of the Way from St James's north – (now St James's Street) which was a quagmire, and also of the Haymarket about *Pigudillo*.'

In February Elizabeth Queen of Bohemia had died in London, the night before a tremendous gale which had blown down trees and chimneys, but the Queen Mother was still in England and in mid-August, with her attendants, she visited Evelyn at Sayes Court – and 'was pleased to honour my poore *Villa* with her presence, and accept of a Collation, being exceedingly pleased and staying' till very late in the evening, and the next day 'Lord Chancellor Clarendon and his Lady (his purse, and Mace borne before him) ... likewise Collation'd with us and was very merry. They had all ben our old acquaintances in Exile.' On his returning the Queen Mother's visit by paying his respects, she 'recounted to me many observable stories of the Sagacity of some Dogs that she had formerly had'.[9]

By the end of August, following medieval and Tudor custom, an elaborate river pageant was staged on the Thames, to bring the new queen from Hampton Court to Whitehall – 'exceeding in my opinion all the *Venetian Bucentoro*'s etc. ... when they go espouse the *Adriatic*'. And on the 29th the king received the Fellows of the Royal Society at Whitehall.

In October 1662 Evelyn had a visitor whose brilliance he characteristically found disconcerting. Sir George Savile, afterwards Marquess of Halifax and known as 'the Trimmer', who would play so important a part in the Revolution of 1688, seemed 'a witty Gent, if not a little too prompt, and daring'.

On 15 October Evelyn delivered his 'Discourse Concerning Forest Trees' to the Royal Society, which, published as *Sylva* in 1664, won him his greatest celebrity in his lifetime.

Thankful as he was to hear Church of England services again, John disapproved of the French fantastical light way in which a consort of violins 'better suiting a Tavern or Play House' had ousted the 'ancient grave and solemn wind musique' in one of the royal chapels, but he approved 'the strange, and wonderful dexterity of the sliders in the new Canall in St James's Park', who in the new fashion could use *Scheets* – Skates – on the ice 'after the manner of the *Hollanders*'. That December of 1662 was bitter, John going home to Deptford by water, 'not without exceeding difficultie ... great flakes of yce incompassing our boate'.[10] It was an appropriate season for the visit of the Muscovy ambassador, with his fur-capped retinue in 'embroidered tunics, bearing sumptuous gifts for the King' – sable, black fox, ermine, Persian carpets, walrus ivory, superb hawkes, Persian horses.

So ended 1662, with memorable pageantry at Court, and John, taking stock of his situation, thanking God for a good year.

Young John now needed a tutor, and his father selected Edward Phillips, at '£20 a year and other accommodations'; 'this Gent; was a Nephew to *Milton*, who writ against *Salmasius*'s *Defensio*, but not at all infected with his principles'. It seemed safe to engage him. So concluded for Evelyn the first phase of an unlooked for and tremendous change, which had brought the king into his own again, the Church of England back to its former authority, and John himself into a new social prominence high in the king's favour at Court, a favour which had been most constructively displayed in the monarch's patronage of a reconstituted and Royal Philosophical Society, now one of John's principal interests.

# CHAPTER TWELVE

# Sylva and the Gard'ner's Almanack

By the middle of February 1664 Evelyn presented to the Royal Society the book which would win him his contemporary fame. *Sylva or a Discourse of Forest Trees and the Propagation of Timber in His Majestie's Dominions* had originated in the autumn of 1662 in a discussion in the Royal Society on the planting and preservation of timber in view of the needs of the Commissioners of the Navy. The problems had been referred to Evelyn, the American John Winthrop, Governor of Connecticut, and to a couple of clergymen, Drs Goddard and Merret. Of the resulting papers Evelyn had made a digest originally for the Commissioners, the most important recipients, since the future of the fleet depended on the conservation of the English woods.

To this main concern Evelyn had added conclusions on the cultivation of apple trees for cider and a gardening calendar, but owing to formalities and printing delays only in 1664 had the first complete edition become available.

Evelyn had long been an enthusiast for the new continental fashions in gardens and parks. As far back as 1652, when he had first resided in part of Sayes Court, he had transformed the garden of the old-fashioned manor house, realizing French and Italian ideas and incorporating a fountain, an aviary and the transparent beehive admired by Charles II and Pepys. He had planted a big lilac hedge, set up a laboratory with a pillared portico and created an oval garden with clipped box hedges and promenades, following the contours of the land and commanding fine views. He had also planted an elaborate grove with French walnuts and a great variety of native English trees. Sayes Court had already come to set new standards for English gardens, superseding the stiff and enclosed Tudor and Jacobean designs and realizing the latest continental fashion of a garden as the open and spacious scene of 'all terrestrial enjoyment'.

Evelyn had also long been working on the vast treatise on gardening, much of it completed and all of it planned by 1659, though, swamped by uncontrolled notes and interlineal additions, most of it would remain unpublished in its author's lifetime. Entitled *Elysium Britannicum*, it depicted the perfect garden, chiefly for the diversion of princes and noblemen rich enough to create large pleasure gardens, though also, the author hoped, useful for less exalted persons who owned or merely enjoyed lesser existing gardens.

Like *Sylva*, the *Elysium* is extremely thorough; 'Amongst all the instruments belonging to our Artist,' writes Evelyn, 'the *Spade* is the principall';[1] and he enumerates – and himself depicts – rakes, hoes, mattocks, 'Planting Sticks, Dibbers' and 'planting Lattices' in the French style. He recommends marble rollers for gravel walks, preferably obtained from the 'old Columns of diminish'd Antiquities' in the Levant, though the best of all, made of cast iron, can be bought in Holland, or from 'our own furnaces where gunns are cast'. Evelyn thought of everything, including shears and pruning knives, watering pots, baskets, bird scarers, and mole traps; he dealt with nursery gardens and the germination of seeds and the mice which in autumn 'prodigiously devour them'. Hedges, tree-lined walks, waterworks, pools and fishponds, are described, as well as grottos and 'mounts'; silk worms and mulberry-trees are recommended; and a wide range of flowers – of which the most fashionable and expensive were tulips – includes carnations, geraniums, gladioli, wallflowers and stocks. Shrubs include jasmine, honeysuckle, clematis and a wide variety of roses.

Most of Book II and all Book III of the *Elysium* have been lost, though part of them appear in *Sylva*, in the *Kalendarium Hortense* or *Gard'ner's Almanack*, and also in a *Discourse on Sallets*, published long after in 1699. But descriptions of the 'pensile Gardens of Babylon', of Montezuma's floating gardens, and of Wilton, Wotton, and Sayes Court, have all vanished. It was thus with both wide experience of continental travel and over ten years of practical and theoretical study of gardening behind him that Evelyn came to write his most celebrated work.

## II

*Sylva or a Discourse of Forest Trees and the Propagation of Timber in his Majestie's Dominions, as it was delivered to the Royal Society on the 15th of October 1662 Upon occasions of Certain Quaeries propounded to that Illustrious Assembly by the Honorable the Principal Officers and*

*Commissioners of the Navy*, by John Evelyn F.R.S. is a massive work, showing its author's formidable ability.[2]

The handsome folio volume is very well planned, comprehensive and thorough, and soon sold out a thousand copies of the first edition; it is dedicated to Charles II – *nemorensis Rex* – the king of the grove, – 'as having once your Temple and Court too, under that sacred oak which you consecrated with your presence and we celebrate ... for your preservation', and as to one who has since proved 'another Cyrus exceeding all other Monarchs by his example in Planting'.

The preface to the reader denies that a subject which so much concerned Solomon, Cyrus, Cato, Cicero and the Plinys is uncultivated or rustic: on the contrary, to preserve, repair and propagate woods and plantations is an art, not to be left to mere rustics, and one which the author intends to present to His Majesty and the world both from advice recorded from others and 'observed myself, and most industriously collected from a studious propensity to serve as one of the least intelligences ... of our illustrious Society and in a work so necessary and important'. As Evelyn candidly states, he was often summarizing the conclusions of other writers; in fact he was elegantly serving them up for his own influential Court and gentry public. Indeed, in 1670 he wrote in a foreword to *England's Improvement Reviv'd* by the former parliamentarian Captain John Smith, now a Royal Forester, 'I am glad to find my own conceptions Fortified, by a Person of so great a Talent and Experience beyond me'.[3]

There had, in fact, been many books on husbandry, apart from the well-known works of Tusser and Gervase Markham, which included the subject of timber, but during the Interregnum the radical ideas of the refugee Hartlib, had taken on, advocating impracticable 'planning' by a centralized government incapable of such responsibilities, and Evelyn was naturally careful not to propagate radical theories, uncongenial both to himself and his public. *Sylva* thus embodied just the ideas and experience that Court and gentry could take and act upon and helped to establish the Royal Society as a centre of practical as well as theoretical studies. It is not too much to say that Evelyn's book on forestry contributed to the 'wooden walls' of Nelson's navy.

The opening chapter is topical and effective:

Since there is nothing which seems more fatally to threaten a *Weakening*, if not a *Dissolution*, of the strength of this famous and flourishing *Nation*, than the sensible and notorious Decay of her *Wooden Walls*, when, either through *Time*, *Negligence* or other *accidents*, the present navy shall be worn out and impair'd,

we need immediately to reflect upon 'an impolitic diminution of our timber and disproportionate spreading of our Tillage' leading to 'an epidemical devastation'.

So Evelyn surveys the nation's needs: in 'solid and dry timber' – Oak, Elm, Beech, Ash, Chestnut and Walnut; in 'light timber' – Maple, Lime, Birch and Hazel; and in 'aquatical', Poplar, Alder and Willow. Within this comprehensive scheme, all the variations of timber are thoroughly examined, for their qualities, suitable soil, and particular contributions.

After planting and transplantation, questions of soil and seed, and the 'sedulous extirpation of old roots and ancient stumps', have been analysed and the advantage of a southern aspect portrayed, along with a picture of a winch known as a 'German Devil' designed to eradicate large roots (p. 22), Evelyn warns the reader that it is unwise to buy growing timber simply on appearance, for defects are often concealed, so that 'a timber tree is a merchant adventurer, you shall never know what he is worth till he be dead'.

He then launches into a panegyric, almost a prose poem, on the splendid qualities of the oak – *quercus silvestris*. It yields far the most lasting timber; houses and ships are built with it; it also makes wheels, and hafts for knives, as well as producing mast 'for the fatting of hogs and deer' and pheasants. Moreover, it flourishes best in our own temperate climate, if planted with room to spread, and in ancient times men indeed had hearts of oak – (an early use of the famous phrase), 'I mean not so hard, but health and strength' (p. 26). Moreover, young oaken leaves decocted in wine make an excellent gargle. Finally, translating Rapinus, Evelyn breaks into clumsy verse:

> When ships for bloody combat we prepare
> Oak affords plank, and arms our Men of War,
> Maintain our fires, makes plows to till the ground
> For use no timber like the Oak is found.

Having thus contributed to the English feeling for the oak, Evelyn turns to the elm.

Of *ulmus* the elm (Chapter IV),

there are *four* or *five* sorts, ... two of these kinds are most worthy of our culture; the vulgar, *viz* the *mountain Elm* ... being of a less jagged and smaller leaf; and the *vernacula* or *French Elm*, whose leaves are thicker and more florid, glabrous and smooth, delighting in lower and moister grounds, where they will sometimes rise to above an hundred foot in height, and a prodigious growth, in less than an age.

The elm tree is 'a Tree of *Comfort*, *sociable* and so affecting to grow in company that the very best that I have ever seen, do almost touch one another: this also protects them from the winds and causes them to grow to an extraordinary height', though they thrive better in hedgerows than in forests. The elm easily suffers transplantation, so that it can be expeditiously used by great persons for planting accesses to their houses. Philip II of Spain imported English elms for the Escorial, 'no tree, whatever, becoming long *Walks* and *Avenues*, comparable to this Majestic plant'.

It delights in sound sweet and fertile land something inclined to loamy moisture where it can be refreshed with springs, but not in sandy and hot grounds. It is also the least offensive of trees to corn and pasture and affords 'benign shade to cattle'. But when you fell one, take care that it is not ruined by its own weight.

Its timber is most singular in use, for mills, ladles, pipes and pumps, and ship planks below the water line. It is also good for axle trees, chopping-blocks for the hat-makers, and for shields and statues. Even its leaves relieve cattle in winter, when fodder is dear: and swine in Herefordshire devour them, though they are bad for bees and 'Obnoxious to the Lark'. Elm bark, decocted and mixed with a third part of aqua vitae, is 'a most admirable remedy for the hip pain'.

Turning to alders and willows, Evelyn finds a surprising amount to be said for the former. It is 'a faithful lover of water and boggie places', and needs profound fixing in deep mud to preserve it steady; it is good for grass and for strengthening river banks, and so tough that it formed the foundations of the Rialto bridge in Venice. Its wood is excellent for hop poles and trenchers, and its fresh leaves, applied to the naked sole of the foot, infinitely refresh the suburbated traveller; moreover, the bark, macerated in water, makes a black dye usable for ink, and 'being beaten with vinegar, it heals the Itch'. In a pre-industrial economy, Evelyn and his readers made the most of everything.

The sallow, or white willow, for example, with its 'Wondrous swift growth', is particularly useful in thatching, as well as for rakes and pike-staves, while oziers provide twigs for baskets, hampers, cradles, coach-bodies and all wicker and 'twiggie' work, particularly cooper's hoops for barrels; indeed they can be worth £20 an acre, and are thus 'in esteem of knowing persons'.

The garden willow, too, though simply 'an hortulan ornament', affords 'a wonderful and early relief to the industrious bee', as well as hurdles and hives, while 'of all the trees in nature' they 'yield the most chaste and coolest shade in the hottest season of the day'.

Having dealt in detail with all the variety of deciduous trees from oak to willow, Evelyn now (Chapter XXI) deals with fences and hedges. These, as Tusser pointed out when he wrote:

> If Cattel or Cony may enter to crop
> Young Oak is in danger of losing his top,

are very important; yet most landlords neglect them. 'Are five hundred sheep worth the care of a shepherd,' asks Evelyn, 'and not five hundred oaks the fencing?'

Hawthorne (or Heithorne) makes a good hedge, and he advises in detail when and how best to plant it: even broom and furze have their merits.

In Devon, the seat of the best husbandry in the world, they sow in the worst land (well ploughed) the seeds of the rankest furzes, which in 4 or 5 years become a rich wood: The young and tender tops of furzes, being a little bruis'd and given to a lean and sickly horse will strangely recover and plump him.

Spindle wood, being very hard, is good for 'toothing of organs' as well as for spinning, and its berries 'purge by vomit' – a sad aspect of their coral colouring. The American yucca, already acclimatized, can make 'palisadoes'.

Turning now (Chapter XXII) to fir trees and pines, Evelyn plunges into the technicalities of Spanish firs, of Prussian and Norway spruce, much esteemed by the Dutch for masts, and of the enormous New England spruces, so large that they are hard to transport. By an odd decree of providence, pines, so useful on ships, grow on mountains, but they have many uses, not least to provide pitch and tar, while 'that enormous stratagem, the so famous Trojan horse, may be thought to be built of that material'. As for plane trees (Chapter XXIII), they were much esteemed by the Greek philosophers, and planted in groves near the 'Palaestritae' where young athletes exercised; they are easy to grow – all they need being plenty of water – and unsurpassed for shade. As for the lotus tree, besides providing pipes for music, it has one extraordinary property: it can cure the bite of a mad dog if the victim so much as handles it. But the Cypress is the 'most pyramidal and beautiful' of all.

The infirmities of trees (Chapter XXVII) are various, according to the rustic rhyme:

> The Calf, the wind-shoc and the Knot
> The Canker, Scab, Scurf, Sap and Rot,

and other 'enemies not seen' make 'many a bargain of standing wood ... very costly'. It also is essential to extirpate weeds, 'dog-grass, bear-bind etc.'. Fern is best destroyed by striking off the tops, as Tarquin did the heads of poppies – a better way than mowing or burning. Woodpeckers, knocking with their bills, indicate worms, and woodlice, if reduced to powder, are good against the jaundice and scurvy, purify the blood and clarify the sight.

In hard winters, deer, conies and hares destroy bark, but are put off if the tree is annointed with human dung and urine, or better still by tanner's liquor, used to dress hides. Ivy, the destruction of many fine trees, should be destroyed at the roots, fungi diminished by exposure to the sun. Tar preserves trees from 'the envenom'd teeth of goats' and destroys hornets, but moles, which 'do much harm by making hollow passages which grow mustie', must be trapped, though they can be driven for a time from their haunts by garlic and other heady smells. Ants can be destroyed simply by scalding water, or by laying soot or refuse tobacco in their runs, though caterpillars are best got rid of by burning them off with wisps of dry straw. Rooks should be shot and their nests demolished, and birds that rob fruit discouraged by clappers or caught in wire mouse traps with teeth, baited with 'rusty' bacon.

Evelyn then turns to the planting and preservation of coppices (Chapter XXVIII), a long-term art, on which he gives much technical advice, and then to the pruning or 'figuration' of trees (Chapter XXIX). 'Tis a misery,' he remarks, 'how our fairest trees are defac'd, and mangl'd by unskilful wood-men and mischievous *Bordurers*, hacking and chopping with short hand bills all that comes their way ... Good husbands should be asham'd of it.'

Pruning is extremely important. Evelyn quotes from 'honest Lawson's' *Orchard*,[4] which insists that trees should not be overladen with boughs and suckers which waste the sap, growth concentrated in the best shoot and pruning done when sap is ready to stir. Woodwards should be daily vigilant, stopping gaps, impounding trespassing cattle, chasing out deer; trees preserved by proper pruning and conservation will be more valuable in twelve years than 'all other imaginable plantations (accompanied by our usual neglect)'.

Felling should not be undertaken until the tree has 'arrived at his perfect Age'. Fruit trees of solid substance, not damnified by heat or cold, can live to enormous ages, and timber trees, particularly yew, box, oak, walnut and cedar, are 'capable of very long duration'. Evelyn cites many classical examples, as a vine which Pliny mentions as six hundred years old, and a ruminal fig tree lasting, as Tacitus calculated, for 840 years, and as Tiberius's larch, and the float that wafted Caligula's obelisks out of Egypt, four fathoms in circumference. And consider all the capacious hollow trees in our own country, as the oak at Kidlington Green in Oxfordshire where vagabonds and malefactors were imprisoned before being removed to the county gaol.

Evelyn writes (Chapter XXX) of the immense trees in New England, in Cyprus, in Sicily, and of a 'Certain fig in the Caribby Islands which emits such large buttresses that they provide planks for tables without harming the tree', and a tree in 'Guchu' in China called the tree of a thousand years which sheltered 200 sheep under one branch alone. 'That goodly trees were of old ador'd and consecrated by the Dryads [Druids?] I leave to Conjecture from the stories of our ancient Britains.'

Evelyn has even now only just received from Sir Thomas Browne a description of a lime tree near Norwich eight yards and a half round and the roots fifteen in circuit. It is thirty yards high, and Sir Thomas had christened it Tilea Colossae Depehamensis – from its native village of Depeham. Evelyn cannot resist comparing 'its measurements with those of the prodigious lime tree at *Neustadt an der grossen Linden* in Würtemberg', and even leaving out several more as 'too tedious to recite', he cites the dimensions of a huge oak in Worksop park belonging to the Duke of Norfolk, and 'that goodly birch tree at the Palace of Augustburg' whose branches can cover 365 tables, one for each day of the year. Indeed, he gives elaborate detailed particulars, with figures attested by ancient inhabitants and by woodwards, at Sheffield Lordship and Worksop.

He concludes by setting problems – ('a tree being 68 inches about, find out how much therof in length will make one foot *square*') and giving the solutions, ending the chapter in a welter of technicalities, doubtless fascinating to experts, if not to most readers.

As *Sylva* draws gradually to its close, Evelyn's native pedantry

or love of learning swamping the original and businesslike
purpose of the book, he ranges into legends of classical antiquity
about woods, groves and sanctuaries, but in his final chapter
(XXXV), he extricates himself from the Druids – 'in this island of
ours, extremely devoted to trees' – from Indian 'Brachmans' and
ancient gymnosophists, to denounce the sacrilegious purchasers
and disloyal invaders of the late Civil Wars,

in this Iron Age amongst us, who have lately made so prodigious a Spoyl
of those goodly Forests, woods and trees, to gratify an impious and
unworthy avarice, which, while being once the treasure and ornament
of this nation, were doubtless [getting back to the point] reserved by our
more prudent ancestors for the repair of our floating castles, the
safeguard and boast of this renowned Island.

Confessing that he 'has hardly power to take off his Pen on the
delightful subject of woods', Evelyn concludes with pious
reflections on the power that created the lofty fir tree and the
spreading oak, the tall elms, the planes and cypresses, the
immense variety of trees, the propagation of their seeds, the
diverse uses for which they provide, and on the miraculous and
elaborate ingenuity of the Creator of the world.

The annexed 'Pomona or an appendix concerning Fruit-Trees,
in relation to Cider: the making, and several ways of ordering'
aims at substituting cider for the still relatively new-fangled beer
made with hops, which was then ousting ale. 'It is a little more
than an Age, since Hops (rather a medical than an alimental
vegetable) transmuted our wholesome Ale into Beer; which
doubtless much altered our constitutions.' But if hops preserve
drink, they bring disease, so we ought to 'abate our fondness' for
beer.

Cider is the best alternative; and already large orchards have
flourished since 'one Harris, fruiterer to Henry VIII', planted
them in Kent and Lord Scudamore planted in Herefordshire,
where cider is already the most popular tipple.

Apart from this rather unconvincing *Appendix*, *Sylva* is a
powerful and thorough work, a round-up of essentials in
forestry, published at just the right time. It shows a formidable
grasp in handling an immense subject, as well as the two sides of
Evelyn's mind: the 'modern', capable of lucid planning and
hard hitting commonsensical argument as demanded by his
terms of reference; and the 'ancient' running uncontrolled after
recondite and curious learning for its own sake. In this aspect, as
in his life, Evelyn representatively spanned his century.

## III

In 1664 Evelyn also published his *Kalendarium Hortense* or *The Gard'ner's Almanack, what he is to do throughout the year and what Fruits and Flowers are in Prime.*[5] It is dedicated to the poet Abraham Cowley – 'This Hortulan Calendar is yours' – who responded with appropriate verse.

Even the Garden of Eden, Evelyn points out, had to be 'dressed and kept', and no life is more laborious and useful than a good gardener's, whose labours, full of tranquillity and satisfaction, are perennial. He had therefore devised 'synoptic tables for monthly use', so thorough that dedicated modern gardeners find them fascinating, but here too detailed for more than summary description. Many readers will be surprised at how many familiar flowers and fruit were already being cultivated and enjoyed.

January, Evelyn begins, is the time to trench the ground, and prepare the soil, particularly the asparagus and strawberry beds; to prune fruit trees, particularly those on walls or palisados, and to clear trees of moss. Then, as now, January flowers 'in prime' include winter aconite, anemones, and winter cyclamen. February is the month to sow beans, peas, carrots, onions and garlic, to set traps and baits for vermin, and 'air your housed carnations'. March sees early daffodils, and plants now need water, but 'water gently newly planted things from a convenient distance' – advice still often disregarded. You should now stake-bind your weakest plants against the 'fare well frosts and east winds, which will prejudice your choicest tulips'. It is best to cover them with mats of canvas, and even to cover with straw your cypress tips and exposed evergreens, for it is the 'cruel winds and never the hardest frost and snow which do the mischief'. And when you remove the covering do it with caution to avoid the 'sudden darting of a scorching sun'. By the end of March you may set your orange trees, lemons, myrtles and oleanders in the open porticos, windows and doors of your greenhouses, 'to acquaint them gradually with the air'.

By April the flowers in prime are crocus, iris, 'junquils', 'narcissus with large tufts', primroses, 'precoce tulips', almond and peach blossom. You can now clip lavender and rosemary, prune strawberries and wall-tree peaches, and sow 'holyhocks' and scabius. 'Plant now the Spanish jasmin.' Cowslips, white violets, lilac are in prime: wisteria unknown.

In May, when the mulberries open their leaves, bring your orange trees 'boldly out of the conservatory',[6] but look carefully at your melons. Flowers in prime by June are antirrhinum, clematis, honeysuckle, carnations, pinks, pansies and roses; while by July gladioli, musk roses, cornflowers, holyhocks, lupins, jasmin and delphinium are all in flower, and strawberries, raspberries, plums, cherries, pears and peaches are in season.

In August remember 'to clip roses now done bearing', while heliotrope and oleanders are out, and the tawny and red roman apricots are ripe, along with the imperial blue plums, cluster grapes, mulberries, figs and melons. The familiar September flowers, chrysanthemum, sunflowers, nasturtiums, and passionflowers are all listed (there were no dahlias), and Evelyn concludes in October by advice to 'prune roses down to a standard' and to 'plant the ranunculus's of Tripoly'. It is important to sweep up 'all autumnal leaves fallen, lest the worms draw them into their holes and foul your garden' – shrewd advice.

As November days draw in, 'be careful not to over water' your 'hous'd plants': if the leaves shrivel they want watering, but if they become pale and whitish they are being swamped. This advice (still relevant) is important, because, Evelyn concludes with a flourish, 'in the secret of seasonally refreshing consists the health and even life of your housed curiosities'.

Such is the range, here only briefly glimpsed, of a thorough and comprehensive treatise which, supplementing *Sylva*, won Evelyn well-earned celebrity in his time. It shows how far gardening in England had already come since the reign of Elizabeth, and what a variety of flowers and fruit Evelyn's more prosperous contemporaries already enjoyed.

# IV

Following up the theory of *Sylva* with practice, in the spring of 1664 Evelyn 'planted the homefield and West field about Says Court', 'with Elmes, being the same Yeare that the Elmes were also planted by his Majestie in Greenewich park'. In March he recorded with resignation the death of his infant son, another Richard, probably 'overlayne' by his nurse, 'to our extreame sorrow, being now againe reduc'd to one: God's will be don'.[7] And in August George Evelyn's second wife died 'unexpectedly' so that John and his brother Richard went down to Wotton to comfort him.

More public responsibilities were accumulating: Evelyn was now on the commission 'about regulating the Mint' and 'striking the new Milled Coins both of white money and *Ginnies*', and on another for 'regulating the *Hackney Coaches* of Lond: and highways'. But that autumn he accompanied Clarendon's son, Lord Cornbury, in a coach and six to help in planting Cornbury Park at Charlbury, in Oxfordshire, where, passing through Woodstock, they observed the destruction wrought in the park there by the 'late Rebels'. He found Cornbury in a 'Sweete dry Park walled with a Dry-wall', and the house built of excellent Cotswold freestone, with 'the paving of the hall admirable for the close laying of the Pavement'.[8]

From Cornbury they visited Ditchley Park, then a 'low antient timber house, with a pretty bowling greene', and after attending a great entertainment at Shotover, where their hostess was the affluent heiress of bishop Ussher of Armagh, they stayed with the principal of Magdalen Hall (since Hertford College) at Oxford, who was a Hyde related to Lord Cornbury. Here they inspected the Sheldonian Theatre, then under construction at Archbishop Sheldon's expense and following the design of Sir Christopher Wren, who showed Evelyn the model, 'not disdaining' his advice.

Back in London, John encountered the king in the Privy Gallery at Whitehall, who 'caused [him] to follow him alone to one of the Windows', and asked 'if [he] had any paper about [him] unwritten and a *Crayon*'. Evelyn presented him with both, and then, 'laying it on the Window stoole', the king with his own hands 'designed to me the plot of the future building of White-hall', 'which royal draft, though not so accurately don, I reserve as a rarity by me'.

# V

Happily married and well established at Sayes Court, John Evelyn had become at once courtier, country gentleman, virtuoso and writer. While not a genius in an original way, and so not at the mercy of moods of wayward creativeness, he was both versatile and indefatigable in his treatment of most of the subjects which interested his contemporaries, not least in forestry and gardening. While hardly at all ambitious, he had a strong sense of public duty, which was at last given scope after the Restoration through contacts with the king and court. And he was so fascinated with life that he was determined conscientiously and thoroughly to record it with a sharp eye and often a vivid pen.

# CHAPTER THIRTEEN

# The Second Dutch War and the Plague of London

While Evelyn had been launching *Sylva* and the *Gard'ner's Almanack* and frequenting the Restoration Court, the Second Dutch War of 1665–7 had been looming up. It was a war for commerce and colonies, already, in fact, begun off West Africa; and by the winter of 1664 Commissioners were being appointed to take care of 'such sick and wounded & prisoners at war as might be expected upon occasion of a succeeding Warr and Action at Sea',[1] and Charles II nominated Evelyn to the Commission.

His district was Kent and Sussex, with power to appoint officers, physicians, surgeons and Provosts Marshal, and 'dispose of half the Hospitals through England'. It was a responsible and arduous appointment, bringing a salary of £300 a year, and that evening Evelyn 'dined at Guildhall, the feast said to cost £1000'. He was placed near various magnates, Lord Chancellor Clarendon, the Duke of Buckingham, the Duke of Albemarle and other great officers of state. There were healths drunk with trumpets and drums sounding, 'cheere not to be imagin'd for the plenty and rarety – an infinitie of Persons at the rest of the tables in that ample hall' – 'so,' concludes John, characteristically, 'I slip'd away in the crowd and came home late'. That year at Sayes Court he 'planted the Lower grove next the Pond'.

By mid-November the Commission was getting under way choosing a treasurer, clerks and messengers; Evelyn devised its seal – a Good Samaritan with the motto *fac similiter* (do likewise), and by 1 December they were reserving half of St Thomas's hospital, Southwark, for casualties from the fleet.

It was a cold winter: Evelyn listened to a sermon 'on preparation for Christ's last appearance', then attended the launching of a new ship with two bottoms, invented by Sir William Petty. The king cautiously named her the *Experiment*, and next year she was lost in a storm. All these activities had not prevented Evelyn from translating and conflating topical books,

La Nouvelle hérésie des Jésuites by the Jansenists A. Arnould and P. Nicol (1662) and L'Hérésie Imaginaire by Nicholas (1664). He entitled the work The Mysterie of Jesuitism, never before published in English, and, save for specialists in seventeenth-century theology, it is not exciting.

## II

More importantly, besides publishing Sylva, his masterpiece, and the popular Gard'ner's Almanack, Evelyn, in 1664, had added to his translation of Fréart de Chambrey's Parallel of Ancient Architecture with Modern, his own Account of Architects and Architecture,[2] which would prove opposite when, in 1666 the Great Fire of London gave Wren his opportunity to build in the new neo-classical style. It is relentlessly conventional, comprehensive and thorough, dogmatically intolerant of all but classical architecture. But, then most usefully in England, it particularly claims high status for architects, who should not be regarded as 'mere illiterate mechanicks', but in high Renaissance fashion as accomplished and versatile men of the world. In its practical common sense, the book owes much to Vitruvius, laying down principles of proportion and convenience which the neo-gothic and eclectic architects of the nineteenth-century would blithely disregard, and which are deliberately ignored by the perpetrators of modern pseudo-Aztec monstrosities and tower blocks.

A good architect, Evelyn insists, must be skilful in design, literate, docile, ingenious, expert in optics, ancient history, philosophy, music, law and astrology; a trained humanist competent in military, naval and civil architecture; and his subject should be recognized and taught in universities.

Having boldly stated the architect's claim to standing and respect, Evelyn, before exhaustively laying down the rules, sharply disparages gothic architecture, which, he insists, came in only after the decline of Classical Civilization. It was the Goths and the Vandals, he declares, who introduced this fantastical and licentious manner of building, – these 'heavy, dark, melancholy and monastic piles', without any just proportion use or beauty compared with the truly ancient. The gothic is distracting and confusing; full of expensive carving, 'fret', and lamentable imagery.

After thus clearing the decks, Evelyn dogmatically asserts that gentlemen ought not to build on old foundations, but choose a new site, and that to join a new style of building to an old style is always wrong. Tirelessly and tediously he proceeds to capitals, caryatids, columns and cupolas, and to the correct size of pilasters; he expatiates on borders, dentilles and modillions, and on where Doric, Corinthian, or Ionic capitals are appropriate. He spares a word of commendation for the Tuscan style, since, deriving from the primitive beam on top of forked posts, it is singularly strong; and he expatiates on domes. Finally, after an exhaustive and comprehensive exposition of the technical terms of architecture, Evelyn pays a deserved tribute to Vitruvius and to Claude Perrault, the contemporary builder of the east front of the Louvre. He had indeed derived most of his ideas from them; and he concludes, still with the scorn of a cosmopolitan intellectual for the English, 'May this suffice in a country where for the saving of a little charge, they seldom consult an experienced architect besides the neighbouring brick-layer and carpenter'. The broadside contributed to the strict and sometimes stifling conventions which would dominate eighteenth-century architecture, and by reaction, provoke the gothic revival. Immediately, it prepared public opinion to give Wren a free hand when the chance came.


## III

In the bitter January of 1665, Evelyn, now aged forty four, was bustling about Kent, appointing officials to deal with the wounded or prisoners of war, and ranging from the North Foreland to Rochester, Canterbury and Dover, where he was well entertained at the castle. He visited Deal and Sandwich and returned to Chatham after a 'cold buisy but not unpleasant journey', thankful to return even to a sermon on the circumcision of Christ. He continued in high favour with the king, who came to him 'standing in the Withdrawing roome', and thanked him for the *Mysterie of Jesuitisme*, which he said he had carried for two days in his pocket and read it – 'at which,' comments the author, 'I did not a little wonder'.

By Ash Wednesday (8 February) Evelyn visited his first batch of prisoners of war at the site of modern Chelsea Hospital; their only complaint was that 'their bread was too fine', the already insipid white English kind being unsatisfactory to Dutch appetites.[3] Next day, returning to scientific interests, he examined the throat of a pelican in St James's Park – 'a fowle between a Stork and Swan – a melancholy Water foule; brought from *Astracan* by the Russian Ambassador'. It was diverting to see how it would 'tosse up and turne a flat-fish'; but the penguin of America was even greedier: 'I never saw so insatiable a devourer. I believe it is the most voracious creature in nature; it was not biger than a *More hen.*' There were already many other 'curious kinds of poultry' in the Park, 'breeding about the Decoy'.

That spring, Evelyn dined with secretary Bennet (now Lord Arlington), at Goring House, on the site of what would be Buckingham House and Buckingham Palace: he thought it 'capable of being made a pretty Villa'.[4] In April he found himself the only Commissioner left in London to deal with prisoners of war and wounded and with the important admiralty business, including the disposal of Admiral Evertsen's son, 'Young Evertse ... taken in fight'. Evelyn asked the king how he wished him treated, and Charles commanded him to bring the 'Young Cap: to him, and take the Dutch Ambassadors word for [another] that ... he should not stir without leave'. Evelyn presented 'Young Evertse eldest sonn of Cornelius, Vice Admirall of Zeeland', to the king, who gave him his hand to kiss and allowed him his liberty, for Charles was not unmindful of the many civilities he had formerly received from the captain's family during his exile. Moreover, he commanded Evelyn to give the captain 50 pieces in board gold and accorded similar treatment to another captain taken in fight. Thus, on the higher levels, seventeenth-century war was mitigated. But Evelyn had to tell the king in council that his organization was costing £1,000 a week.

By the end of May he was taking young John to Dover, where he had business, and the boy 'went to sea but was not sick', and in June Evelyn was asking the king and Albemarle for horse and foot guards for the prisoners of war, and the Duke of York and the Council for as much as £20,000 and the disposal of the Savoy hospital for the sick and wounded. On 3 June 1665 the battle of Lowestoft proved a disappointing victory, which, Evelyn considered, might have 'ended the Warr, had it been pursued', but it meant casualties and prisoners and Evelyn at once waited at the coast on the Duke of York, as he came 'triumphant from the fleete, goten in for repaire', and, with the king's support, obtained the necessary money.

IV

In the midst of these heavy responsibilities which he proved well able to discharge, Evelyn, like the rest of the country now faced the horrors of the Great Plague. By the end of July 1665 deaths were mounting in London, the disease, like that of 1348, being spread by fleas from black rats; but along with Lord Sandwich, Admiral of the Blue, Evelyn was visiting the fleet at the Nore in the mouth of the Medway; and on board the *Prince* (1,299 tons, 86–92 guns, 500–600 men) they were impressed by 'the good order, decency and plenty ... in a vessel so full of men'.[5]

The king himself, the duke and Prince Rupert came aboard and, although in a general council of flag officers the decision was taken that York[6] – dynastically too important – 'should adventure himselfe no more this summer', and resign his command, Evelyn came away encouraged, 'having seen the most glorious fleete that ever set saile'. As he returned with Lord Sandwich in the king's yacht, he could not know that within a year the *Prince* would be captured by the Dutch, then burnt in action.

The plague had now got such a hold (by mid-July there had been 1,843 deaths) that, totally ignorant of its cause, on 2 August the government proclaimed a series of fasts 'to deprecate God's displeasure against the land'. Charles II and the Court retreated to Hampton Court, then to Salisbury, finally to Oxford and, until the worst of the plague was over, did not return. Evelyn took young John and his tutor down to Wotton; but he himself returned to London where he waited on Albemarle and found the tough old soldier also resolved to stay, though the death roll had now mounted to 2,817 plague deaths in a week and by August to nearly 4,000. By the end of the month 'the Contagion growing now all about us,' Evelyn records, 'I sent my Wife and whole family (two or three of my necessary Servants excepted) to Wotton ... being resolved to stay at my house my selfe, and to looke after my Charge, trusting to the providence and goodnesse of God'.[7] The risk was not quite so great as he imagined, for the plague was fiercest in the crowded, filthy and rat-infested dwellings of the poor, but his decision showed courage and characteristic independence. He continued his routine inspections by coach, returning in early September to find 'perishing now neere ten-thousand [in fact about seven thousand] poore Creatures weekly'. But the streets from Kent street to St James, were a 'dismal passage and dangerous', with 'so many Cofines exposd in the streetes and the streete thin of people, the shops shut up and all in mournefull silence, as not knowing whose turn it might be next'.

But on 17 September good news arrived from the fleet: Lord Sandwich had intercepted part of the Dutch convoy from the East Indies and taken two East Indiamen and other rich prizes. In the general tension the news led to what Pepys termed an 'exstasy of joy', and at a dinner party at Greenwich which included old Sir John Minnes, Evelyn for once brilliantly let himself go, his freakish wit being 'inspired by such a spirit of mirth, that in all my life,' writes Pepys,

I never met with so merry a two hours as our company that night was. Among other humours, Mr Evelyn repeating of some verses made up of nothing but the various adaptations of *may* and *can*, and doing it so aptly ... and so fast, did make us all die almost with laughing.

He completely outdid Sir John Minnes, whose 'mirth to see himself undone was the crown of our mirth'.[8] After completing his business at Greenwich with the Commissioners for the Navy, Evelyn went down to Wotton still so strung up that, on his return by his brother's house at Woodcote, he fainted at dinner. But the next day he was dealing with another 3,000 prisoners of war. He was now closely collaborating with Pepys to remedy the neglect of the great officers of state, their masters, 'about all business especially that of money; having now some thousands of prisoners kept to no purpose at great charge, and no money provided almost for the doing of it'.[9]

So when, on 23 September, Lord Sandwich and Evelyn again called on Albemarle, Evelyn was 'peremtory that unlesse we had 10,000 pounds immediately the Prisoners would sterve'; and on 27th Pepys recorded:

To Mr Evelyn, where much company and thence in his coach with him to the Duke of Albemarle by Lambeth ... who tells us that the Dutch do stay abroad and our fleet must go out again, or be ready to do so: Here we got several things ordered as we desired for the relief of the prisoners and sick and wounded men.

In spite of contrasting temperaments, the collaboration of Pepys, the steady professional administrator, and Evelyn, the brisk perceptive amateur, would lead to life-long friendship.

It was now proposed that the king's share of the captured East Indiamen should meet the expense of the prisoners; but since the decision was for the King's Council, an 'expresse' was sent 'to his Majestie and Council to know what they should do', while the prisoners were kept in five vessels with competent guards.

Albemarle had backed the sale of the prizes for cash, and Evelyn now had to hand over the Dutch merchant, Vice-Admiral Burckhorst, to the Marshalsee prison, recording how exceedingly he pitied this 'brave unhappy person, who had lost with these Prizes 40,000 pounds after 20 yeares negotiation in the *East Indies*'. Dining in one of the Dutch ships, he found it 'full of riches'.


## V


The plague, meanwhile, had passed its peak, and on 1 October, 1665, in the same red chamber at Wotton where nearly forty-five years earlier he had himself been born, Evelyn's wife gave birth to a daughter ('after 6 sonnes'), who was christened Mary. After visiting Wotton for the ceremony, he had to traverse London on return and, descending several times from his coach on business, still found himself 'invironed with multitudes of poore pestiferous creatures, begging almes; the shops universaly shut up, a dreadfull prospect'. But he dined with Albemarle, obtained another £10,000 and 'guards to carry both my selfe and it', and so 'through Gods infinite mercy', returned home.[10]

# CHAPTER FOURTEEN

# The Fire of London

In December 1665 Albemarle had superseded Sandwich as 'General at Sea', following a scandal about the embezzlement of prize plunder by flag officers and false accusations of cowardice. But Albemarle, thought Evelyn, had himself been over-confident of 'confounding the Hollander', whom 'upon a more disloyal Interest', he had confounded before. After Christmas, spent by the Evelyns at Wotton, the king returned from Oxford, where the courtiers had thoroughly upset the more pedantic dons, to Hampton Court. Here, presented by Albemarle, Evelyn again found himself in high favour; for the king 'ran towards me, and in most gracious manner gave me his hand to kisse, with many thanks for my Care, and faithfullnesse in his service, in a time of that greate danger, when every body fled their Employments.'[1]

By early March, 1666, it seemed safe for Mary Evelyn and her children to return to Sayes Court, and Evelyn resumed his project for a permanent infirmary, now taken up by Charles II and the Duke of York, who were very earnest that he should 'set about it speedily'. But of course, though the project would have saved the Crown thousands, they could not raise the money.

The Royal Society had also now reassembled, and again elected Evelyn to its Council, an office he refused on plea of other public business. They were now concerned with the unpromising project of a 'saddle on springs, to make a Trotting Horse go Easier to the rider'; more sensibly, Evelyn, who had hired Leeds Castle in Kent for his prisoners of war, 'flowed the drie moate and made a new draw bridge, brought also Spring Water into the Court of the Castle to an old fountaine and took order for the repaires' – a turning point for this still famous building.

The naval war in which the French had now joined the Dutch, had come to a new crisis in the battle of the First of June 1666 or 'Four days Battle'; and being in his garden and 'hearing the Great gunns go thick off', Evelyn at once rode to Rochester and to the coast, but there being 'no noise or appearance' at Deal,

returned to London, where he found the king impatiently expecting news in St James's Park. Back at Sayes Court on 3 June,
Evelyn heard 'the Gunns still roaring very fiercely', and by the
5th the news at last came through that 'our losse was very greate
both in ships and men'; Albemarle had been forced to retreat,
though he had done so 'like a *Lyon*', and the *Prince* had been lost.

The action had proved 'exceeding shattring of both *fleetes*', for
'both being obstinate', had 'parted rather for want of amunition
and tackle than Courage'.[2] Albemarle, Evelyn considered, had
overreached himself, having 'once beaten the Dutch in another
quarrell' and being ambitious to out-do the Earl of Sandwich,
'whom he had prejudice [to], as defective of Courage'.

In mid-June Evelyn again went down to visit the fleet, and
from Sheerness could see the sad spectacle,[3]

namely more than halfe of that gallant bulwark of the Kingdome
miserably shatter'd, hardly a Vessel intire, but appearing rather so
many wracks and hulls, so cruely had the *Dutch* mangled us ... none
knowing for what reason we first engagd in this ungratefull War.

'Weary of this sad sight,' Evelyn concludes, 'I returned home.'

But the war, in fact crucial for trade and colonies, pursued
him. Early in July the king in council nominated him a
commissioner for the supply of saltpetre for gunpowder
throughout the kingdom, the only time he was expected to be
officially knowledgeable about his family business. And when, at
the end of the month, the English narrowly defeated the Dutch
in the 'St James's fight', Evelyn had to visit the wounded in the
Savoy hospital.

He found a more congenial task as one of the surveyors for the
repair of Old St Paul's, going about with Wren 'to survey the
generall decays of that ancient and venerable Church, and to set
downe the particulars in writing, what was fit to be don'. They
found the steeple so far decayed that they both insisted on a new
foundation, and planned a 'noble' (and incongruous) cupola –
not as yet known in England: they even drew up a 'draught and
estimate' and tried to appoint a committee of able workmen to
examine the existing foundation.

## II

Their plan had soon to be scrapped for one far more
comprehensive. On 2 September 1666, 'this fatal night, about
ten, began that deplorable fire, neere Fish-streete in Lond:'; in

four days it would reduce the Cathedral and much of London to smoking ruins. 'After dinner the fire continuing, with my Wife and Sonn took coach and went to the bankside in Southwark where we beheld that dismal speectaccle; the whole Citty in dreadfull flames neere the Water side ... and so returned exceedingly astonish'd.' The fire increased during the night – 'if I may call that night which was as light as day for 10 miles round after a dreadfull manner' – fanned by a 'fierce Eastern Wind, in a very drie season'. Returning next day on foot to Southwark, Evelyn[4]

saw the whole South part of the Citty burning from Cheape side to the Thames, and all along Cornhill *Tower-Streete, Fen-church*-Streete, ... and so along to Bainard Castle, and ... now taking hold of St *Paules-Church*, to which the Scaffalds contributed exceedingly.

The conflagration, with what Pepys called its 'horrid malicious bloody flame'[5] so staggered the people that they 'hardly stirr'd to quench it ... running about like distracted creatures, without at all attempting to save even their goods'. The flames even seemed to have 'ignited the air' and leapt from street to street devouring everything. The Thames was covered with floating goods, boats and barges all laden, while carts were carrying what they could out into the fields, where tents were put up to shelter the people and what they had saved: 'all the skie were of a fiery aspect, like the top of a burning Oven', the light seen 'above 40 miles round for many nights'. 'God grant mine eyes,' wrote Evelyn, 'may never behold the like.' He saw 'above ten thousand houses all in one flame', he heard 'the noise and crakling and thunder of the impetuous flames ... the shreeking of Women and children, the hurry of people, the fall of towers'. He saw the billowing smoke reaching 'neere 50 miles in length'. '*London*,' Evelyn summed up, 'was, but is no more.'

On 4 September the fire was still raging; Evelyn, riding in from Sayes Court, found it had reached the Inner Temple, and that the stones of St Paul's were flying like grenades, while the molten lead from its roof poured down streets whose very stones glowed fiery red.

The king and the Duke of York had all along personally led the fight against the catastrophe 'even labouring in person, and being present, to command, order and encourage workmen, by which [the King] shewed his affection to his people, and gained theirs', and Charles himself commanded Evelyn to look to the quenching of Fetter Lane and that part of Holborn. Some stout seamen had early argued that only systematic demolitions could stop the fire spreading, but the householders ('Aldermen etc') had refused: now belatedly, demolition was enforced. So many houses were blown up, which clearance along with three days of devastation, now made gaps enough for the fire to be contained; then the east wind abated so that Evelyn could leave the 'smoking and sultry heape which mounted up in dismal clowds night and day', at least with relief that his own charge, the Savoy hospital, had just survived, and return with a sad heart to his own house, thanking God for his 'distinguishing mercy ... to me and mine', who 'in the midst of all this ruine' were 'safe and sound'.[6]

When, three days after the fire had been extinguished, Evelyn on foot traversed the worst areas of damage, including Fleet Street, Ludgate Hill, St Paul's and the Exchange, he had to clamber over mountains of smoking rubbish in intense heat, and was 'infinitely concerned to find that goodly church St Paules now a sad ruin', with the new portico put in by the late king 'split in sunder', its massive columns and capitals of Portland stone 'calcin'd', and six acres of leaden roof totaly melted. 'Thus lay in ashes that most venerable Church, one of the ancientist Pieces of Early Piety in the Christian world.' Evelyn could only pass through the widest streets, the by-lanes being filled with rubbish, and the air still so hot that his hair was almost singed and his feet 'surbated' (sore). Out at Islington he saw an enormous crowd of fugitives sitting by the few possessions they had retrieved. The government had issued a proclamation for 'the Country to come in and refresh them with provisions', but a rumour got loose that the French and Dutch had landed and were entering London, so that 'uprore and tumult' broke out and the 'Clamor and perill grew so excessive that the whole *Court* amaz'd at it' and troops had to restore order.

As the Court virtuoso of architecture, Evelyn at once presented the king with a survey of the ruins and a 'plot for a new Citty'; whereat Charles sent for him to the queen's bedchamber, 'her majestie and the Duke only present,' and they 'examined each particular and discoursed for a full hour, seeming to be extreamly pleased with what I had so early thought on'. Evelyn had already backed Wenceslas Hollar, the fine Czech refugee artist appointed His Majesty's Designer at the Restoration, to enable him to complete his map of London, a project interrupted by the plague; and he now helped him to become the king's Scenographer, after he had made a new map leaving the burnt portion blank, a useful prelude to any plans for rebuilding. But the careers of most artists, then as now, were very precarious, particularly if they were good ones, and in 1677 Hollar aged seventy, would die in penury, only asking his creditors not to remove his bed first.

By October, Evelyn, feeling unwell, 'entr'd into a course of steele against the Scorbut' (scurvy) – hardly a good remedy, and on 10 October another national fast was proclaimed, 'upon the late dreadful Conflagration added to the Plague and War'. He considered all 'highly deserved for our prodigious ingratitude, burning lusts and abominable lives' after all God's favour in 'restoring the Church Prince and People from our late intestine calamities'. The preachers had also been taking occasion 'to mind us how we ought to walke more holilie' and to show the 'justnesse of God's judgements'. More usefully, in the Deptford parish assembly, a collection was made for 'the poor distressed loosers in the late fire and their present relief'.


### III

The war with the Dutch and French led the king to abandon his customary French fashion of dress; putting himself solemnly into the *Eastern fashion*, 'changing doublet, stiff collar and Cloake into a comely Vest after the Persian mode with girdle or Shash. ... resolving ... to leave the French mode which had hitherto obtained to our greate expense and reproch.'[7] Some of the courtiers betted the king heavily that he would not keep up this change – nor did he for more than five years –; but Evelyn took some of the credit, having described the elegance of Persian clothes in his own pamphlet, already described, *Tyrannus or the Mode*, published in 1661. The monarch having set a new style, the Court gaieties resumed, and Evelyn, much as he disapproved the new fashion of actresses ('women now (and never 'til now) permitted to appeare and act, while inflaming some noblemen and gallants, became their whores and to some their wives'), had to attend Lord Orrery's tragedy, *Mustapha*, at Court.

Back at Deptford the vicar continued to inveigh against sin, and on the severity of God's judgments, and on how it was Jesus, as the second person in the Trinity who had overthrown Sodom for 'dishonouring the nature he was to assume', etc. But Evelyn as a good subject and courtier, now wore 'the new fashion of vest, surcoat and tunic, after his Majestie had brought the whole Court to it'.

In November he made another circuit of his district and
ordered better provision for about 600 French and Dutch
prisoners in Leeds Castle, and, returning to Chatham, his chariot
upset, cutting him about the head and threatening worse injury
to young John. The Royal Society had resumed its autumn
meetings, now at Arundel House in the Strand, and Evelyn, as a
friend of the late Lord Arundel, the collector, now arranged that
his Howard grandson, Lord Henry, afterwards Sixth Duke of
Norfolk, 1678–84, presented the Society with 'that noble Library,
which his grand-father and all his Ancestors had collected' ...
'this Gent: having little inclination to books'. They were thus
also preserved from 'imbezilment'.

By 1667 young John, though only twelve, was due to go to
Oxford, so Evelyn presented him to Clarendon, the chancellor of
the university, and by the end of the month he was in London to
see about his boy's journey. Being very early taught Greek and
Latin, and 'prompt to learn', John was committed to the care of
the President of Trinity, though his tutor came from New
College. On 30 January he set out to Oxford with his tutor.


## IV


These literary and academic concerns, carried on while peace
negotiations with the Dutch had been afoot since the previous
year, were now dwarfed by public disaster. On 10 June 1667 a
Dutch fleet took Sheerness, on the 12th it had entered the
Medway, then it blockaded the Thames. On the 11th Evelyn
recorded,[8]

Alarm'd by the *Dutch*, who were falln on our Fleete, at Chattam by a
most audacious enterprise entering the very river with part of their
fleete, doing us not onely disgrace but incredible mischiefe in burning
severall of our best Men of Warr, lying at Anker and Moored there ...
and all this thro' ... our negligence in setting out our fleete in due time.

Fearing that the Dutch would 'adventure up the Thames even to
Lond: which with ease they might have don, and fired all the
Vessels in the river, too', Evelyn even removed all his best
valuables from Sayes Court.

As usual, Albemarle was called in, along with Prince Rupert
and the Duke of York; but 'the resolute Enemy' broke through
all the improvised defences, and continued to blockade the
Thames: Evelyn went to see a battery at Woolwich commanded
by Prince Rupert and designed to prevent the Dutch coming up

river. prepared at Deptford, now in flames, and the people panicked, convinced that the Dutch had landed. At Chatham on 28 June Evelyn was horrified to see 'how triumphantly their whole [Dutch] fleet lay within the very mouth of the Thames', from the North Foreland to the Nore – a 'Dreadfull Spectacle as ever any English men saw, and a dishonour never to be wiped off. Those who advised his *Majestie* to prepare no fleete this Spring, deserv'd I know what!'⁹

Off Chatham lay the 'carcasses' of the best ships – the *London*, the *Royal Oak* and the *Royal James* 'yet Smoking'. And when on 31 July 1667 treaties were at last signed at Breda ending the Second Dutch War, they marked a peace of exhaustion, in which the English apparently came off worst. In fact, the Dutch with lesser resources, had suffered more; they surrendered New Amsterdam which became New York, as well as New Jersey and Delaware, a loss which more than offset their retaining most of the forts on the West African coast and Guiana in South America.

Strategically the war had been less disastrous than Evelyn believed, but its tactical disasters had been occasioned by that 'fatal duality of sovereignty which paralysed England's action from the Restoration to the Revolution'¹⁰ and by the inadequate resources allowed the king. Shortage of money and credit that summer had in fact prevented the fleet putting to sea, but the disgrace now came home to Clarendon, since the Restoration principal minister and Lord Chancellor. Already unpopular for his old-fashioned formal arrogance, increased by his being father-in-law to York, and belonging to a relatively high-minded generation who had grown up before the Civil Wars, he was not at ease in the raffish and cynical court of Charles II, who himself found him worthy but tedious.

Evelyn had known him well in Paris, and late in August 1667, soon after the king had ordered Clarendon to surrender the Great Seal, he visited the fallen magnate: 'I found him in his bed-Chamber very Sad.' The parliament had accused him and he had enemies at Court, especially the 'boufoones and Ladys of Pleasure, because he thwarted some of them'. He had also disappointed many leading cavaliers and was thought to have 'advanced the old rebells that had money enough to buy places', but he had been Evelyn's 'particular kind friend in all occasions'. John dined with the old chancellor, still 'pretty well in heart', then attended the audience for the Russian envoy from the Tsar Alexis Romanov, who spoke 'in the Russe language alowd, but without the least action or motion of his body ... which was immediately interpreted by a *German* who Spake Good *English*'. Half of the speech consisted in 'repetition of the *Zarr*'s titles which were very haughty and oriental' ... 'but their real errand was to get money'.[11]

On 13 September 1667, John's wife bore a second daughter, christened at a family gathering Elizabeth; then Lord Henry Howard, who had already presented his great library to the Royal Society, also made the sumptuous gift to Oxford university of the 'Arundelian Marbles – Those celebrated and famous Inscriptions in Greeke and Latine, with so much cost and industrie gathered from Greece by his Illustrious Grandfather ... my noble friend while he lived'. The monuments had been 'miserably neglected and scattred up and down' and impaired by the corrosive London air, and Evelyn had 'procured [Howard] to bestow them on Oxford'. That September he also procured from the king Chelsea College, hitherto used for prisoners of war, which was handed over to the Royal Society.

The university of Oxford were delighted at the gift of the 'Arundel Marbles' (about 130 inscribed stones), and the vice chancellor sent Dr Bathurst, the President of Trinity, to call on Evelyn and receive directions about their transport. The Provost of the Queen's College also arrived on the same errand, followed in October by a formal decree of thanks from Convocation in Latin. Evelyn, at forty-seven, had become a major benefactor.

## V

Nor had he neglected learned pseudo-academic controversy. In February he had published a *Tract on Publick Employment with an Active Life with all its appenages, such as Fame, Command, Riches, Conversation etc. preferred to Solitude.*[12] by J.E. Esq. F.R.S. (London, 1667).

It is conventional, flowery and self-conscious, directed against another pamphlet entitled '*A Moral Essay, preferring Solitude to Public Employment*' (Edinburgh, 1665), by Sir George Mackenzie of Rosshaugh (1638–91), known to the Covenanters he had prosecuted as 'Bloody Mackenzie'. As a king's advocate in Scotland, Mackenzie, born in Dundee, had seen many unattractive aspects of public life, to which he had himself contributed; but he had managed to write *Aretina, or a Serious*

*Romance* describing the Civil War in, of all places, an Egyptian setting.

Evelyn's reply is voluminous, stuffed with classical learning, suggesting the work of a rather ordinary mind with a trenchant pen, showing off. Sir George, he alleges, had argued that private repose was Godlike: or that 'to resemble God' we are to 'sit still and do nothing'. 'Be that our faith,' saith Lactantius, 'then farewell religion!' On the contrary, Evelyn points out, God has always been intensely energetic, not permitting the world to remain an idea only, but creating it with a great deal of trouble.

Men, in fact, only praise retirement when incapable of action, and a merchant does not make money to end up in solitude, but with a 'fair lady, a rich coach, a noble retinue, good german wine and to make more noise among his jolly friends than ever he did at sea or in camp'.

Nor do the best princes want to play all day at retirement, just give audience to buffoons, or even sport with apes; they 'give laws to kingdoms, and march before legions'. Consider the illustrious duke (Albemarle) 'who so resolutely unnestled the late *Junta* of Iniquity'.

Besides, solitude is bad for anyone; whenever men abscond themselves, human miseries and their own vices find them out; the blackest treacheries are excogitated in gloomy recesses; and close, stagnated, and covered waters stink most. Look at the Fifth Monarchy Men!

After some shrewd jibes at over-bookish scholars, pedantically morose and unpolished, who have spent solitary lives speculating 'how many oars Ulysses' galley carried', Evelyn declares roundly that a life spent in theories and abstractions is better for bedlam and a potion of hellebore; and he concludes with a contrast, 'landskip for landskip', between the public life of a great hierarchy, with the sovereign in parliament making laws, the Lord Chancellor and judges dispensing them, the secretaries of state receiving intelligence, the statesmen counteracting plots, the generals embattling their forces, the poor set to work, the naked clad; on the other hand, he portrays a prince on a cushion picking his teeth, country gentlemen taking tobacco after a gorgeous meal, a contemplative private man like a ghost in a churchyard or poring over a book while his family starves, a gallant ogling his pretty female, an anchorite at his beads or a young poacher with his dog trampling the corn. It is an effective sensible and conservative conclusion to an artificial controversy.

## VI

In October 1667 Clarendon was again being attacked in parliament. He was impeached by the Commons of high treason, an accusation which the Lords refused to consider, and though Clarendon wrote abjectly to the king, 'I do upon my knees beg your pardon for any overbold or saucy expressions I have ever used to you', and begged Charles to allow him to retire beyond the seas, Charles, not daring to give him a pass for fear of the Commons, merely remarked that 'he wondered the Chancellor did not withdraw himself'.

But Evelyn still stood by his old friend and patron, and found him in the garden of his 'new built palace' which had so infuriated his enemies, 'sitting in his Gowt wheele chare.... He looked and spake very disconsolately.'[13] By the night of 29 November Clarendon had left for France, and Lords and Commons combined to pass an Act to banish him for life. Had he simply retired to Cornbury and 'lay quiet', Evelyn considered, parliament might have been satisfied; but Clarendon had seen too much political murder, and, being under both indirect pressure from the king and direct pressure from York, he was taking no chances.

Impervious to politics, that December, the Royal Society was experimenting with transferring blood from a sheep to a man – presumably with fatal results; at Christmas the vicar at Deptford preached on God's inexpressible love for mankind, and made a parallel between Isaiah and our Blessed Lord, and, as usual, Evelyn gave thanks for the Almighty's mercies to himself and his family this year past.

# CHAPTER FIFTEEN

# Politics, Encaenia and 'a rare Discovery'

In spite of the popular goodwill and rejoicing of the Restoration and the apparent success of a realistic settlement, the position of the monarch was extremely difficult. Charles II was not yet a constitutional king, but the representative of a 'mixed' monarchy in which the initiative and responsibility remained in royal hands, but in which financial and military power was in the hands of an Anglican, landowning and mercantile oligarchy, who had brought in the king to consolidate their own position against the army, the nonconformists and the radicals. The revenues voted to the king for life were quite inadequate for the needs of government, and the Crown depended on parliament for essential supply, but the constitutional question had not yet been solved of making the king's ministers responsible to a majority in parliament, while there was no regular system of credit whereby the inevitably large expenditure on the navy could be financed. Charles II, moreover, a cosmopolitan king, Scots-Danish on his father's side, Bourbon-Medici on his mother's, retained the idea of divine right prevalent on the Continent, and remarked in his casual and succinct way that he 'did not think he was a King as long as a company of fellows were looking into all his actions'. No more than his father was he content to be the 'mere painted sign of a King', and in so far as he had any religious belief, he inclined to Catholicism, the religion of the greatest monarchs abroad, and one which, unlike Presbyterianism, he considered was fit for a gentleman.

Not that, like his father, he was ready to die for his beliefs: he was a cunning politician, hardened in penurious exile, and determined on two things – 'not to go on his travels again' and to preserve the legitimate succession of his dynasty, even for the politically inept and now Catholic Duke of York.

With the fall of Clarendon, a statesman of pre-war vintage, who had managed the Restoration settlement with much skill and was not responsible for the Anglican intolerance of the

Clarendon Code, Charles II had to govern through shifting cliques of 'King's men' who, between them, tried to manage a factious and restive parliament, subject to gusts of religious fanaticism; Charles thus became the first monarch who tried to manage parliament, a tradition which continued intermittently into the reign of George III, and was necessary if government was to be carried on. But he was regularly frustrated in minor and salutary projects, as diminishing the smoke of London or building a regular hospital for seamen, both of which Evelyn had put up to him.

During the interregnum, in a more complex and modern society a rudimentary civil service had emerged out of Tudor and early Stuart foundations; it needed development and money, and Pepys, who reorganized the administration of the navy, and Evelyn, in his lesser responsibilities, were constantly handicapped by lack of funds. The perennial problem facing the king and government, and constant in most of Europe since the late sixteenth century, was how to finance and make effective the authority of a new sort of sovereign state, which roused much provincial resentment and had exacerbated the English Civil Wars, yet was necessary in the current social and economic context. And in Restoration England resentment was worsened when the increasingly money-minded establishment was shocked by the casual Frenchified lavishness of the Court. Only in North America, where, once the effects of the English Civil War had been overcome, the Crown had a freer hand, could the later Stuarts work comparatively untrammelled; in England Charles II, on whom the responsibility of government remained without the means of financing it, was driven to use his freedom in foreign policy to blackmail Louis XIV for subsidies that made him periodically independent of parliaments hostile to the French.

After 1667 and the fall of Clarendon, the coalition of king's parliament men which came to be labelled the Cabal, and the regime of Sir Thomas Osborne, Earl of Danby (1673–9), now formed the political setting of Evelyn's life. They were both strongly royalist governments, politically tainted with Catholicism, and with the fall of Danby, following the panic over a bogus 'Popish Plot' in 1679, Charles II's first 'Long' or 'Cavalier' parliament was dissolved.

The relatively incoherent factions of the former parliament now began coalescing into the rudiments of 'party' political organizations – Whig and Tory, both with their origins in the religious strife of the Civil War. The Whigs (from Whiggamore, Scots Covenanters of the 1640s) drew their strength from the remnants of the 'Good Old Cause', the dissenters and small artizans, and were afterwards led by aristocratic politicians, great landowners and city magnates with wide commercial horizons; the Tories (from Catholic extremists in Ireland) drew their strength from the Court, the royalist lesser gentry and the High Anglican clergy, some even supporting 'non-resistance' to a monarchy by divine right.

The first major crisis between the two 'parties' or factions arose when the Whigs attempted to exclude James Duke of York, from the succession, and Charles II, supported by subsidies from Louis XIV, had to fight a skilful rearguard action against his second and third parliaments, both predominantly 'Whig', and dissolved the last in 1681, so defending his brother's rights against the Whig candidate for the succession, his own eldest bastard, the Protestant Duke of Monmouth.

Such are the political facts which now formed the background of Evelyn's life and of the developments of the far-flung oceanic trade and settlement which made England a power of far greater consequence, superseding the Dutch and challenging the French.

II

In 1668 constitutional problems were hardly Evelyn's main concern. He produced a translation of *An Idea of the Perfection of Painting* by Roland Fréart, Sieur de Cambray, and even ventured into the dangerous field of art history with a Preface which he had composed himself.[1] It was orthodox and applauded by the standards of his time.

Evelyn judges art by Cartesian rationalism and Baconian common sense. Making no allowance for their contexts, he condemns most of the old masters out of hand for ignorance of perspective, though he singles out Raphael and Alberti as accurate about antiquity, praises Poussin for his indefatigable study of the Greeks and Romans, and considers Bernini 'our now living and universal Master', comparable to 'our own' Christopher Wren. The greatest painters and architects, he declares, are the masters of Design.

Titian, Giorgione, Tintoretto and Paolo Veronese, on the other hand, are all condemned for historical inaccuracy: how ridiculous to depict Pharaoh's daughter with Moses in the bull rushes attended by Swiss Guards, to paint Adam and Eve with navels, and place an artificial stone fountain in the Garden of Eden! Even the great Rubens, regardless of context, made most of his figures 'brawney Flemings'.

Apart from translating Fréart, Evelyn had faithfully recorded the brisk critical standards of his time. His outlook is also revealingly displayed in a long letter to Pepys, written much later, in 1689, in which Evelyn protests that he is himself 'unfit to appear among Pepys's pictures of illustrious men', and goes on at length ('methinks I hear you cry out what a ramble has Mr E made') to deplore that 'great painters have wasted their talents painting some porter or squalid chimney sweepes ... I am in perfect indignation at this folly!'[2]

'Give me,' he continues, 'Carolus Magnus, a Tamburlaine, a Scanderbeg, Solyman the Magnificent, Math: Corvinus, Lorenzo, Cosimo Medicis, Andrea Dorea ... the effigies of Cardan and both the Scaligers, Copernicus, Galileo.' Evelyn preferred the official celebrities of history; he was indifferent to the poetry elicited by great artists from the light of common day.

In mid-February 1669, Evelyn was presenting the king with 'my history of the foure Imposters', a derivative work of ephemeral interest, and Charles took this occasion to 'tempt' him to write about the late Dutch Wars in order to counteract the propaganda of the French and Dutch. But the laborious project long hung fire, and when in 1674 the king raised the subject again, all Evelyn could do would be to send him a Preface on *Navigation and Commerce*, which was immediately published, then 'called in'.


## III


In March 1669 Evelyn went down into bucolic East Anglia: dining in Norfolk, he recorded:[3]

the Servants made our Coachmen so drunk, that they both fell-off their boxes upon the heath, where we were faine to leave them, and were driven to Lond: by two Gent: of my Lord's [Lord Henry Howard]. This barbarous Costome of making their Masters Wellcome, by intoxicating the Servants had now the second time happn'd to my Coachman.

Evelyn's family circle was now increased by the return of young John, still only fourteen, from Oxford; and in May by the birth of a third daughter, christened Susanna; but his younger brother Richard was now 'afflicted with the stone'. So Evelyn's friend

Pepys, who had early been successfully cut for the illness, carried his own stone 'as big as a tenis ball' to Richard to encourage him.

Then in June Evelyn went down to Oxford to attend the first Encaenia in the new-built Sheldonian. It was celebrated with the utmost 'splendor and formalitie', marred only by the academic spite of the Public Orator who made 'malicious and undecent reflections on the Royal Society as underminers of the University' but 'the rest was in praise of the Arch Bish: and [Wren] the ingenious Architect'. There followed loud music, 'divers Panegyric Speeches both in prose and verse by the young students', and the whole ceremony, which lasted from eleven in the morning to seven at night, concluded with bells ringing, and universal joy and feasting.

But next day Evelyn was distressed by the gross jests of the *Terrae Filius* or 'Universitie Bouffoone' – 'more licentious lying and railing than ... wit' – and plainly expressed his disapproval to the vice chancellor and several heads of houses: 'In my life,' he concludes, 'I was never witnesse to so shamefull entertainement.' Tone was restored by more music and by professorial orations, and a final panegyrical oration by the vice chancellor.

But the Arundel marbles, now in place, were being scratched by idlers, and Evelyn advised that a holly hedge, low enough for them to be seen, be planted to protect them; a project which the vice chancellor promised to carry out. Finally, robed in scarlet, Evelyn himself received an honorary doctorate, according to a ritual which still continues, 'So formal a Creation of Honorarie *Doctors*' had 'seldome ben seene', and they were all sumptuously entertained by the president of St John's College.[4]

Back in London, Evelyn resumed his usual routine of visits, meetings of the Royal Society, and analysing sermons. On 14 November he attended the funeral of Mrs Pepys, who had died, aged only twenty-nine, to the desolation of her husband; and at Christmas he recorded, 'Hardly was ever felt so great cold in England for many years.'

By March 1670 Richard Evelyn was in 'such exceeding torture' from the stone, that John set apart a day to 'beg God to mitigate his sufferings' and 'prosper the only meanes which yet remained for his recovery'; but though in 'convulsion fits' and most wasted, Richard remained 'averse from being cut', and though the operation was prepared, he could not face it. So on 6 March, towards five in the morning, Richard died. He had been a 'sober, prudent, and worthy Gent': he had married a great fortune, but left but 'an onely daughter, and a most noble seate at Woodcot'.

The autopsy revealed a stone not much bigger than a nutmeg, but that his liver was badly diseased and 'his kidnis almost quite consum'd'. Cutting for the stone would not have saved him. He was interred at a very well-attended funeral, with 'about 20 Coaches of six-horses'.

In May Evelyn managed to escape the promised office of Latin Secretary to the king: it was worth only £80 a year and a 'place of more honor and dignitie, than benefit'; then in June, reluctantly and 'forced to accompanie some friends', he visited the Bear-Garden,[5]

Where was Cock *fighting*, Beare, *Dog-fighting*, Beare and *Bull baiting*, it being a famous day for all these butcherly Sports, or rather barbarous cruelties: The Bulls did exceedingly well, but the Irish Wolfe dog exceeded, which was a tall Gray-hound, a stately creature in deede, who beate a cruell Mastife. One of the Bulls tossd a Dog full into a Ladys lap, as she sate in one of the boxes ... There were two poore dogs killed; and so all ended with the Ape on horse-back, and I most heartily weary, of the rude and dirty passtime.

In July, Richard Evelyn's daughter and heiress married William Montagu, son of the attorney general to the queen, 'with a magnificent entertainment, feast and dancing', and Evelyn made an excursion by coach and six to Burrough Green near Newmarket, where his friend Henry Slingsby, Master of the Mint, intended to build a house, and thence rode out to see the 'great meere or Levell of recover'd Fenland' around Ely. They also looked over the king's new-building house at Newmarket, which Evelyn thought 'meane' and 'hardly capable for a hunting house'. 'Many of the roomes above', moreover, 'had the Chimnies plac'd in the angles and Corners, a Mode introduced by his Majestie which I do at no hand approve of, and predict it will Spoile many noble houses and roomes if followed'. But the king's fine horses were kept up at vast expense 'with all the art and tendernesse Imaginable', and after watching draining engines at work by Soham Mere, and riding about the vast level 'pestered with heat', Evelyn returned over Newmarket heath ... 'being mostly sweete turfe and down, like Salisbury plaine, the *Jockies* breathing their fine barbs and racers, and giving them their heates'. On the way back to London they visited Audley End 'in Saffron Walden parish, famous for that useful plant'; it is indeed, he commented, 'a cherefull piece of Gotic-building, or rather *antico-moderno*, but placed in an obscure bottome: The Cellars and Gallerie very stately.'

By September 1670 the king, following the secret anti-Dutch

Treaty of Dover with Louis XIV, had again been urging Evelyn to
write a propagandist piece about the Second Dutch War, and in
late August at Windsor had taken him 'aside into the *Balconie*
over the Tarice', apparently pleased with the little he had told
him of the enterprise, 'enjoying me to proceede vigorously in
it', and said that he had ordered the secretaries of state 'to give
me all necessary assistance ... and enjoyning me to make it a little
keene, for that the *Hollanders* had very unhandsomely abused
him, in their pictures, books and libells, etc.'.[6]

Windsor, being 'exceedingly ragged and ruinous', was now
under repair; and Prince Rupert as Constable had begun to
'trim up the *Keepe* or high round Tower' and 'handsomely
adorn'd his Hall, with a furniture of Armes'. His bedchamber,
by contrast, was hung with tapestries and 'curious and
effeminate Pictures ... extreemly different from the others which
presented nothing but Warr and horror'. Charles, at Windsor,
spent most of his time stag hunting or walking in the park which
he was planting with avenues of trees, of which some have
survived into this century. Back in London, Evelyn saw the
twenty-year-old Prince of Orange, his future sovereign as
William III, and marked his intelligent expression and
resemblance to his uncle, the late Duke of Gloucester.

## IV

On 18 January 1671 John told the king of one of the happiest
discoveries of his life. Walking by a poor and solitary thatched
house in a field near Sayes Court, he observed a young man
inside 'carving that large ... *Crucifix* of *Tintorets*', a copy of which
Evelyn had himself brought back from Venice. 'I asked if I might
come in, he opned the doore civily to me, and I saw him about
such a work, as for the curiosity of handling, drawing and
studious exactnesse, I never in my life had seene before in all my
travells'.[7] Asked why he worked in such an obscure and
lonesome place, young Grinling Gibbons replied that he did so
to work 'without interruption', and when asked if he were
'unwilling to be made knowne to some Greate men', answered
modestly that he was 'as yet but a beginner, but would not be
sorry to sell off that piece'. He named his price at £100 – but John
thought the exquisitely carved frame of flowers and festoons
alone well worth the money. He also found that this young
Anglo-Dutchman, born in Rotterdam, was 'musical, sober and

discreete': 'of this Young *Artist*', he concludes, 'together with my manner of finding him, I aquainted the King'.

A monarch of taste in an age of fine craftsmanship, Charles at once declared that he would go to see Gibbons himself, and on 1 March Evelyn had the artist bring his carving to Court. 'I advertized his Majestie, who asked me where it was. I told him, in Sir R. Browne's (my F in Laws) Chamber', and offered to have it brought in. ' "No" says the King: "shew me the Way, Ile go to Sir *Richard*'s Chamber" ', which his Majestie immediately did, walking all along the Enteries after me.'

Charles was astonished at the excellence of the work, discoursed with Gibbons, whom he allowed to kiss his hand, and commanded the carving to be carried to the queen's bedchamber, where, having to attend a Council, he left it, thinking that, 'it being a Crucifix', the queen would buy Gibbons's work. But one of the queen's French pedling women, began to find faults with the masterpiece, 'which she understood no more than an Asse or Monky'.[8] And finding the Portuguese queen 'so much govern'd by an ignorant woman', Evelyn in a kind of indignation had the work carried back where it had come from; so Gibbons, 'this incomparable artist' (had) 'the labour onely for his paines', and was 'faine to send it downe to his cottage again'. Not long after, he sold it, not for £100, but for £80, but Christopher Wren promised Evelyn that he would employ him extensively. So, after all, Grinling Gibbons was launched into his memorable career. He was a meticulous craftsman, very particular about what woods he used: lime wood for carving fruit, flowers, festoons and game; oak for church stalls and panelling; boxwood for medallions. He worked for Wren at St Paul's and decorated the superb library at Trinity College, Cambridge. He lived until 1720 and adorned Chatsworth, Petworth and Blenheim and many other great houses; he remained 'Master Carver in Wood' to successive monarchs until the reign of George I.

## V

Charles II had now nominated Evelyn to one of his more important appointments. At the end of February 1671 he was made one of the king's new Council for Foreign Plantations, with the then substantial salary of £500 a year. The terms of reference of this Council, which already included the Lord

Chancellor, the Lord Treasurer and the secretaries of state, were wide: to find out the condition and potential of all and each of the plantations (colonies), to enquire into the conduct of their governors and councils and in general find out the facts; moreover, it had been now enlarged by the appointment of the Duke of York, Prince Rupert, the Duke of Buckingham, Ormond, and Lauderdale. In September of 1672 the Council, renamed the Council for Trade and Foreign Plantations, would be given yet further scope.

So on 10 March 1671 Evelyn went to London about 'passing my grant for my sallerie of 500 pounds per ann as one of the Standing Council on Plantations; a considerable honour'. Evelyn thus became included in the most constructive and lasting enterprise of the later Stuarts – the development of the colonies, and the change over of England from a late medieval economy, excessively dependent on the cloth trade, to an *entrepot* of oceanic commerce deriving mainly from the West Indies, the North American plantations and the East Indies as well. Untrammelled by the political warfare which at home almost crippled government by factions still deriving from religious hatreds of the Civil Wars, Charles, York and Prince Rupert could take a modern initiative in North America, while the expanding oceanic commerce with India as well as the plantations would gradually give the English something better to think of than the politico-religious strife which had created so much havoc and misery during the mid-century.

## VI

Not that the king's versatile abilities were concentrated in a bourgeois way on such purely practical objectives: they were incidental to his relentless pursuit of pleasure, his laziness and his enslavement to women. Evelyn had long disapproved of the goings-on at Court, and now, walking with the king through St James's Park to the royal garden, lately laid out east of St James's Palace, he was even more shocked at his sovereign's intimate conversation with Nell Gwyn, when he 'both saw and heard a very familiar discourse betweene ... and Mrs Nellie, as they cal'd an impudent Comedian, she looking out of her Garden on a Tarrace at the top of the Wall, and ... standing on the greene Walke under it: I was heartily sorry at this scene.'[9]

The king, distributing his civilities impartially, then proceeded to call on Lady Castlemaine, now Duchess of Cleveland, another 'Lady of Pleasure and the curse of our nation'. Evelyn could only feel deep regret at these frailties in the Lord's Annointed.

# CHAPTER SIXTEEN

# Foreign Plantations: *Navigation and Commerce*

The first plenary session of the Council for Foreign Plantations occurred in May of 1671: first it directed an agreed form of circular letter to all the plantations and territories of the West Indies, ordering them to give a full account of their present state, then the council insisted on finding out 'in what condition *New-England was*'.[1] The colonists were already 'appearing to be very independent as to their reguard to Old England, or his Majestie, rich and strong as now they were'. The question was 'in what style to write to them', for it was feared they 'might altogether break away from all dependence'. The king himself had particularly directed the council's attention to the question.

New England had already taken advantage of the Civil Wars and the interregnum to become almost free of the old country, and it was urgent to find out the facts. While some of the Council wished to write a menacing letter, others who better understood the 'touchy and peevish humor of that Colonie, were utterly against'. On a note of caution the council adjourned.

Evelyn still had other official responsibilities: since the previous December he had become involved in a lawsuit with George Cooke, Treasurer of the Commission for the Sick and Wounded, who had been late in rendering his accounts, and he now sought the advice of William Jones, KC of Grays Inn. On 27 May he obtained a trial before the Lord Chief Justice Hales for money owing: but 'after the Lawyers had wrangled sufficiently, It was again referred to a new Arbitration'. 'This,' Evelyn comments, 'being the very first Suite at Law that ever I had with any Creature before, and Ô that it might be the Last!' Perhaps it was a relief even to hear the vicar of Deptford on who and what were to be the precursors of the Last Judgment.

The council business was brisker: on 6 June 1671 they heard 'a most exact and ample Information of the state of *Jamaica*, and of the best expedients to reduce *New-England*, on which there was another long debate'. It was concluded that, if any, there should at first be sent 'onely a conciliatory paper ... since we understood that they were a people almost upon the very brink of renouncing any dependence of the Crowne ...'. Evelyn then introduced a Colonel Midleton of Shelter Island east of Long Island in America, to Lord Sandwich, the president of the council, to advise him about the state of New England. Colonel Cartwright, one of the Commission sent out then in 1664, also gave evidence; on which the council concluded that 'if policy would not reduce the disaffected there, force should'; and although 'in the first place a letter of amnestie would be dispatch'd, a certain Iland in the mouth of the chiefe river' should be fortified, while the king bought part of Fernando Gorges's (grandson of Sir Fernando, the original proprietor of Maine) estate, which would 'inable him to curb Boston'.

The council was now in full stride, and Lord Arlington announced that the king proposed that they should all 'contribute 20 pounds a piece towards the building of a new council chamber and conveniences some where in White hall', so that he could himself come and hear their debates. The money was to be repaid out of the contingent £1,000 a year set aside for them. The proposition was, of course, agreed, and on 29 June came the news of Captain Henry Morgan's exploit in capturing Panama in January. On 4 July the letter to New England and the proposals to Gorges were drafted and agreed, and by the 24th the surveyor brought them a 'plot' for the building of a Council Chamber at Whitehall, to be erected at the end of the Privy Garden – 'which', without delay, 'was wel don'.

Early in August, the Council meeting in full session, continued to discuss a tough line with 'them of the Massachusets' and whether to send a Deputy to New England to see justice done to the colonists who had petitioned the Council, with secret instructions to find out just how strong the New Englanders really were. Colonel Midleton asserted roundly that they 'might be curbed by a fear of his Majestie's 5t rate freghats [frigates] to spoile their trade' with the West Indies, and it was agreed to advise the king to send out such a formal commission to adjust boundaries and investigate.

That Sunday at Deptford Evelyn was edified by his vicar's sermon 'shewing how far Christians might enjoy the refreshments of this life without offending God', and on 19 August the Council were edified by letters read from the Governor of Jamaica fully relating the 'exploit of Panama'. Morgan had taken and burnt the whole town and 'pilag'd it of vast Treasures, ... Such an action had not ben don since the famous Drake'. Next Sunday the vicar enlarged his theme 'shewing that all sinn was madnesse', and described 'the miserable slavery of debauch'd men etc.'.

At the Council, however, original sin caused a warm contest between the president and the secretary 'about some unkind expressions'. Evelyn, disedified, returned home.

## II

It was now September, 1671, and on the 9th Evelyn again went down to Newmarket with Arlington, the Lord Treasurer, in a coach and six, 'the King and all the English Gallantes being here for the autumnal Sports'. On the heath they saw a great race between the king's horses *Wood-cock* and *Flat-foot* and the horses of the Keeper of the new King's House, before many thousands of spectators – and 'a more signal race had not ben run for many years'.[2] Evelyn spent the night with Arlington at Euston, which the Treasurer had recently purchased and rebuilt and which, through the marriage (in 1672) of Arlington's heiress to the Duke of Grafton, the king's illegitimate son by Lady Castlemaine, would come to his FitzRoy descendants. At the moment it was 'Madam Carwell', the new French mistress, who was in the ascendant, but Charles often stayed at Euston, where 'it was universally reported that the faire Lady (Louise de Kéroiialle, a Breton maid of honour to the King's sister, Henriette Anne, Duchess of Orléans) was 'bedded one of these nights and the stocking flung, after the manner of a married Bride':[3] 'I acknowledge,' wrote Evelyn, that 'she was for the most part in her undresse all day, and that there was fondnesse, and toying with that young wanton', and though Evelyn never saw the ceremony, he concludes that, though he thought the rumour false, ' 'twas with confidence believed that she was first made a *Misse* as they cald those unhappy Creatures, with solemnity at this time, etc.'.[4] An agent of Louis XIV, she became the most expensive and permanent of the king's mistresses, and mother to the Duke of Richmond.

During the rest of September Arlington entertained a concours of East Anglian magnates and gentry: 'in the morning we went hunting and hauking', then at 'cards and dice almost till morning, yet, I must say, without noise swearing quarrell or confusion'. Evelyn, no 'gamster', made conversation with the French ambassador, went riding with the ladies, and 'idly passed the time', but 'not without more often recesse to my prety appartment, where I was quite out of all this hurry'. He thought 'no man more hospitally easy to be withal' than Arlington.

But Evelyn's judgment of an estate remained objective: though he considered Euston, as rebuilt, 'very magnificent and commodious', he thought the soil 'miserably sandy'. Asked by Arlington for his advice about plantations, he urged him to bring them nearer the house, and the advice was accepted.

From Euston Evelyn accompanied the Catholic Lord Henry Howard to Norwich – 'my lord and I alone in his Flying Charriat' with six horses – and called upon the recently knighted Sir Thomas Browne, author of *Religio Medici* and *Pseudodoxia Epidemica (Vulgar Errors)*. He found the Doctor's house and garden a 'Paradise ... of rarities, where Medails, books, Plants, natural things, did exceedingly refresh' him. Browne had an immense collection of birds' eggs, especially from 'the promontorys of Norfolk' frequented by birds that never went further inland; he also showed Evelyn the 'venerable' Norwich Cathedral. Stately churches and buildings of Norfolk flint, of which, he declared, the craftsmen had now lost the art of squaring. He consulted Evelyn about extensions to his house.

After returning to Euston, Evelyn again traversed royal Newmarket where he 'found the jolly blades, Racing, Dauncing, feasting and revelling, more resembling a luxurious and abandon'd rout, than a Christian Court'. The Duke of Buckingham, since boyhood an intimate of the king and now in highest favour, had brought down the Countess of Shrewsbury, 'that impudent woman, ... with his band of fidlars etc.'. It was with relief that Evelyn returned to London, and on 31 October at Sayes Court, being 'now arrived at my fifty one yeare of age', thanked God for his 'many many mercies'.[5]

By mid-November 1671 the Council for Foreign Plantations were considering the 'indiscreete managements' of Sir Charles Wheeler, governor of the Leeward Islands and resolving to advise the king to remove him. But by March 1672 they were seriously debating whether the new governor, Colonel Stapleton, should be subordinate to Barbados or not, since the French were threatening the islands and they might need an independent command.

In February Evelyn had sustained a severe loss with the sudden death of Dr Breton, the vicar of Deptford, whose sermons he had long so assiduously recorded – the vicar having long been of a 'plethoric habit of body'.

Never had Parish a greater losse, not only was he an Excellent Preacher, and fitted for our great and vulgar Auditory, but by his excellent life and Charity his meekeness and obliging nature ... I lost in particular a special friend, and one that had an extraordinary love to me and mine: God's will be don.


## III


Evelyn now had again to provide for more wounded from the fleet. In March 1672, following the king's secret commitment to Louis XIV, the third and disastrous war was declared against the Dutch, who were already fighting off a massive French invasion. Evelyn thought the whole quarrel 'slenderly grounded and not becoming Christian neighbours', particularly as the English, desperate for plunder, had attacked the homeward-bound Dutch convoy of sixty-six merchant ships from Smyrna, before war had even been declared. The English commanders, however, had divided their forces, and most of the convoy had got through to Holland. So the piratical enterprise had failed to stave off the near bankruptcy of the government, which by a 'Stop of the Exchequer' had suspended the repayment of two and a half million pounds worth of loans and failed to pay regular interest, thus, according to Evelyn, 'ruining many *Widdows* and *Orphans* and the reputation of the King's Exchequer forever. ... The Credit of this bank being thus broken, did exceedingly discontent the people.' So Evelyn at Gravesend had to visit 'divers wounded and languishing poore men that had ben in the Smyrna conflict', and he sailed to Sheerness in an admiralty yacht to inspect fortifications there and at Gillingham. He also had to watch the amputation of a gangrened leg – 'the stout and gallant man induring it with incredible patience', though he himself had hardly the courage to be present. The gangrene remained unchecked, and the 'stoute man ... but a common sailor', suffered in vain: a second amputation, higher up, killed him. 'Lord ... what confusion and mischiefe dos the avarice, anger, and ambition of Princes cause in the world!'[6]

There were more wounded at Margate, whom Evelyn visited with the king's chief surgeon, 'taking such order for the accommodation of the Wounded as was requisite', and returning through a part of Kent he thought the best cultivated he had ever seen anywhere, which 'infinitely delighted me, after the sad and afflicting specctacles and objects I was come from'. Having organized another centre for prisoners of war at Rochester, he returned to report progress to the king, and to observe the Easter 'fopperies of the Papists' at York House.

By mid-April, he was again at a session of the Council for Foreign Plantations, preparing the commissions and instructions for the governor of Barbados and the Windward Islands, and then for Colonel Stapleton to go as governor to St Christophers in a separate command. Young John, back from Oxford, was now specially admitted to the Middle Temple by the King's Solicitor-General, his father's intention – unfulfilled – being that he should seriously apply himself to the study of the law. The Third Dutch War continued.

Suddenly ordered to attend the king, Evelyn found him[7]

in the *Pal Mal* in St Ja: Park, where his Majestie coming to me from the companie, he commanded me to go immediately to the Sea-Coast, and to observe the motion of the Dutch Fleete and ours, the *Duke*, and so many of the flower of our Nation being now under saile coming from Portsmouth thro' the *Downes*, where 'twas believed there might be an encounter.

So, at Dover, Evelyn saw combined English and French squadrons of 170 ships – over a hundred men of war – passing up the Channel against the Dutch who lay off the North Foreland – 'Such a gallant and formidable Navy never I think spread saile upon the seas, it was [a] goodly yet tirrible sight to behold them as I did passing by the straits.'

But the sequel on 28 May 1672 was the battle of Solebay, when De Ruyter, taking advantage of an east wind, surprised the English fleet; Sandwich was killed and his flagship burnt, York's flagship disabled, and the Dutch regained the initiative in the North Sea.

It brought much grief to Evelyn: Edward Montagu, First Earl of Sandwich, Pepys's distant cousin and patron, had long been a friend and also President of the Council for Foreign Plantations. Before putting to sea as Admiral of the Blue, he had remarked to Evelyn that he 'thought to see him no more' – 'no, says he, they will not have me live'. Albemarle, ignorant of naval tactics, had unjustly reflected upon his courage, and the Duke of York had traduced him: 'thus this gallant Person perish'd to gratify the pride and envy, of some I named', though a 'true noble man, an ornament to the Court, and his Prince'. After a formidable resistance, Sandwich's flagship, *The Royal James*, had been grappled by a fireship and blown up; and ten days later, Sandwich's body had been found in the sea off Harwich. 'I am yet heartily griev'd,' concludes Evelyn, 'at this mighty losse, nor do I call it to my thoughts without emotion.'[8]

The French, who had failed to support their English allies at Solebay, were now frustrated in their massive invasion of the United Provinces. The Dutch turned out de Witt and his brother and lynched them, elected William of Orange as Stadtholder, opened the dykes, flooded the polders and brought the French invasion to a halt. In August 1673 De Ruyter defeated an Anglo-French invading force at the battle of Texel and prevented the interception of their own East Indian Convoy. The French invasion settled down to a frustrating and elaborate routine of sieges, and in February 1674 the third Anglo-Dutch war was concluded by the Peace of Westminster, followed up in 1677 by the epoch-making marriage of William of Orange to York's daughter, the Lady Mary.

Evelyn had felt Sandwich's death the more bitterly because, like Sandwich, he had never approved of the war against another Protestant state, 'for no provocation in the World, but because the Hollander exceeded so in Industrie and all things else but envy'. Moreover, he felt that 'the stresse of both' Dutch Wars had laid far more on himself than on any of the other Commissioners for sick and wounded, the brunt of it falling on his own district. On 12 June 1672 he had to go to London 'to solicit his Majestie for money for the sick and wounded, which he promised me;' but on the 19th he was soliciting for it again, in mid-July he was 'sent for to Gravesend to dispose of no fewer than 800 sick men etc', and by the end of the month again asking for money in London.

Light relief was provided in September when at dinner at Leicester House, he watched 'Richardson the famous *fire eater*, who before us devour's Brimston on glowing coales, chewing and swallowing them downe; he also melted a beere glasse and eate it quite up'.

On more serious business, in October 1672 the new Patent had been read constituting the members of the Council for Foreign Plantations to be of the Council of Trade as well. It greatly but briefly extended the scope of Evelyn's appointment; Ashley Cooper, Earl of Shaftesbury, the Whig politician, now became chairman, and his protégé, John Locke, the philosopher, 'an excellent learned gent: and a student of Christ Church', became one of the clerks and, in the following year, the secretary. Evelyn himself that November was elected secretary to the Royal Society, a post he held for one year.


## IV

During the Dutch War Evelyn, following the king's previous command in 1669, now renewed, had made his contribution to political warfare. His *Navigation and Commerce Their Original and Progress*, 'containing a succinct account of Traffick in General' (London, 1674, 120 pp.), in fact a Preface to the larger work the king had 'tempted' him to endeavour, is written in a formal, rather grand style. 'I take the Boldness', he begins, 'to Inscribe your Majestie's name on the front of this little History, since your Majestie has named me ... of the Council of your Commerce and Plantations.' But anyone who expects to light on the then latest methods or theory of commerce or on the settlement of plantations will be disappointed. When confronted with a great theme, Evelyn's pen had run away with him, and being better endowed with descriptive than analytic power, and fascinated with his subject, he soon got swamped by his material.

Opening loftily *en robe de parade*, he writes, 'Whosoever shall with serious Attention contemplate the Divine Fabrick of this Inferior Orb ... and above all the Nature of Man, he must need acknowledge that there is nothing more agreeable to Reason than that [it] was ordered for mutual use of communication.' And he follows this resounding and elegant platitude by examples. Consider the Mediterranean; so aptly contrived for intercourse, that the Dutch could not have designed it better. Trees grow on mountains, ready to turn as it were spontaneously into vessels and canoes, wanting but the launching to render them useful, and make great ships ready for any motion 'undertaken to fathom the World and secure the benefits of Commerce', so that no place or country can say they 'have no need of another'.

Then consider the Hollanders: they have no indigenous grain, wine, oil, timber, metal, stone, wool, hemp or pitch: yet by commerce they have obtained them all so that 'the whole world seems but a Farm to them'. And consider the Venetians, who founded a glorious city on a few muddy scattered islands and thence 'distributed over Europe the product of the Eastern World'; or Genoa, developed from a barren rock into a proud city, or the rich Hansa cities of the Easterlings. Seldom had Evelyn's power of phrase been in better form.

Turning now to England, he points out that commerce and navigation originally created our national export – wool, and now 'Asia refreshes us with Spices, Recreates us with Perfumes, Cures us with Drougs and adorns us with Jewells.' From Africa come ivory and gold; from America silver, sugar and cotton; from France, Spain and Italy 'wine, oyl and silk'; Russia 'warms us with furrs', Sweden supplies copper, Denmark masts. All this wealth comes by the sea, which 'makes the world's inhabitants one Family'.

After this fanfare, which almost anticipates Macaulay, Evelyn gets swamped in an historical narrative, going back to the Tyrians and Trojans who revived commerce after the Flood. Lycurgus, indeed, prohibited traffic among the Lacedaimonians, Plato placed his city distant from the sea and the Romans at first despised trade and were 'all for conquest and the sword,' but the Jews and Egyptians had early become expert sailors and pilots, the Greeks launched the Argo and Bacchus came to Greece out of Asia by sea. After the 'piratical wars' of Pompey, and Octavius' victory at Actium, Evelyn sweeps on, irrelevantly, to King Arthur, who got to Iceland; to Charlemagne, the Danes, Columbus and Drake; and only by page 72 comes back to earth by citing the fifteenth-century *Libell of English Policie*. This interlude, however, soon gives place to a panegyric on the defeat of the Invincible Armada and on Elizabeth I, when 'the extraordinary virtue of this brave Virago', thwarted Spain, so that 'what havoc was made in Cales ... her enemies to this day feel'.

The historical narrative then culminates and comes to the point with the reigns of James I and Charles I, and states the 'Inherent Right of the Crown of England to the Dominion of the Seas'. It has long been 'asserted by many abler and famous pens', as against the learned Grotius who had argued that the sea is '*Fluxile Elementum, quod nunquam idem possidere non posse*' – 'you can never anchor in the same billow', and that water is 'free as Air'.

But again Evelyn plunges back into history; to Counts of the Saxon Shore, King Edgar, Canutus, supreme lord and governor of the ocean: the English monarchs, he insists, 'possessed their right to its entire latitude for more than a thousand years' (p. 89). Under Henry V the Lords of the Cinque Ports were 'Lords of both Shores' and from Henry VI to Elizabeth passports have been issued to foreigners who sail our seas. The antiquary

Camden even asserted that we had rights over fisheries up to Greenland and beyond, and foreigners long sued our monarchs for leave to fish.

Now, alas, these rights are being allowed to lapse. The Dutch have no rights to the prodigious emolument they get from poaching our fisheries, so great that there is hardly a beggar in Holland or Zeeland. It is only by 'detestable sloathe' that we have allowed their exploitation; Charles V, more realistic, used to visit the tomb of Beukelsz, who had invented the pickled herring. But we now tolerate Dutch, Hamburgers, Lubeckers and other 'interloopers', while our own people 'daily flock to the American Plantations', where the fisheries, too, are neglected. Yet 'no great magic is needed to reduce our bold supplanters to a more neighbourly temper'. The *Navigation and Commerce*, after its earlier devagations, concludes with the desired case for protecting English fishing rights.

But Evelyn had probably done what was wanted: he had assembled an apparently learned and so prestigious, background to English rights against the Dutch. But he had always looked down on trade, and had no grasp of the new methods of organizing oceanic commerce or credit; unlike Thomas Mun, whose *Englands Treasur by fforaign Trade*, published posthumously in 1664, had shown a grasp of mercantilist economic theory, or Sir William Petty, who had surveyed Ireland, or Gregory King whose *Natural and Political Observation* had pioneered statistical method, Evelyn was an amateur; essentially a writer. He had done his best, and his pen had been allowed a fine run, but the pamphlet – a mere preface perfunctorily supplied – now, with peace concluded with the Dutch, occasioned diplomatic protest. It was therefore suppressed, and though still obtainable, officially quashed. Such, for Evelyn, was the penalty of attempting a singularly ineffective polemic to order, in which the historian had characteristically swamped the pamphleteer.

# CHAPTER SEVENTEEN

# Romantic Friendship: the *Life of Mrs Godolphin*

Long happily and sedately married, Evelyn in middle age now formed a high-minded emotional friendship with a pious girl, of whom in due course, he wrote an edifying life. Margaret Blagge in 1673 was twenty-one, the daughter of a royalist colonel from Suffolk, who had preserved Charles II's George emblem after Worcester, and two years later she married Sidney Godolphin of Breage, Cornwall, afterwards first Earl of Godolphin, Lord High Treasurer of England and the principal politician who backed Marlborough at the height of his success; their son, Francis, would be a close friend of Evelyn's only surviving grandson, Jack, in whose advancement Godolphin would be decisive.

John first mentions visiting Margaret on New Year's day 1673, and afterwards he coyly refers to her by a star or 'pentacle'; in the following months he often dined with her at a time when his mind was particularly running on prayer, since young John was being instructed by the bishop of Winchester before receiving his first communion – 'Ô that I had been so blessed and instructed!' By mid-April John and Mary were both visiting Margaret, in May Margaret and Sidney Godolphin dined with them, and on 17 June Evelyn accompanied her to have her portrait painted by Lely's collaborator, Mathew Dixon, in a demure and attractive pose.

This new interest did not prevent Evelyn's usual political apprehensions, increased when the Duke of York again abstained from the Anglican Communion – a lapse which scandalized the whole nation 'That the heyre of it, and the sonn of a Martyr for the *Protestant Religion*, should apostatize: What the Consequence of this will be God onely knows, and Wise men dread.'[1] One consequence was the resignation of York's supporter, Lord Clifford, from the Treasury, who was said to have hanged himself with his own cravat.

While the Third Dutch War continued to its disastrous end, Margaret Blagge and Evelyn were happily visiting an exhibition called *Paradise Transplanted and Restored*. They saw moveable animals painted on cloth that could even 'roare and make their severall cries', and they both laughed at the pretentious verses declaimed by the showman.

This happy friendship, enhanced by a shared sense of humour, was overshadowed by the mounting political crisis: on 5 November, that Protestant anniversary, the City youths burnt the pope in effigy, provoked by the projected marriage of the Duke of York to the Catholic Maria Beatrice d'Este of Modena, but by the end of the month Evelyn witnessed her appearance as York's second duchess. The Protestants were justifiably scared; for Louis XIV had promoted the match as part of the Jesuit plan for the conversion of England, and the princess had believed it her duty to face the elderly Stuart *roué*, a duty she would amply perform, quickly bearing him two daughters and a son, all of whom died in infancy of smallpox; and then in 1688, James Prince of Wales, the 'Old Pretender', whose belated appearance enhanced the popular belief that he had been imported in a warming pan. Immediately, too, the marriage of the heir to the throne to an Italian *dévote* with her entourage of Jesuits and Catholic confidantes, confirmed Evelyn's worst fears for the dynasty, only briefly assuaged by pulpit eloquence – 'an excellent discourse against the Pope's pretended Infallibility'.

Private life went on. During the spring of 1674 John dined and visited regularly with Margaret; they would together attend communion services for the poor and visit the curios of the Royal Society: then, in an access of entire confidence, Margaret asked John to help her make her Will. So, early in September 1674 he was in London 'sealing writings in trust for Mistress Blagge', and giving her 'deeds for £500 which he had disposed of for her'.

After being in attendance on the first Duchess of York and then on Queen Catherine of Braganza, she had, as she put it, 'escaped from Court servitude' and was now staying with Lord and Lady Berkeley of Stratton at their great mansion, Berkeley House. He was a veteran of the Civil War, who had won his peerage for defeating the parliamentarians at Stratton in Cornwall in 1643 and taking Exeter, but whose advice had led to Charles I's getting trapped in the Isle of Wight. In 1670 he had been appointed Lord Lieutenant of Ireland, he was now manager of the Duke of York's household, and his wife was the daughter of a wealthy merchant in the City. At his hospitable board the piratical Colonel Morgan from Jamaica gave Evelyn a glowing account of his famous raid on Panama, and declared roundly that 10,000 men could easily conquer the entire Spanish Indies. With more boats he could have captured far more gold as the Spaniards were transporting it to their ships, and when he had ravaged widely round Panama the local Spaniards had proved so supine and undisciplined that they had been afraid to fire their own 'great gun'. Next day, on his fifty-third birthday, Evelyn, in contrast to Morgan, confirmed his resolution to lead a more holy life.

Though concerned with retrieving English prisoners still held by the Dutch at Surinam since the Second Dutch War, he had time to hear an Italian violinist who made his instrument 'speake like the Voice of a man', and in December to hear another Italian, one of the best masters of the harpsichord in Europe. Margaret, too, was becoming less exclusively pious, reluctantly acting in a Court comedy with the Lady Mary and the Lady Anne, and, like them, 'all covered with Jewels'. When, on a great occasion, she wore £20,000 worth, and lost one worth £80, Evelyn merely commented that it was a wonder she lost no more.

This worldly behaviour culminated in the following year, when on 16 May 1675 Margaret secretly and without Evelyn's knowledge, married Sidney Godolphin with whom she had been in love since childhood, and whom Evelyn had already advised her to marry. But she still lived with the Berkeleys; and when Berkeley of Stratton was appointed ambassador extraordinary to the Court of France to help negotiate the Peace of Nymegen, she decided to accompany the Berkeleys to Paris. Though apparently unable to face owning up to her marriage but having already given Evelyn a power of attorney to manage her affairs, she now also persuaded him to the much heavier task of looking after Berkeley's affairs in England as well – 'more than enough,' he commented, 'to employ any drudge in *England* ... but what will not friendship and love make one do!'[2] By way of return, young John was to accompany the ambassador to acquire greater experience of the world, 'safe' under Margaret's 'inspection'.

Before leaving Dover, Margaret and the ambassador both handed over their wills to the patient and reliable John: they then all took leave of one another on the beach, 'and so I parted with my Lord, my sonn, and the person in the world I esteemed as my own life Mrs *Godolphin*; being under saile, the Castle gave them 17 Gunns'.[3]

So it was not until April 1676, after recording 'came my dearest friend to my great joy' back from France, that John discovered that his adored girl was married. And then obliquely by chance, when her sister, Lady Yarburgh, referred casually to the fact. Even John's complacency was shaken, and he so far lost his usual composure as to expostulate with Margaret about the 'concealment'. He was as wax in her hands; she somehow persuaded him that she had 'never meant deceit' and he continued to look after her interests about a lease in Lincolnshire, while, to his father's relief, young John returned from Paris, apparently unharmed by its temptations.

Reconciled to the *fait accompli*, Evelyn resumed his dinners with Margaret Godolphin and attended a great feast at Trinity House in honour of Pepys, now chosen Master. He helped both Godolphins over building their apartment in Whitehall, and went obediently with Margaret to buy chimney pieces in Lambeth; in the autumn she stayed with the Evelyns at Sayes Court. During the better winter of 1676–7 John regularly dined with Margaret, and continued to record sermons – on the 'Tirriblenesse of Christ's appearing to the wicked', on the 'Joys of the Righteous', the dangers of hypocrisy, and the sin of taking physic which prevented one attending church on the Lord's Day. But the entanglement with Berkeley had to be cleared up. On his return from the Paris embassy, Evelyn had at once handed over the account of his great trust, when he had dealt with £20,000, 'with no small trouble and loss of time, and all purely at Mrs Godolphin's request'. Dining with her at the Berkeley's, he was 'abundantly thanked', and, the troublesome business ended, at last felt delivered from an 'intollerable servitude', with 'liasure to be somewhat more at home and to' himself.[4]

## II

Having visited his brother in Wotton, that August Evelyn again stayed with Arlington at Euston, killed a fat buck and went hawking. He even found the monastic gate house at Bury St Edmunds 'a vast and magnificent Gotic structure', and greatly approved Arlington's elegant new church in Euston Park. He dilates on the elaborate house, so well placed for hawking, hunting and racing, where the hospitable magnate lived at vast expense. Indeed, Arlington, who by way of Westminster School and Christ Church had risen entirely by his own abilities, was a brilliant, much-travelled man, fluent in Latin, French and

Spanish and 'the most courtly person His Majesty [had] about him'.

When Evelyn returned in September 1677 to London, the Prince of Orange's important marriage to the Lady Mary had been announced, and he again saw much of Margaret Godolphin. Ever solicitous for his son, he presented young John, now nearly twenty-three, with 'instruction how to govern his youth'.

The political setting to these mild activities was now more tense. The spirited royalties at Windsor on both sides had long been spoiling for a fight; in August 1674 Monmouth, fresh from the siege of Maestricht, and the Duke of York had together been playing elaborate war games below the castle, with great guns fired and grenades thrown, mines set off and 'prisoners' taken, to the delight of many spectators – but, surprisingly, without accident; and in June 1678 on Hounslow Heath Evelyn now saw a large army supposedly raised against the French, but the subject of great suspicion by parliament. Charles II was reviewing it himself, and it included a new sort of soldier called '*Grenadiers* ... dextrous to fling hand grenados', with 'furr'd Capps with coped crownes like Janizaries', which 'made them look very fierce'.[5]

Trying to disregard these portents, Evelyn persevered with one of his best projects – transferring the magnificent library inherited and collected by his old acquaintance, Thomas, Earl of Arundel, and little appreciated by its present owner Lord Henry Howard, later Sixth Duke of Norfolk, to the Royal Society. The Society itself was happily engaged on its usual miscellaneous hobbies: being assured, for example, that the Greenland whale – 'that vast fish' – when harpooned hastens to the shore, while the Bermuda one, being 'smitten', hastens out to sea, so that a whale hunter, half drunk, leapt on a wounded one's back and so hacked it that before it could escape it succumbed – a method, it was alleged, since widely practised in Bermuda. Evelyn returned to Deptford to hear the new vicar on the more edifying subject of the saints in Heaven.

### III

A typical seventeenth-century tragedy now hit him hard. On 3 September 1678 Margaret Godolphin bore a 'lovely boy' and appeared quite well. But soon a letter from Sidney Godolphin appraised the Evelyns at Sayes Court that she was dangerously ill; they at once took boat to Whitehall, but found her in the delirium of malignant (puerperal?) fever. The doctors, as usual, were helpless, and the paroxysms increasing to agony, on 9 September, aged only twenty-five, Evelyn's beloved Margaret died.

Recording the disaster, his habitual reticence breaks down, and he writes of 'unexpressable affliction to her deare Husband, and all her Relations; but of none in the world, more than my selfe, who lost the most excellent, and most estimable Friend that ever liv'd'. 'My very Soule,' he continues,[6]

was united to hers and ... this stroake did pierce me to the utmost depth: for never was there a more virtuous, and inviolable friendship, never a more religious, discreete and admirable creature; belov'd of all, admired of all. ... Ô the passionate, humble, mealting disposition of this blessed Friend! how am I afflicted for thee! my heavenly friend.

Utterly prostrated, Sidney Godolphin relied entirely on the dependable Evelyn to deal with the funeral, the embalming, the distribution of the legacies and mementoes that Margaret had providently arranged; then, exhausted, Evelyn returned for two days of solitary reflection at Sayes Court.

IV

Margaret Godolphin was given an elaborate funeral – 'costing her deare husband not much less than 1000 pounds, (Ô that ten thousand more might have redeemed her life!)'. Evelyn accompanied the cortege as far as Hounslow and it proceeded nearly three hundred miles to the Godolphin vault in Cornwall. On his return from Hounslow he found that their mutual friend old Lord Berkeley of Stratton was also dead.

John's love for Margaret had been so profound that he was irresistibly impelled to record her perfections. Four years later in 1682 he began *A Life of Mrs Godolphin*, which, completed in 1684, he would present to Lord Godolphin in 1702.[7] Since Evelyn here reveals himself rather more than in most of his generally guarded writings it is worth attention.

The work, first published in 1847, went into a second edition in the following year,[8] and is preceded by an unctuous dedication to Edward, Lord Archbishop of York (the Hon. Venables-Vernon Harcourt (1757–1847),[9] by the editor, bishop Wilberforce. Having discovered someone with apparent claims to be almost an

Anglican saint, Wilberforce rubs in the lesson: 'The light of such an example as [these pages] exhibit ought not to be concealed'; and 'you may rejoice to know that you have lived to see a British Court which in purity of morals and domestic virtue affords the most blessed contrast to those evil days through which Margaret Godolphin was enabled to live in the brightness of Godly purity, and to die in peace'.

An apparent honorary early Victorian, 'her lot was cast in the darkest days of England's Morals; she lived in a Court where flourished in their rankest luxuriance all the vice and littleness' that arose from 'French Gold and foreign influence', culminating in 'a day of heartless merriment,' for which the bishop cites Evelyn's own account of the king toying with his concubines, (see p. 187), 'upon which fell suddenly a night of blackness, which swallowed up its crew of heartless revellers' following the demise of Charles II. In a 'general reign of Wickedness,' writes Wilberforce, here more in command of his subject than when bandying arguments with the scientist T. H. Huxley, it is refreshing to find such a model of female virtue.

After these saponaceous platitudes, it is also refreshing to turn even to Evelyn's own extreme humility, as he disclaims the talent to describe the virtues of Margaret Blagge: 'It would become a steadier hand than mine and the penn of an Angell's wing,' he writes, 'to describe the life of a saint.' Born in 1652, she had been the youngest daughter of a distinguished royalist, a gentleman of ancient Suffolk family, Groom of the Bedchamber to Charles I and commander of the Wallingford garrison during the Civil War; taken to France by the Duchess of Richmond, she had early resisted attending Mass and, aged twelve, had been Maid of Honour to the first Duchess of York. At an early age she had 'loved to be at funeralls', would 'never trick or dress herself up', and avoided talking to gallants and young men.

Evelyn had at first found it hard to believe that anyone of her solid virtues could be found at Court; 'I minded my bookes and my garden and the circle was big enough for me. I aspir'd to no offices, no titles, no favours at Court.' But Margaret turned out not to be the 'pert' Court lady he had expected. Indeed, he found her 'conversation was a treat', and her wit, beauty and vivacity reproved his own 'moroseness'. 'This creature, I would say to myself, loves God.' Then one day when she was nineteen, to his surprise, she complained that 'She had never a friend in the world', and when Evelyn declared that that could not be possible for anyone so charming, ' "Pray leave your complimenting"

(said she smiling) "and look upon me henceforth as your child." '
' "Well" said I, "Madam, this is a high obligation." ' So between
'jest and ernest', the girl drew up a solemn engagement in
writing, and from this moment the middle-aged Evelyn 'looked
on her as his child indeed'.

He was fascinated by her vivacity, her intelligence, her piety –
her sheer goodness. She had always, he discovered, been careful
not to give the least liberty to the gallants of the Court in
conversation; yet she had 'kept her pretty humour while making
it impossible for any to introduce a syllable which did not comply
with the strictest rules of decency', 'preferred to entertain ladies
and not talk foolishly to Men' – and, wisely, 'more especially [to]
the King'. Indeed, one of her rules was 'Goe not to the Dutchesse
of Monmouth above once a weeke and be sure never to speake to
the King'. In fact, it was best to 'talk to men as little as maybe',
and 'when they speake filthyly, tho' I be laughed at, looke grave'.

These rules, in particular the precaution of avoiding the
monarch himself, had enabled her to survive uncontaminated
the bawdy atmosphere of the Caroline Court, until she
persuaded the Queen (generally known as 'Lisbon Kate')
reluctantly to release her. Having dismissed the pleasures of a
Court for the sake of doing good, she had become 'sedulous in
many acts of Charity', turning from the company of princes to
that of 'poor necessitous wretches'. 'What,' she would say, 'loose
money at cards, yett not give to the poore – 'Tis robbing God!.'

In spite of her pious ways, Margaret Blagge's charm made her
greatly missed at Court; but, recalled to take part in the Court
comedy with the Lady Mary and the Lady Anne, in which she lost
a valuable diamond belonging to Lady Suffolk, she read a work
of divinity in the intervals instead of her lines, being by no means
'transported by splendid follys and gay entertainments'. Indeed,
being 'forc'd to be an Actoress … put a mortification on her',
and she soon 'slipped off like a spirit to Berkeley House to her
little oratory'.

She was now, at twenty, suffering agony of mind over whether
or not to marry Sidney Godolphin, being 'inclined to retire from
the world', and to declare 'My Saviour shall be my Husband'.
Evelyn, unselfishly, dwelt on the blessings of family life and
pointed out that such a marriage to an old friend would not be
like those of people who, blinded by sudden passion, became
entangled in family toils, then fall into satiety and aversion.
' "Marry, then, in God's name" said I.' She replied that she
would 'essay how her detatchment from Royal Servitude would

comfort with her ... before entering another change'. But when at last, in May 1675, she secretly married Godolphin, 'her not aquainting me with this particular,' writes Evelyn, 'occasioned a friendly quarrel between us', she having even written from France, when in fact married, 'Butt Mr Evelyn, if ever I return again and do not marry, I shall retire and end my days among you'.

The marriage, based on a childhood affection, turned out well, and in 1676 she was writing happily of 'perfect health of body, cheerfulness of mind, no disasters without nor grief within, my tyme my own, my house swette and pretty, all manner of conveniencys for serving God': ironically, she longed only for the child which would kill her. Her native good sense and kindness became apparent in a touching letter she soon wrote to her husband: 'My deare, not knowing how God Almighty may deal with me I thinke it my best course to settle my affaires ... in case that I be to leave this world.' Her first concern was with her child – 'Pray, my dear, be kind to that poore child I leave behind for my sake, who loved you so well': if Godolphin remarries, the remains of her fortune (of £4,000) should be settled on it, and it was to live with one of her sisters in case her 'successor be not too fond of it'. The letter continues with detailed arrangements and bequests for servants and the poor.

Here, in spite of the austerity of her religion, a natural benevolence shines through, which along with the demure physical charm apparent in her portrait, explains Evelyn's devotion. In the concluding 'picture' he describes how she arranged to be woken by a tug of a thread at her wrist through a key hole for Sunday communion; how every meal was a day of abstinence with her, for she seldom ate of above one or two dishes, even when there was great plenty, how she would very rarely have any sauces, and commonly chose the leanest morsels, 'frequently have I known her deny her appetite things which I was certain she lov'd'.

Though clever at cards, she hated winning, and frequently broke off in time for public prayers; moreover, she would read, and note, edifying books. When reading she could be a good mimic. In sum, she was a loyal wife as a consummate Christian, of exquisite natural beauty, piercing apprehension, sparkling wit, with a gentle and agreeable voice. She even inspired Evelyn to verse, never his happiest medium.

> A crowne of Rayes
> And never fadeing Bayes

Such as Heaven's Parnassus grows
Deck thyne Angelick Brows
A Robe of Righteousness about thee cast,
Bathed in Celestial Bliss, thou that dost tast
Pleasures at Gods Right hand,
Pleasures that ever last.

A happy married life and the rewards of a family would perhaps have assuaged the more forbidding aspects of her religion; the death of Margaret Godolphin in raging delirium, tortured by erysipelas and 'cupping by pigeons', at twenty-five was an unmitigated tragedy, not least for John Evelyn.

CHAPTER EIGHTEEN

# The Popish and Protestant Plots

While Evelyn had been so deeply concerned with the personality and fate of Margaret Godolphin, the tension over the attempted exclusion of the Catholic Duke of York from the succession had been mounting even higher in parliament and country. It now, in the winter of 1678, came to a climax of hysteria, fear and fanaticism over the alleged 'conspiracy', as Evelyn put it, 'of some Eminent Papists, for Destruction of the King, and introducing Popery; discovered by one *Oates*'.[1]

Titus Oates, who falsely claimed to be a Doctor of Divinity of the University of Salamanca, was the son of a Norfolk Puritan clergyman; he had attended Merchant Taylors' School, from which he had soon been expelled, then won a scholarship at Gonville and Caius College, Cambridge, whence he had transferred to St John's there, but had left without taking a degree. He had managed, however, to become vicar of Bobbing in Kent, and to become a curate at Hastings, where he had soon become a chaplain on a warship bound for Tangier, and then served the Catholic Duke of Norfolk as chaplain to the Protestants in his household. He had also taken up with a rabidly anti-Catholic clergyman, Israel Tongue, Fellow of University College, Oxford and Rector of Pluckley, Kent and, to further their common purposes, in 1677 professed his conversion to Catholicism. After a brief attendance at the Jesuit College at Valladolid, which he soon had to leave, Oates was admitted to the English seminary at St Omer in France, whence, duly expelled in June 1678, he had returned to London and, at a 'bell founders' at Vauxhall, converted Tongue, a talented but credulous crank obsessed with alchemy, to belief in a Jesuit 'plot' to kill the king. Warned of it in August, Charles II refused to take it seriously; so in September Oates applied to a well-known London magistrate, Sir Edmund Berry Godfrey, and made his dispositions before him on oath. Godfrey (1621–78) was the son of a Kentish landowner of Sellindge; educated at Westminster

School and Christ Church, Oxford, he had become a prosperous timber merchant, a zealous but tolerant Protestant and reputed the 'best J.P. in England'. The 'plot' had so far made little impression, but it flared up into a conflagration of public panic when, in October, Godfrey was found murdered.

Evelyn was already acquainted with Tongue, having himself in 1667 translated Nicole's *The New Heresie of the Jesuits*, and now visited him in Whitehall where he and Oates were established. He thought Oates 'a bold man and in my thoughts furiously indiscreete', which indeed he was; but 'everybody believed what he said', so that Oates was encouraged and 'everything he affirm'd (taken) for Gospel.' 'The Truth is,' comments Evelyn, 'the *Roman* Chath: were Exceeding bold, and busy every where'.[2] The barbarous murder of Sir Edmund Berry Godfrey found strangled (and transfixed by his own sword) about that time, in a ditch near Hampstead, as 'was manifest', he thought, 'by the Papists', had 'put the whole nation in a new fermentation against them'.

On 5 November 1678, Dr Tillotson, preaching before the House of Commons, alleged that the Catholics were even denying that there had ever been a Gunpowder conspiracy; but, restoring morale, the archbishop of Canterbury preaching before the Lords on the 13th, showed 'how safe the Church and People of God were under wings of the Almighty'. Evelyn records that by the Queen's birthday he had never seen 'the Court more brave or the nation in more apprehension'.

Meanwhile, Edward Coleman, a Jesuit secretary to the Duchess of York, had added fuel to the flames. He had been accused by Oates of participating in the 'Plot', his letters to the almoner of Louis XIV had been seized, and on 23 November he was tried for high treason before Lord Chief Justice Scroggs. Oates swore that he had conspired to raise rebellion in Ireland and suborned a well-known physician to poison the king. Nothing was proved, save that Coleman had urged payment to be made to Charles by the French to insure that he would dissolve the anti-French parliament, but the jury found Coleman guilty, Scroggs sentenced him to death, and on 3 December 1678 he was executed.

After this, writes Evelyn, '*Oates* ... grew so presumptuous as to accuse the *Queene* for intending to Poyson the *King*; which certainly that pious and vertuous Lady abhorred the thought off, and *Oates* his Circumstances made it utterly unlikely in my opinion.'[3] It was probable, he added, that Oates sought to please some who would have liked the king to have a 'more fruitfull Lady', but that 'the king was too kind an husband' to think of such a thing. But parliament now passed a Test Act excluding all Roman Catholics except York from sitting in Lords or Commons, an Act which would remain in force until 1829.

Uneasy about it, Evelyn consulted the Bishop of Ely on whether the Mass was in truth, as described in the Act, 'idolatry': the bishop reassured him that it was, though 'he wished' the Act had been 'otherwise worded'. It had certainly expressed prevalent majority opinion, now running so strong against Danby's government that, to save him from attainder following impeachment, on 25 January 1679 the king dissolved his eighteen-year-old 'Cavalier' parliament – to the frustration of most of the politicians. In the ensuing election, George Evelyn of Wotton was returned to the Commons as Knight of the Shire for Surrey, an occasion when his supporters, by 'a most abominable custom', ate and drank him out of nearly two thousand pounds.

The new parliament proved as violently Protestant as its predecessor, and in March 1679 the Duke of York, '*Voted* against by the Commons for his Recusancy', retired with his Duchess to the Spanish Netherlands. A committee of the House had also, quite unjustly, committed Pepys, as secretary to the admiralty, to the Tower on charges of corruption, and in July, having sent him some venison, Evelyn dined with him there: 'the people and Parliament,' Evelyn commented, had 'gotten head through the vices of the greate ...'.

Politics now pervaded all. In July Evelyn attended the trial of Sir George Wakeman, one of the Queen's doctors, and of three Benedictine monks, accused of plotting to poison the king; but Oates's evidence was so obviously unconvincing that after nine hours the jury brought them in not guilty; a great setback for Oates, whom Evelyn now regarded as a 'vaine, insolent man, puff'd up, with the favour of the Commons'. Afterwards he supped with the judges and excused himself in his diary for having attended the trial; he had wished at first hand, he explained, to form an opinion of a cause which had so alarmed the nation. Fastidiousness had, in fact, given place to the curiosity and descriptive power that gave him his touch of genius.

## II

It now being high summer, Evelyn went down to Clivedon on

the Thames, then the property of the Duke of Buckingham, on the same site as the house erected in 1851 and still extant; he thought Buckingham's house rather like Frascati, with '*Cloisters*, Descents, Gardens, and avenue ... august and stately', but told Charles II, when he asked how he had liked it, that he much preferred Windsor: Clivedon was on barren land, 'producing nothing but ferne', though it 'answered the most poetical description'.[4]

During August Charles had been ill at Windsor; early in September York had returned to Court, and by mid-September Charles had ordered Monmouth, this time, to go abroad; such was the tension about the succession, aggravated, thought Evelyn, by 'various bold and foolish discourses'. But the king was soon well enough for his 'Newmarket recreations', and early in November he attended the second formal marriage of his natural son Henry, Duke of Grafton, to Arlington's daughter and heiress, Isabella, now aged twelve. Lady Arlington, who shared Evelyn's misgivings, told him 'the King would have it so, and there was no going back'; but Evelyn, who thought the girl a paragon, could only 'pray God the sweete Child find it to her advantage'. At supper when the king sat between the Duchess of Cleveland, 'the incontinent mother of the Duke of Grafton', and the bride, Evelyn beheld 'all this with regret'. He thought Grafton, 'a boy that had ben rudely bred', might emerge as a 'plaine, useful, robust [sea] officer', and 'were he polish'd, a tollerable person, for he [was] exceedingly handsome, by far surpassing any of the King's other naturall Issue'.[5]

Following seventeenth-century custom, which he had himself escaped, Evelyn was now planning young John's marriage to a Martha Spencer, step-daughter to Sir John Stonehouse Bt, of Radley,[6] and daughter of Richard Spencer, a London merchant, and by February 1680 he had the jointure and contracts settled and sealed by the lawyers. Martha Spencer was to contribute the substantial sum of £5,000 capital, in return for £500 a year present maintenance, with another £500 after Evelyn and Mary Evelyn's decease, which would probably be increased by another thousand a year. So the young people would be very substantially provided for, and Evelyn, a little self-righteously, adds 'I pray God make him [John] worthy of it, and a comfort to his excellent mother, who deserves much from him.' Evelyn did not allow 'young' John to marry without overwhelming him with intimate advice. He warned him against 'filthy lusts even with your own wife', and against 'inciting [his] fancy with nakedness and unnatural figures and usages of yourselves, for they will breed impudence loathing and contempt'. 'Be none of those', he continued, 'who brag how frequently they can be brutes in one night, for that intemperance will exhaust you and ... create importunate expectations ...'.[7] He warned 'young' John against 'carnal caresses upon a full stomach, or in the day time', or in very hot or very cold weather, and stressed that 'too frequent embraces dulls the sight, decays the memory, induces the Gout ... and shortens life'.

On 24 February, Shrove Tuesday, 1680, Evelyn recorded 'was my *Sonne married* to Mistress *Martha Spencer*, daughter to my lady Stonehouse by a former gent: at St *Andrews* in *Holborn* by our *Viccar*'. After the ceremony and dancing they were 'beded' at Sir John Stonehouse's lodging. 'I would fain,' adds Evelyn, 'have had the marriage deferr'd til after the Lent',[8] but it had been 'left to the disposall of her friends.' No comment on the girl's personality or on the feelings of 'young' John. By March Evelyn was in London to collect £3,000 of the bride's portion, paid in gold.

That spring he visited Cassiobury Park in Hertfordshire at the invitation of Arthur Capel, first Earl of Essex of the new creation, after the Devereux earldom had become extinct with the death of the parliamentarian army commander in 1646. Evelyn thought his host, formerly ambassador to Denmark, Lord Lieutenant of Ireland and a Commissioner for the Treasury, 'a sober, wise, judicious, and pondering person, not illiterate' (in classical learning) 'beyond the rate of most noble-men in this age',[9] indeed, a worthy son of Lord Capel, the royalist executed after escaping from the Tower to which he had been consigned after the siege of Colchester in the Second Civil War. With all his old flair, Evelyn examined the house, with one room parqueted in yew, chimney mantles of Irish marble, and the large and sumptuous library; but he thought little of the situation, built on the site of the former mansion.

That summer of 1680 the preachers were particularly fierce; the vicar on how God generally chastized men's posterity for their ancestors' sins, and a 'stranger' illustrating the pains of hell from the Egyptian custom of cutting malefactors in two and placing the upper half on a hot plate.

At Court his old friend the Earl of Ossory, having taken physic and so wanting to be private, took Evelyn aside to air a bitter grievance. When he had been appointed governor of Tangier after Lord Inchiquin, who had almost lost it to the Moors, secretary of state Lord Sunderland had told the king, to Ossory's face, that the town could not be held, but that it was fit to send him with a token force to take the blame. Ossory declared that he would not 'beare up' against such treatment, and the following week died of grief and a malignant fever. 'O unhapy *England*!' Evelyn comments, 'at that illustrious person's loss'. Ossory had been a friend for thirty years, since they had both been in Paris – and Evelyn had stayed by his bedside to his last gasp 'to close his deare eyes'.

## III

That August Jean Chardin, a Huguenot who had made a fortune out of jewels from Persia, produced many drawings of Persian antiquities from Baghdad, Nineveh and Persepolis for the inspection of Evelyn and Wren on behalf of the Royal Society. He alleged that Persia was infinitely 'fertile' and discoursed of Japan and China and the gross errors of geographers about them. All this Evelyn and Wren reported to the Society to which Chardin two years later was elected. Evelyn then had the chance of inspecting Charles II's own library at Whitehall. There were about a thousand books, mainly those presented or dedicated, and 'few if any' important or unfamiliar. But there were a great many maps and sea charts and 'Pieces relating to the Navy', and some rare Romish breviaries with exquisite 'monkish' miniatures, including one inscribed by Henry VII to his daughter Margaret, afterwards queen of Scots, and a meticulously written exercise book of Edward VI, which showed him 'stupendiously knowing for his age'.

On 30 October 1680, his fifty-ninth birthday, Evelyn very solemnly, introspectively and piously, tried to review his entire life, and to confirm his peace with God in the hope of making his calling and election sure. This puritanical strain had increased with the years and he now spent a whole week asking to be forgiven his faults. He became even more assiduous in recording sermons.

Out in the world he assisted in electing the Hon: Robert Boyle, the chemist, to be President of the Royal Society and the panic about the Popish Plot continuing, early in December attended the trial of the Catholic peer, Lord Stafford, second son of Evelyn's old friend and patron, Arundel, in Westminster Hall.

The elderly victim had been impeached, and now stood trial

before king and Lords. Elaborate ceremonial was laid on, conducted by Thomas Cheke, the Lieutenant of the Tower, the axe-bearer and his guards, and the charge was nothing less than the attempted murder of the king. Jesuit doctrines on tyrannicide were raked up; Stafford made a confused defence, but Evelyn disbelieved the testimony of the inevitable Oates as coming from such a hypocrite, who had already 'so deeply prevaricated' that the 'witnesse of such a profligate wretch ought not to be admitted against the life of a Pere'; indeed, his testimony 'should not be taken against the life of a Dog'.[10] 'From this moment foreward,' he adds, 'I quite lost my opinion of Mr *Oates*.' The accused flatly denied the charge; but such was still the anti-Catholic panic that Stafford was found guilty by fifty-five peers against thirty-one, the axe was turned towards him and he was sentenced to be hung, drawn and quartered for treason. Evelyn was deeply concerned; was it possible that anyone of Stafford's advanced age and experience could have plotted with men whom he had never seen before to murder the king? Characteristically, he concluded, that only God, who searches hearts, could know the truth and to Him the question must be left.

He was even more disquieted when he saw a comet which reminded him of the one which had appeared in 1640, preceding the Great Rebellion and about the time of the trial of the great Earl of Strafford: 'I pray God avert his judgements ...'. Comets, Evelyn concluded, though they appeared from natural causes, might be warnings from God. His fears were widely shared: on 22 December a solemn public fast was held throughout England petitioning that God would prevent all Popish plots, avert his judgments and give a blessing to the (anti-Catholic) parliament which struck at the succession of the Duke of York. So on new year's day, 1681, Evelyn had more than usual cause to 'beg the blessing of Almighty God on me and mine'.

The blessing seemed effective when, in February, George's son, John Evelyn of Wotton, married the daughter and heiress of a Mr Ersfield of Surrey with a portion of £8,000: the ceremony being performed by the Bishop of Rochester in Henry VII's chapel, Westminster Abbey.


## IV


It was an extremely cold spring, with frost and snow long lying, and in March 1681 all the political nation was looking to Oxford, whither parliament had been summoned, 'in great expectation of his Royal Highnesse's case as to succession'. But suddenly the king dissolved it, the last of his reign, and saved his brother's prospects, and the Whig extremists had been given enough rope to hang themselves.

Turning to more congenial interests, Evelyn invited Sir Christopher Wren to dine; he had now completed the 'column' or monument commemorating the Great Fire, and was designing St Paul's and fifty City churches – 'a wonderfull genius had this incomparable Person'. More important for his own old age, Evelyn next year on 1 March 1682 heard of the birth of 'young' John's second son, his own grandson, Jack.

At Court, early in 1682, the solemn dignity of the ambassador of Morocco, who brought two lions and thirty ostriches to Charles II (who laughed and said he 'knew nothing better to return for them than a flock of geese'), and came to negotiate about peace over Tangier, proved very impressive. The Moors, who wore 'cassocks' beneath great woollen mantles, were horrified at the disorder and tumult at the English Court, being accustomed to dignified silence before royalty, but they managed to retain a 'courtly negligence' even when seated among 'Portsmouth, Nelly etc.; Concubines, and catell of that sort, as splendid as Jewells ... could make them', and imperturbably sipped milk, water, and 'jacolatte'. They won more prestige by brilliant horsemanship in Hyde Park, standing up in their stirrups and flinging up and catching their lances at full gallop. The Moors made a great impression on Evelyn, who thought the Russian ambassador a clown compared to these 'Civil Heathen'.[11]

The king now determined on building a 'Royal Hospital for Emerited Souldiers', which would become Chelsea Hospital, with money lent by Sir Stephen Fox, who had risen from being a choirboy at Salisbury Cathedral[12] to the management of Charles's and Clarendon's households in exile. After 1660 various high offices had brought him immense wealth ('honestly got and unenvied'), and he now bought the land for the hospital from the Royal Society. Fox himself projected further great benefactions, – 'as well it became him, who had gotten so vast an estate (as Pay Master General) by the Souldiers etc', and Evelyn gladly collaborated.

In Fox's study they planned the staff and salaries of the institution; Evelyn insisted on a library and suggested several books, since a few of the old soldiers might possibly be 'studious'.

Evelyn was afterwards delighted when Pepys showed him a large book on shipbuilding made by the Master Shipwright, complete to the last detail; indeed, he 'esteemed this book above any of the Sybillas'. And at the king's chapel, that February, a preacher 'outdid himself' on the Second Coming of Christ, dilating on the depravity of mankind, particularly in England, and on how the end of the world could not now be long and how it would come suddenly. Moreover, John had an 'admonition' of 'fits', cured only by sitting up to the knees in very hot milk and covered in blankets. So he made a new will.

By May 1682 Fox, Wren and Evelyn took the completed design of Chelsea Hospital to Lambeth for the approval of the archbishop, and Evelyn, hearing that the East Indian ambassador from Bantam had arrived, went to consider other exotic guests. He found the Indonesians less impressive than the Moroccans; very hard favoured, much resembling 'some sort of *Munkeys*', though dressed in 'rich Indian Silks flowred with gold, with caps like fruit baskets'. They wore poisoned daggers, the haft carved with devils' heads, and they sat cross-legged like Turks, nails and teeth black as jet from betel nut. They ate rice pilaw dextrously with their fingers.

Now in his sixty-third year, John was even more careful of excess, and after attending a great reception by the Swedish ambassador with the Earl of Ailesbury, whom he had known years before as Lord Bruce in Venice, and with Lord Castlehaven, 'the sonn of him who was executed 50 years ago for Enormous Lusts, etc', he wisely stole away and left the company when they rose from table; he ended the year well 'by the Blessing of God' by selling his East India stock of £250 to the Royal Society for £750.

Early in 1683 Mary's father, Sir Richard Browne, aged seventy seven, died of gout and dropsy at Sayes Court. The vicar pronounced an elaborate, funeral eulogy, stressing his achievement as ambassador in Paris during the interregnum, and 'so ended this honorable Person after infinite Changes and tossing too and froo, in the same house and place where he was born'. By a clause in his will, Sir Richard had commanded that he was to be buried in the churchyard, since he disapproved of the new fangled custom of burial within the church, which made churches 'Charnel-houses'. He left all his property to Mary Evelyn.

Evelyn felt less respect for the newly rich merchant Sir Josiah Child, whose big estate he visited in Epping forest, in a barren spot, 'as commonly these over growne and suddainly monied men in the most part seat themselves'. From an ordinary merchant apprentice, Evelyn records with some scorn, he had become worth £200,000 and lately married his daughter, with an enormous dowry, to the eldest son of the Duke of Beaufort. Evelyn thought Child, governor of the East India Company, who had declared that the laws of England were 'a heap of nonsense, compiled by a few ignorant country gentlemen incapable of regulating foreign commerce', 'sordidly avaricious': nor did he approve the enterprise of Shape, His Majesty's farrier, who had opened a new tavern at the bowling green near Blackheath, frequented only by far too many 'drinking people' from London. And when the philistine Duke of Norfolk (formerly Lord Henry Howard) asked to sell his cartoons by Raphael, replied that he would sell anything for money except the Duchess, Evelyn acidly remarked that were he in the Duke's condition she would be the first thing he would part with.

But, preaching before some knowledgeable seamen, the vicar of Deptford committed himself all too heavily about Noah's Ark, probably the 'first ship ever made'. He agreed with the late Dr Wilkins of Wadham and Chester, who had thought it had been flat-bottomed, without mast or sail, and had never stirred far from where it had been built. This amateur theory was ill-received.

## V

By the summer of 1683 the panic over the Popish Plot had diminished, 'through the folly, knavery, impudence and giddynesse of *Oates*'; but there was now 'as they call'd it, a *Protestant-Plot* discover'd'. It was to assassinate both the king and Duke of York as they were returning from Newmarket, and timed to coincide with a general rising of Protestant extremists. This 'Rye House Plot' had been, it was alleged, originally concocted by Shaftesbury before he had fled to Holland, where 'the fox had died', and William, Lord Russell, eldest son of the Earl of Bedford, the republican aristocrat Algernon Sidney, and Evelyn's friend, the Earl of Essex, were all arrested. Evelyn considered that Essex at least was innocent, and in July he was horrified to hear that on the very day while Russell was being tried and sentenced to death, Essex had cut his own throat in the Tower – an 'accident' that amazed Evelyn since Essex had been of sober and religious deportment, and particularly as he had cut his throat so thoroughly that an executioner 'could hardly have don more with an axe'. Charles II characteristically commented that 'he wondered that the earl should destroy himself'; really Essex 'might have tried his Mercy' (for his father Capel's loyalty) since he 'owed him a life'.

Russell, prosecuted under the shadow of Essex's suicide, which influenced the jury against him, was a Puritan intellectual and incongruously a grandson through his mother of Robert Carr, Earl of Somerset; he had been ardent in promoting the exclusion of York, and had 'grudged' Stafford's being beheaded instead of being hanged, drawn and quartered; he was condemned and on 21 July beheaded with 'three butcherly strokes', himself to become a hero of Liberal historians.

The 'Protestant Plot' created widespread consternation: Evelyn writes that the king was 'very melancholy, not stirring without redoubled Guards'; nor were prospects abroad propitious. The Turks were advancing on Vienna, and the French, in pursuit of universal monarchy, had 'almost swallowed' all Flanders. Evelyn thought that the English had a heavy responsibility for having betrayed the Dutch, being 'Wanton, madd, and surfeiting with prosperity ... and never constant to anything'. 'The *Lord* in mercy,' he concludes, 'avert the sad *Omen*; & that we do not provoke him farther, 'til he beare it no longer.'[13]

# CHAPTER NINETEEN

# 'Le Roi est Mort: Vive le Roi'

'All engines at worke to bring in Poperie amain'

In July 1683 Evelyn first encountered Prince George of Denmark, newly arrived to marry York's second daughter, the Lady Anne. The prince was blond, heavy and taciturn; he spoke French badly, and Charles II remarked that he had 'tried him drunk and tried him sober, and, odds fish, there was nothing in him', but he proved an amiable consort to the future queen. Evelyn now chronicled great events abroad; how in September John Sobieski of Poland and the Bavarians relieved Vienna from the Turks and diminished the pressure on the empire, while at home Charles II, profitably uncommitted on the Continent, was now peacefully concerned, following a fire at Newmarket, with commissioning from Wren a new palace at Winchester, where Evelyn thought the air and prospects superior than at Newmarket for the king's 'outdoor recreation'.

He was not so keen on the monarch's indoor amusements: following Charles into Louise de Kéroüalle, Duchess of Portsmouth's dressing room, where her maids were combing her hair, he found the furniture more interesting than the lady. It was much superior, he observed, to the queen's; superb French tapestries, Japanese cabinets, great vases of wrought plate, some of the king's own best pictures; 'disquieted' and 'surfeited' with such luxury, he returned contentedly to his own 'poore but quiet' and already celebrated 'villa'. He became even more mindful of the vicar's edifying sermons, on religion as the only bridle to keep the wicked in awe, and on the 'unreasonableness' of dissent; but, now over sixty, John was apt to be surprised by sleep in church, – and 'not so attentive as I ought to have ben. The Lord Jesus pity me!'[1] On the anniversary of the Gunpowder Plot, the vicar ploughed on about perseverance and advocated not the furious zeal of Jehu, but the vigilance of the eyes of the winged beasts in Revelation: religion should be wary constant and sedate.

That winter Evelyn brought most of his household, including

'young' John and his family, to Villiers Street in London,
convenient for business and the education of his own daughters.
'Young' John, newly married and supposedly still studying the
law, remained without employment; he had wanted to attend at
Court, but Evelyn warned him that a courtier's life was
'anxiously tedious', and at best may have agreed with the
opinion of Lord Berkeley with whom John had served in Paris,
that he would 'never dance, nor make a leg well, nor have his
periwig and cravat in good order, or be *à la mode*, but he will
prove an honest, solid and judicious man and be very good
company.' Reading 'young' John's immensely laborious
commonplace books[2] and his often spirited letters, one cannot
deny him industry or talent; but he was too easy-going;
overburdened, as well, with his righteous and exacting father's
expectations. These would finally focus on John's son, Jack, but
were now also wrapped up in Evelyn's most talented and
attractive daughter Mary. Meanwhile, Evelyn was delighted
when Arlington's daughter, the young Duchess of Grafton, over
whose marriage he had been apprehensive, gave birth to Charles
FitzRoy, who became the Second Duke of Grafton; and he made
a point of visiting Danby, still, after four years, detained in the
Tower, where his lady 'railed' at his long imprisonment.

The winter of 1683–4 was insufferably cold, and by January so
bitter that streets of booths were set up on the frozen Thames;
John himself walked through cold and thick air over the ice from
Lambeth to the Horseferry leading to New Palace Yard. An
enterprising printer, from his press on the ice, printed off
visitors' names with date and place, making, it was said, £5 a
day; while bear baiting, horse racing, tippling and 'worse',
created a 'bacchanalia'. The very seas were locked in ice, and the
London coal smoke taxed lungs and blanketed vision. The
garden at Sayes Court was hard hit, only the cypress 'like to
endure it out', and the river remained unnavigable until mid-
February.

But life went on. Danby, under the new Habeas Corpus Act of
1679, at last emerged from the Tower on bail. Tenison devised a
fine project, backed by Evelyn, for the first public library in
London; it was to be near Leicester Square where it would keep
young clergymen from taverns; and eleven years later, when
Tenison was archbishop of Canterbury, it would be built and
endowed.

That Easter at Court John watched Charles II conduct three of
his young bastard dukes to holy communion; royal boys on the

right, bishops on the left. Northumberland, Richmond and St
Albans were respectively the offspring of Portsmouth, Cleveland
and 'Nelly', all 'prostitute creatures'; John thought
Northumberland 'the most accomplish'd and worth owning' –
extremely handsome and perfectly shaped, and the others both
very 'pretty boys with more wit than most of the rest'. Given the
king's outstanding sexual powers, it was a sad freak of fate that
he was denied legitimate offspring.

With the spring of 1684 the Evelyns moved back to Sayes
Court, though 'young' John, as his father records with
disapproval, stayed in London 'under pretence of studying
harder at the law'. To start the season well, Evelyn 'took Physick
and a Vomite', which greatly restored him; he also wrote a
memorandum for the Royal Society on the terrible effects of the
past winter. The belated spring then turned to such a drought
that 'the leaves dropt off the trees', and not until well into
August, after 'such a drought as no man living had known',
came the rain.

But Evelyn's prospects were now improved when his close
friend, Sidney Godolphin, was created a baron and First
Commissioner of the Treasury; indeed in the long run his
patronage would be decisive for both Evelyn and for his
grandson Jack. More immediately exciting to John's still eager
curiosity and accurate descriptive powers was his first sight of a
live rhinoceros (or 'Unicorne'). She 'more resembled a huge
enormous Swine, than any other Beast amongst us', her small
eyes were in the centre of her cheeks and head, 'Eares ... very
much pointed, her Leggs [about] the size of a man's wast', her
feet 'like an elephant's' and her body 'at least twenty feet round'.
She 'had a set of dreadfull teeth', and most peculiar of all, a
'loricated' skin that hung in folds 'like Coach leather'. Lying
down, she seemed as big as a coach, but she 'rose nimbly as ... a
horse ...they fed her with Hay and Oates, and gave her bread'.[3]
An apparently amiable beast, she was sold for no less than
£2,000; in contrast, though the Indian crocodile in a tub of warm
water only seemed tame, it was fed on flesh and in fact 'promised
to be dangerous'.

Apart from exotic animals, the Court always presented
curiosities to Evelyn's observant eye and vivid pen. Three
splendid Turkish horses, for example, taken from a 'Bashaw' at
the relief of Vienna, were paraded before King Charles. They
were 'spiritous and proud', 'trotted like Does as if they did not
feel the Ground', no one 'in these parts' had seen their like, and

their accoutrements were unexampled. But the Court, as always, had its dissolute side, and Evelyn in a celebrated passage afterwards recorded that he had never seen such profuse gaming and 'luxurious dallying and prophanenesse', the king 'Sitting and Toying with his Concubines, ... a French boy singing love songs'.

## II

But Charles II's days of dalliance were over. By 4 February 1685, he was 'surpriz'd in his bed chamber by an Apoplectical fit' – the symptom of kidney disease and uraemia. His senior physician promptly let him 'bloud in the very paroxysme', and soon the king was again 'cupped, [and] let bloud againe in both jugularies'; he was then given vomits and purges. His fever unalleviated by 'Jesuits' powder' (quinine), he complained of pain in his side, whereat they drew another twelve ounces of blood. In great pain and struggling for breath, he died on 6 February at eleven in the morning, the victim of incurable disease, grossly aggravated by misguided remedies.

He had recommended all his natural children, save Monmouth, now in exile in Holland, to the Duke of York, 'Spoke to him to be kind to the Duchesses of Cleveland and Portsmouth', and that 'Nelly might not sterve'[4] 'Thus died King Charles 2d, of a vigourous and robust constitution and in all appearances capable of a longer life.' He was only fifty-four.

From first hand observation, Evelyn sums him up.[5]

A Prince of many Virtues and many greate Imperfections, Debonaire, Easy of accesse, not bloudy or Cruel: his Countenance fierce, his voice greate, proper of person, every motion became him, a lover of the sea, and skillfull in shipping, not affecting other studys, yet he had a laboratory and knew many Empirical Medicines and the easier Mechanical Mathematics: Loved Planting, building, and brought in a politer way of living, which passed to Luxurie and intollerable expense. He had a particular Talent in telling stories and facetious passages of which he had innumerable ... An excellent Prince doubtlesse had he been less addicted to Women. ... His too Easy nature resign'd him to be menag'd by crafty men ... He was ever kind to me and very gracious ... and therefore I cannot without ingratitude but deplore his losse, which in many respects (as well as duty) I do with all my soule.

Summoned by the Sheriff of Kent to assist at proclaiming the new king, James II, Evelyn, having attended the pompous ceremonies in London, repaired to the bishop of Rochester's palace at Bromley, and attended the proclamation in the market place. At Court, he was glad to find, the atmosphere had at once changed into 'more solemne and moral behaviour', the new King James 'affecting neither Prophaneness nor bouffoonery'; but on the very day of his brother's funeral in Henry VII's Chapel in Westminster Abbey, he went in public to Mass in the little oratory by his old lodgings; and Evelyn was soon grieved to observe a new pulpit in the Catholic oratory in Whitehall, mass being publicly celebrated and 'the Romanists swarming at Court more than ever seen in England since the Reformation'.

These public apprehensions were now dwarfed for him when on 14 March 1685, John's intelligent and accomplished daughter Mary died of smallpox; she had a particularly sweet voice, 'nobody living read prose, or Verse better and with more judgement', and she used to read for hours in Evelyn's study: 'ô how desolate hast Thou left us, Sweete obliging, happy, Creature!' Her mother wrote that though she 'submitted to her loss as a Christian, she was apt to murmur at the decree when all her engaging ways return to my imagination': Mary was only eighteen.

So affected were the Evelyns that, not wishing to leave his wife alone, John did not attend the coronation of the new king; but he was present early in May at the trial of Titus Oates in Westminster Hall for perjury. It proved very tedious, and he did not hear the sentence – that this 'man of an ill cut', with his broad Norfolk accent and nasal drawl, should be whipped from Newgate to Aldgate and then to Tyburn with a whip of six thongs, pilloried five times a year and imprisoned for life.[6] But by chance Evelyn from his coach observed the culprit, after his first whipping at the cart's tail, dragged on a sledge to Tyburn, being unable to walk, and whipped again all the way, 'a punishment but what he deserved'.

Meanwhile John had secured a place in the House of Lords 'very commodiously' below the bishops, to hear the new king make his speech to parliament. He declared that he would call a new parliament, defend the Church of England as by law established, and invade no man's property. In return, he asked for his revenue to be settled for life, rather than that he should be 'supplied from time to time'; he also alarmed them by the timely news that Argyle had landed from Holland in the Western Highlands with treasonous intent. The Commons thereupon promptly went into committee and unanimously voted the king his revenue for life.

## III

The nation was now much further alarmed by the Monmouth rebellion. On 11 June 1685, Monmouth landed at Lyme Regis in Dorset, and by the 20th he was proclaimed king at Taunton in Somerset. The French, hoping to be rid of the Protestant claimant, but in fact clearing the way for the much more dangerous Prince of Orange, had not interfered with the hopeless project, and James reacted swiftly. On 16 June Monmouth was proclaimed a traitor with £5,000 for his capture alive or dead.

Unperturbed by these ill-boding events, Evelyn, the next day took the chair as Vice-President at the Royal Society, and by the 28th recorded that Argyle had been captured in Scotland and his following dispersed. Then on 8 July of that torrid and hitherto rainless summer, came the news of Monmouth's utter defeat two days before at Sedgemoor, and his subsequent capture in a ditch near Ringwood. He had betrayed his own followers; 'The horse (at Sedgemoor) breaking their owne ranks,' writes Evelyn, 'Monmouth gave it over and fled ... leaving their party to be cut in pieces'. Four hundred men, mostly from Taunton, were killed on the field by Feversham's troops, and two thousand in the pursuit, and Monmouth found, unarmed, sixty miles away 'in a dry-ditch cover'd with fern braken'.

The sequel was grim. Monmouth was brought up to London and interviewed by James II, who wrote coldly to the Prince of Orange that the Duke 'seemed more concerned ... to live and did behave himself not so well as I expected, or as one ought to have expected from one who had taken upon him to be King. I have signed the warrant for his execution to-morrow.'[7] Evelyn alleges that at the execution, the headsman, though heavily tipped, made 'five Chopps before he had his head off'. 'Thus,' he concludes,[8] ended this quondam Duke, darling of his Father, and the Ladys, being extraordinarily handsome, and adroit; an excellent souldier and dauncer, a favourite of the people, of an Easy nature, debauched by lust and seduced by crafty knaves ... Se what *Ambition* and want of principles brought him to!

The life of official London carried on. Later that July Evelyn attended a grand meeting of Trinity House, where Pepys, as secretary to the admiralty, was a second time chosen Master: they all heard a sermon on the benefits of navigation both for commerce defence and the propagation of Christianity; it concluded suitably, with 'an exhortation to the sea-men (especially the vulgar) to holiness, and reproving their universal prophaneness – not sparing their Commanders'. The meeting then proceeded up the Thames from Deptford to London, where they all had a 'magnificent feast' – over eighty at one table.

The public danger from Argyle and Monmouth was over, but following the death of their beloved Mary, the Evelyns now sustained another shock. While they were all asleep, their daughter Elizabeth stole away and eloped with a young nephew of one Sir John Tippet, originally only Master Shipwright at Portsmouth, if now Surveyor of the Navy. She was seventeen, and without telling either of her parents, married him the next morning. Yet, having been 'bred-up with the utmost Circumspection', she had hitherto appeared entirely docile, until her 'passion for this young fellow had made her forget her duty'. 'The Affliction,' writes John, 'went very neere me and my wife', but they both thought it a further chastisement from God to which they must humbly submit. John felt so 'discomposed' that he even could not go to church, and promptly altered his will so that she could 'see what her undutifullness had deprived her of'. But young Elizabeth's emancipation was brief. By mid-August she was stricken with smallpox, and though her parents, relenting, risked contagion to comfort her, God was soon 'pleased to take her out of this vale of misery'.

From these domestic tragedies and masochistic religious reflections, Evelyn was distracted by a signal and fairly lucrative honour. His friend, the Second Earl of Clarendon and the Lord Privy Seal, having been appointed Lord Lieutenant of Ireland, nominated him as one of the Commissioners at £500 a year to administer the Privy Seal office in London during his absence. So Evelyn went down with Clarendon to Windsor to kiss hands on the appointment, and records King James saying that he was glad to have the chance of showing the kindness he had for him. 'Abundance of great men', the Earl of Rochester, Lord Peterborough, Lord Godolphin, 'Gave him joy', and in the splendid St George's Chapel, Evelyn heard a comprehensive sermon by a Frenchman on sin.

The king now planned to inspect the fortifications of Portsmouth, and Evelyn and Pepys, as secretary to the admiralty, took a coach and six horses to go down there: they arrived at Winchester to find the king installed in the Deanery, and discoursing about miracles. James declared himself 'extreamly difficult' of them, 'for fear of being imposed on'; but various examples were canvassed, then the phenomenon of 'second sight', especially among the Scots, whereat James spoke of a crucifix, taken by a workman from Edward the Confessor's coffin, which the late king had given him on his deathbed. He then in pious mood suddenly declared that all the negroes on the plantations must be baptized, though their masters had forbidden it.

The party then proceeded to Charles II's new palace on the site of the old castle, already a stately fabric of three sides and a corridor, all of brick, intended for a 'Hunting House', one side having 'an incomparable prospect.' Unfortunately his 'now Majestie' did not 'seeme to encourage the finishing of it'.[9] Evelyn, though it had rained all day, decided to see the Cathedral, 'a reverend pile, and in good repair.'

Early on 17 September while Judge Jeffreys at Taunton was completing his 'Bloody Assize' in the west country, the royal party proceeded to Portsmouth, where the king rode on horseback through large crowds, the women in their best, to be entertained magnificently by the mayor. There were thirty-two men-of-war in the harbour and after inspecting the forts, James rode back to Winchester.

Evelyn and Pepys returned by Guildford to London, Evelyn greatly impressed by the 'infinite industry, sedulity, gravity and greate understanding and experience of affaires in his Majestie'. Indeed, he 'could not but predict much happiness to the Nation, as to its political Government', and thought that if the king would so persist as he was confident he would, he would accomplish the nation's prosperity, 'for such a Prince never had this Nation since it was one'. But he still thought 'nothing could be more desired ... than that he were of the national Religion'.[10]

Early in October Pepys invited Evelyn to dine, adding, 'I have something to shew you, that I may not have again another time.' After dinner, along with a rich merchant of Flemish origin, Pepys confided that the king had told him that Charles II had died a Catholic, and, what was more, shown him two papers in the late king's own hand charging the Church of England with heresy for refusing to acknowledge the authority of Rome. James had even lent Pepys copies, attested by his own hand; but Evelyn, knowing Charles II better, thought that the arguments were too 'well penn'd as to discourse ... to have ben put together by the Late King'. He remained unconvinced.

IV

That autumn Evelyn had his likeness painted by Kneller, and pictures of Mary and their surviving daughter, Susanna, also 'drawn'. He accompanied Lady Clarendon to her estate at Swallowfield, south of Reading, and his eye for a garden approved walks and groves of elms, limes and oaks, 'noble orangeries' and a canal. From fishponds full of carp, bream and tench, they had 'Carps and Pike etc of size fit for the table of a Prince, every meale', and, with a cook standing by, 'at the drag', the visitors 'pointed out what we had most mind to'.[11]

After the summer recess of 1685, the Royal Society was shown a model chariot claimed to be unsurpassed for comfort, speed and safety, but it had disadvantages. It would contain only one person, was apt to catch fire every ten miles and made an almost intolerable noise, so for these failings the Society were asked 'to excogitate the remedies'.

Meanwhile in France the persecution of the Huguenots was 'raging with uttmost barbarity', the French tyrant having abrogated the Edict of Nantes, and Protestant refugees were spreading to England as well as to Switzerland, Germany, and Holland. Louis XIV's decision, by ruining many bankers had diminished his own revenues, but it was feared that his action might set a precedent for England – suspicions fanned when, for the first time in eighty years, bonfires had been forbidden on the anniversary of the discovery of the Gunpowder Plot.

In consequence, when James in his speech to parliament required that his standing army should be continued instead of the militia, the Commons found his demands 'unexpected and unpleasing', and they passed the indemnity of Catholic officers from the Test Act by only one vote. Moreover, the soldiers, dispersed to quarters about the kingdom, were proving 'insolent': with the ominous precedent of persecution in France still raging the year ended in a gloomy Christmas, Evelyn beseeching the Almighty to pardon the sins which had provoked Him to 'discomposse' his own sorrowful family by the death of two daughters, and 'accept their humiliation'.

Nor was Evelyn happy when early in 1686 at the Privy Seal office they had to pass the creation of the king's mistress, Catherine Sedley, of whom Charles II had said that she must have been assigned to him as a penance, as Countess of Dorchester; an honour that the queen took so hard that she almost refused to eat and spoke not a word to the king at two dinners, and which also made the Catholics furious. The lady herself had been long surprised at the former Duke's passion, remarking 'It cannot be my beauty for he must see that I have none; and it cannot be my wit, for he has not enough to know that I have any'.[12]

Evelyn continued to record the 'unheard of cruelties' to the persecuted Protestants of France.

He had long been involved as executor for his father-in-law, with William Prettyman, Mary's uncle, the former occupant of Sayes Court, over bills of exchange allegedly unpaid during Sir Richard Browne's residence in France. The case was at last being heard by Judge Jeffreys, now Lord Chancellor, who violently reproved one of the opposing lawyers, an intervention for which Evelyn heartily thanked God. He was also edified in March when the Provost of Eton preached at Whitehall on the vanity of earthly enjoyments.

But public tensions were now more menacing. As a Commissioner for the Privy Seal, Evelyn feared he would have to authorize the Rev. Obadiah Walker, Master of University College, Oxford, a Catholic convert, to hold office without taking the Test, a dispensation contrary to the king's promise in his first address to parliament; he was relieved that the dispensation was confirmed by letters patent under the Great Seal instead. But 'all engines', he felt, 'were now at work to bring in Popery, amaine', particularly as the Waldenses in Piedmont were now being massacred and driven into exile, following 'a universal designe to destroy all who would not Masse it throughout Europ'.[13]

Evelyn himself was driven to resist, and after consulting with the archbishop of Canterbury and the Lord Treasurer, who advised him to follow his own conscience, he refused to put the Privy Seal to a licence for Walker to publish Popish books. 'How strangely,' he thought, 'is this nation fallen from its ancient zeale and Integritie Ô unhappy, unthankfull people!' In his mid-sixties, Evelyn, like most elderly English people in most centuries, was more than ever convinced that England was going to the dogs.

The king, taking a leaf from his politically inept father's book, was now claiming retrospective fees from baronets created since the Restoration; the army, encamped at Hounslow with nothing to do, were conspicuous for 'great feasting', and Lord Tyrconnell, appointed lieutenant general of the army in Ireland, had gone over there with suspicious intent, while new judges had been appointed, among them a Catholic younger brother of the Milton 'who wrot for the Regicides'. The king's chief physician in Scotland had also publicly apostasized from the Protestant religion.

## V

At the office of the Privy Seal, though the duties were light, Evelyn was well placed to observe the manoeuvres of the king. In July 1686 he had to seal the constitution of Ecclesiastical Commissioners with powers to regulate the church exceeding those of the pre-war High Commission Court, and among the Commissioners, of course, was the Lord Chancellor, Jeffreys. By September the bishop of London was suspended for not reproving an anti-Catholic preacher and illegally overruled and sentenced by the Lord Chancellor, though the archbishop of Canterbury had refused to sit in judgment. Even the standard of sermons at Deptford was going down, although on 10 October a visiting 'stranger' preached well on 'Lot's wife, her disobedience, love of sensual enjoyments etc', and her deserved fate.

In November 1685, the king had prorogued parliament, reckoning it would not withdraw the anti-Catholic laws; but he was still thwarted by the resistance of the great officers of Court and state, while, during the Good Friday service of 1686, a tense congregation was scared when men entered with drawn swords, though they turned out to be only a debtor seeking sanctuary, pursued by bailiffs.

The king, now back from Windsor, reviewed the guards in Hyde Park – Evelyn thought that 'such horse and men could not be braver', and the officers 'wonderfully rich and gallant'. The Evelyns, too, returned to London for the winter, staying with 'young' John in Arundel Street near Norfolk House. Dining in November with Lord Chancellor Jeffreys and three other lawyers, Evelyn was shocked at their stories of how their procrastinations had fleeced their clients: it was as if 'highway thieves should have met and discovered the severall purses they had taken: This they made but a jeast of; but God is not mocked.'[14]

By January 1687 the king's designs had further developed. The Lord Treasurer, Lawrence Hyde, Earl of Rochester, after being assigned £4,000 a year for ninety-nine years out of the Post office and £1,700 a year in perpetuity from Lord Grey's estate forfeited in the Monmouth rebellion, was superseded by a partly Catholic commission and the hopes of Protestants were dashed by the recovery of Louis XIV from a dangerous and painful operation for *fistula in ano*. The magnificent new Catholic Chapel Royal at Whitehall was now opened publicly for the full Catholic service, with Jesuits in rich copes and adoration of the papal arms. Evelyn had to admit that the Italian music was superb, but could hardly believe that he would ever have lived to see such things in the King of England's palace. He put it all down to the furious drive of the Jesuits who could compel even princes to violent courses. It was feared that the highest officers of state would be removed for being Anglican, JPs from the meanest of the people would be established in the counties and judges ignorant of the law would pervert it. 'Jesus,' wrote Evelyn, 'Defend his little flock!' By March a Proclamation was reported from Scotland of universal liberty of conscience and enabling Catholics to hold offices of trust, and Clarendon, superseded by Tyrconnell, returned from Ireland.

The king therefore sent for Evelyn and the other Commissioners of the Privy Seal and promised he would provide for them; he did not, however, restore the seal to Clarendon, but to the Catholic Lord Arundel of Wardour. Most of the other great officers of state were also dismissed, and likewise most of the parliament men in office who would not repeal the Test Act.

The Anglican clergy stood their ground; particularly Dr Ken, bishop of Bath and Wells, who, preaching before the Prince of Denmark, drew an immense congregation at Whitehall, comparing the Catholic priests to scribes and pharisees and worse. Evelyn was also reassured to find at least the routine of Anglican Christ's Hospital unimpaired – 800 boys and girls, 'so decently clad, cleanely lodged, so wholesomely fed, so admirably taught', especially the forty boys with special badges being trained in navigation in the mathematical school founded in 1673 by Charles II. All were taught for particular callings and trades, the girls trained to be good wives and a 'blessing to their generation'. After hearing them all sing a Psalm with cheerful harmony, Evelyn came away with 'infinite satisfaction', having 'never in my life seene a more noble, pious and admirable Charity.'[15] He still felt immense benevolence for the young: by contrast, on the way home, he saw a more up to date spectacle – 'the trial of those devilish murdering mischiefe-doing engines Bombs, shot out of the mortar piece on black-heath'. Their cost, range and destructiveness were already prodigious.

Impervious to the political crisis, Evelyn's own 'great cause' with Prettyman still dragged on in Chancery, and the case, further delayed, was now 'referred to a Master'. Evelyn sought relief with Pepys, where he heard an Italian eunuch sing, esteemed the best in Europe, but he proved 'wanton, effeminate and childish, very coy and proudly conceited in my estimation'.

It was still impossible to escape politics. Dining with the Prince of Orange's envoy, the 'Holland ambassador', Evelyn heard him deplore the stupid folly of the English in having let the French overrun strategic Luxembourg; at last, however, by the end of May, agreement over the Chancery suit was in prospect. Then, early in June, Evelyn obtained £6,000 under the Great Seal for discharging Sir Richard Browne's debt to Prettyman. There remained outstanding another £6,000 due to Evelyn as Sir Richard's executor, but through the favour of Godolphin at the Treasury the Chancery suit had at last been determined. Mary Evelyn felt that her father's credit had been vindicated, and the Evelyns, brother George, young John and William Glanville drank a hogshead of claret at Wotton in celebration.

The king, now courting the Dissenters as a way of including Catholics in a general toleration, now received a loyal address from the nonconformists of Coventry who said that his Declaration of Indulgence had been good for trade. James even put off his hat in acknowledgment and promised to preserve their just liberty of conscience by law; he also accepted an even more peculiar address for a 'sort of refined Quakers called the Family of Love' whose custom was just to read the scriptures and then preach. They were very few, and came from the Isle of Ely; but James brought himself to be civil even to them.[16]

## VI

With parliament still prorogued, James was using the royal Prerogative to control government. James had long alienated the influential Halifax and Danby and had created a permanent standing army, the nightmare of the political nation.

Like many loyal subjects, Evelyn was torn between conscience and fear of civil war. His sympathies, always civilian, were with the moderates led by Halifax, rather than with Danby and his followers, who had now turned so far against the monarch that they were in correspondence with William of Orange. But by then Evelyn had been horrified in his religious feelings when the king had ordered a second Declaration of Indulgence to be read in the churches, and seven of the bishops, including old archbishop Sancroft, had refused to read it, he ordered the bishops to be put on trial. As at the opening of the Civil War, it was religion more than economic interest that drove even moderates into conflict.

With advancing age, Evelyn was becoming more obsessed with religion, more addicted to recording sermons, more penitent, when he fell asleep in church: two sermons a Sunday were his usual fare, and their records swamp his *Diary*, as the ingenious divines sought to refurbish long threadbare themes; indeed this amiable and upright man was increasingly haunted by the projection of an irate God watching his every action and totting up the score of his trivial sins. To Evelyn's pre-Newtonian generation nature did not proceed by rational laws under her own power, but was still a confusion, interrupted by the incomprehensible interventions of divine providence, signifying favour or wrath, and demanding propitiation.

During the backward spring of 1688 with cold easterly winds, by Easter 'almost perpetual', the rumour had run that the king had been perverted by the Jesuits into altering the church establishment, and in May the crisis broke. The bishops of Bath and Wells, Peterborough, Ely, Chichester, Bristol and St Asaph petitioned the king that they could not read the Declaration, because it was founded on a dispensing power that could 'set aside all laws, Ecclesiastical and civil', and which appeared to them illegal.

The king was furious and dismissed their petition. By the 25th Evelyn had forgathered with Dr Tenison, Pepys and other friends 'all the discourse being about the bishops'. The king's injunction had not been drafted in proper legal form, the report was that the Protestant secular lords and nobility would 'abett' the clergy, and violence was expected.

On 8 June Evelyn records that the six bishops, and the archbishop of Canterbury as well, were all sent to the Tower, and 'Wonderfull was the concern of the people for them, infinite crowds of people on their knees, ... as they passed out of the Barge'.[17] Two days later the crisis deepened when Evelyn heard the guns of the Tower discharged and the bells ringing, for the birth of a Prince of Wales. The royal event, he observed, would 'cost dispute'.

By the end of June the bishops, acquitted by a jury, were released. Prelates had not often been popular in seventeenth-century London, but the popular rejoicing was tremendous, the bishops blessing the people who were on their knees by the waterside; there were bonfires and bells pealing. The bishops, who had 'all along' been 'full of Courage and cherefull', had refused even to pay the surly lieutenant of the Tower any fee. And the royalist John Evelyn had entirely and representatively approved their resistance.

# CHAPTER TWENTY

# 'A sad revolution to this sinfull Nation'

Evelyn was always susceptible to intelligent women, and the Countess of Sunderland, born Lady Anne Digby, heiress of the Earl of Bristol, had long been one of them. Her husband, Robert Spencer, Second Earl of Sunderland, was in the full tide of political power and political intrigue; having served Charles II as Secretary of State after the fall of Clarendon, he had been made Lord President of the Council by James II as well as principal secretary, and become a timely convert to Catholicism. He was now trying to restrain the king's political blunders, but was already in touch with William of Orange.

In Augst 1688 Lady Sunderland invited Evelyn and his son down to the Spencers' great house at Althorp; flattered and impressed, Evelyn greatly admired the mansion – 'or rather palace', which 'could become a great Prince', its avenues, canals and fishponds, store of game, and all managed 'without any show of solicitude'. His one reservation was the 'fatal apostacy' of the earl, which would soon end, after a flight to Holland disguised as a woman, in return to the Church of England and high office under William III. The Sunderlands' heir, Lord Spencer, was meanwhile 'rambling about the world', 'dishonoring his name and family', and died that year of drink in Paris; but Evelyn much approved of his brother, Charles, who in 1700 by his marriage to Lady Anne Churchill, Marlborough's second daughter, would become the ancestor of the Spencer-Churchill Dukes of Marlborough.

Evelyn returned to find panic mounting in London, where the Irish troops encamped at Hounslow were rumoured to be murdering Protestants, the Dutch fleet reported as ready to sail, and the French said to have attacked Baden instead of Holland, thus giving William of Orange a freer hand. By 6 October the 'hourly dreate of the Pr of Orange's Invasion' had made the king recall the writs of summons for a new parliament; but he also abrogated the hated Commission for Ecclesiastical Affairs, and restored the ejected Protestant Fellows of Magdalen at Oxford. Yet, despite these concessions, he continued to bring in Irish-Scots troops and place more Catholic officers in his large army, – 'too such a strange temper' was 'this poor nation reduced'. Then on 14 October significantly, Evelyn observed, an anniversary of William the Conqueror's victory at 'Battel', the wind turned east, bringing 'wonderful expectations of the Dutch fleet'; but on Sunderland's advice, James had refused the help of French warships to stop it, and the English battle fleet now lay wind-bound off the gun-fleet south of Harwich, in expectation of a Dutch landing in eastern or north-eastern England.

Now sixty-seven, Evelyn implored the Almighty 'Be thou my protector this following yeare, and preserve me and mine from these dangers and greate confusions, which threaten a sad revolution to this sinfull Nation.'[1] Having seen one Civil War, he did not want another.

## II

By 2 November it was reported that the Prince of Orange had sailed, probably making north-east; then two days later, that, passing through the Straits in an easterly gale, he had landed 'about Portsmouth or the Ile of Wight'. In fact on 5 November he landed at Torbay in Devon, and the news reached London the next afternoon. Evelyn heard eye-witness accounts of the passage of his great fleet in sunshine through the Straits of Dover – 'so dreadfull a sight passing through the Channell with so favourable a Wind, as our Navy could by no meanes intercept ... them',[2] and that the invaders, after a lucky strategic surprise, had 'gotten already into Excester', with 'the season and wayes very improper for his Majesties forces to march so greate a distance'. The king still had an army larger than any Cromwell had controlled; but morale was crumbling. Archbishop Sancroft and a few other lords, spiritual and temporal, summoned to Whitehall to express abhorrence of the invasion, denied that they had known of its imminence; but, saying they were so few, desired to consult the rest of their colleagues and see the prince's own manifesto before making any public declaration. Naturally, this 'did not please his Majestie'.

Far from anticipating the 'Glorious Revolution' of Whig tradition, Evelyn and his like expected civil war for which the king was apparently well equipped – 'the beginning of Sorrows, unlesse God in his Mercy prevent it'. He thought that a free parliament, the only way to a solution, was unlikely with such military force present on both sides, and prayed God to 'direct the King for the best'. Still exerting his thaumaturgic powers, James, accompanied by the Jesuit Father Petre, was touching, apparently unperturbed, for the King's Evil.

Through frosty November weather, as gradually some of the gentry in the mid-west came in to the prince, the king on the 19th joined his troops at Salisbury; but, though he declared that 'he would not see himself deposed: he had read the story of King Richard II', he was 'doubtful of their standing by him'; and already Cornbury, Clarendon's son, had deserted with some cavalry to the prince at Honiton: most importantly on the 23rd Lord Churchill and the Duke of Grafton joined the prince, while in London, Evelyn records, the queen was preparing to leave for Portsmouth to 'attend the issue of the Commotion'.

At the crucial moment, when James, by temperament and experience a fine commander, surprisingly lost his nerve and returned on 26th to London, leaving the prince undefeated to collect more support, and revolt in the provinces to proceed unchecked, Evelyn is laconic. He visited Godolphin, who was proceeding on a Commission from the king with Halifax to the prince at Hungerford, but with little power to negotiate, merely offering to summon a parliament by mid-January; and he records that York, Hull, Bristol and 'all the eminent nobility and persons of quality throughout England' had declared for the prince, Protestant religion and laws, and that the Jesuits were seen to 'flie or abscond', with universal consternation among the 'Popists' in office. Events were in fact making up Evelyn's own royalist mind, and he even instructed 'young' John to present himself to the prince and convey his father's respects.

Writing from Radley in mid-December, John described how a garrison of gentlemen volunteers had secured Oxford for the prince, though 'the Passive Obedience men in the university trembled for the plate and libraries, part of the king's army being still at Little Wycombe Henley and Reading'. 'Of this small garrison in defense of our English Athens,' he continued,

I had the honour to make one ... not without alarms, till his Highness, where he lay at Henley sent us order to disband ... Having thus finished my five days Rebellion in very good company, being in arms for the Nassovian Hero, the Primitive Religion and the liberty of my country

young John concludes that he had found time to salute the prince, who 'seemed to be very grave and deliberate in his

speech and motion, and even when he eats, not unthoughtful ...
Tranquility, order and silence reign among his attendants'. With
the 'Nassovian Hero' John anticipates a spirited note of
eighteenth-century-style mockery, alien to the solemn fanaticism
of the Civil Wars and a salutary sign for the future; then, like
many another Englishman, he goes on to speculate on the
chances of employment under the new regime.

Meanwhile his cousin, George Evelyn's son, the heir to
Wotton, who also took politics less seriously than did the older
generation, had an 'apoplectic fit' through getting drunk to
celebrate the Protestant victory, and in London the Protestant
rabble were happily burning the Spanish ambassador's library.

The king then threw all the moderate loyalists like Evelyn into
agonies of apprehension: at three in the morning of 11
December, having smuggled the queen and the Prince of Wales –
his main concern – into France, he bolted. He had burnt the
writs for a parliament, disbanded the armed forces, and tried to
paralyse government by throwing the great seal into the
Thames. He had then got to sea from Rochester, but,
apprehended and recognized, he had been retrieved amid some
popular acclaim to London, where on 17th Evelyn observed him
dining as usual in public, with a Jesuit in attendance.

The monarch's physical and psychological breakdown is
understandable; attempting to square the circle of being a
Catholic king of a strongly Protestant realm, with Jesuits driving
him one way and a Protestant people another, this Catholic
convert was haunted by his father's fate, and his last gesture of
defiant destruction showed the disgust of a cosmopolitan
Catholic royalty with his insular subjects. Commanding to Lord
Feversham to disband the army, he had written,

having been basely deserted ... I could no longer resolve to expose
myself to no purpose to what I might expect from the ambitious Prince
of Orange and the associated rebellious lords, and therefore have
resolved to withdraw till the violent storm is over, which will be in
God's good time.

And to Lord Dartmouth, disbanding the fleet, James also wrote,
'and this I may say, never any Prince took more care of his sea
and land men as I have done, and been so very ill repaid by
them'.[3]

Impervious to such gestures, however damaging in theory,
most of the pragmatic English establishment – king or no king –
rallied to the authority of parliament and of their version of the
constitution. By 18 December the prince's Dutch guards

occupied Whitehall and St James's, where Evelyn saw him, 'very stately, serious and reserved', holding great court. Shepherded by Dutch guards, James had taken the royal barge for Gravesend, and soon after midnight on 23 December again left Rochester for France, where he arrived, by English reckoning, on Christmas Day.

Ingloriously the English Revolution was being muddled through, with 'Divers reports and opinions, what all this will end in'. First the Lords, then the Commons surviving from the last parliament of Charles II, formally accepted the prince as the only effective authority, and petitioned him to take on the government until a convention of Lords and Commons could assemble. William had already taken control of the army; he knew his own mind, and at once declared he would summon a new parliament. Winter set in with bitter cold, and Evelyn, with the Thames freezing over, had to walk home through deep snow.

The politically conscious nation was still characteristically confused: some were for making the Princess Mary queen outright, many others were for a regency, with government still working in the name of the king; some Tories wanted James back under conditions; others a republic with the prince 'like a Statholder'. Dining with archbishop Sancroft and five other prelates, Evelyn found they were all wanting to have it both ways through the fiction of a regency – thus furthering the calling of a parliament according to existing law. The archbishop of Glasgow, frightened that the whole episcopal hierarchy in Scotland was in danger, begged Sancroft to intercede with the prince: Evelyn took leave of them, recording a prayer that 'God ... would settle truth and peace amongst us againe'.

William had not taken great risks to create a regency or a republic, so he had promptly and simply assumed the executive power, and summoned a convention parliament for 7 January 1689. He had also remarked that he was 'not prepared to be his wife's gentleman usher', and by 7 February, faced with this resolute and decisive continental soldier and diplomat, the Lords and Commons of the convention had to combine to determine what Evelyn calls 'the greate question about the Government'. So the Commons resolved that

King *Jam*: 2d, having by the advise of Jesuites and other wicked persons, endeavoured to subvert the Lawes of church and state, and Deserting the Kingdome (carrying away the Seales etc) without taking any care for the manegement of the Government, had by demise, abdicated himselfe and wholy vacated his right.

They then,[4]

desired the Lords' Concurrence to their vote, to place the Crowne upon the next heires: the Prince of Orange for his life, then on the Princesse his wife, and if she died without Issue on the Princesse of Denmark, and she failing to the heires of the Pr: Excluding forever all possibility of admitting any Ro: Cath:

The Lords' proposal for a Regency backed by twelve bishops (Sancroft being discreetly absent) was only narrowly defeated; according to Evelyn who, as usual ubiquitous, got near the door of the Lobby, only by three votes, many peers naturally 'aledging the danger of dethroning' which put all hierarchy at risk; some even argued that in law 'the King could do no wrong'. But despite the bishops, the three votes put both Houses in agreement and the settlement was sanctioned by the convention parliament.

Thus, by a narrower margin than since widely realized, the *fait accompli* was recognized, and at the cost of the glamour of divine right, the English retained a Protestant, if not for long a Stuart, monarchy.

## III

It now looked as if 'God had so composed the crisis that', as Evelyn representatively put it, 'we may at last be a Nation and a Church under some fixt and sober establishment'. At Deptford they held a service of thanksgiving for deliverance by the Prince of Orange, with prayers purposely composed. On 13 February William and Mary, who had joined him the day before from Holland, were jointly proclaimed king and queen, with 'Wonderfull acclamation ... Bonfires, bells Gunns etc'. Mary in fact much distressed for her father, put of a forced gaiety, coming to Whitehall 'as to a Wedding, riant and jolly'; indeed, she at once resumed the Court routine, a gesture which gave a false impression that she 'took nothing to heart', while the prince, with his formal continental manners, seemed, after the intermittently charming Stuarts, 'wonderfull serious and silent'.

He had plenty to think about. On 22 February the convention declared itself a parliament, and a throng of office-seekers besieged the new monarch. Danby became president of a Council of Thirty and Halifax Lord Privy Seal; but troubles threatened in Scotland and in Ireland, fomented by the prospect of French invasion. The country seemed in no condition for a major war, though the battle fleet, rehabilitated under the former king by Pepys and his administration and prevented from attacking the prince's expedition, was still powerful and intact.

But there were still many who 'had not expected to see the government assum'd without any regard to the absent King', or without 'proving a spontaneous abdication' or that 'the Pr of Wales was an Imposture etc', and five 'non-juring' bishops had refused to take the oath of allegiance; so to 'gratify and sweeten the people', the hearth money or chimney tax established in 1662 was remitted.

By March 1689 there was still 'a wonderful uncertainty where King James was', and things appeared to Evelyn still 'far from the settlement that was expected'. He blamed 'the slothful sickly temper' of the new king, and the 'unmindfulness of the Parliament as to Ireland'.

But on 11 April the coronation of William and Mary took place with traditional ceremony, including the 'ceremony of the Champion'; but though the feast was magnificent, only the archbishop of York and six of the bishops attended. When the following day, Evelyn visited archbishop Sancroft at Lambeth, and urged him to discourage baptism in private houses and the burial of the dead inside churches – both legacies of the Civil Wars and Interregnum – he found the archbishop 'not so fully satisfied with the Conventions abdicating the late K. James'.

## IV

James, it was now reported, was certainly in Ireland, supported by the French; but the Scots, reckoning he had forfeited his right by maladministration, had declared for William and Mary. Evelyn thought they had managed better than the English, who had 'precipitated all things to the great Reproch of the Nation', undermined all future succession to the Crown and the prosperity of the Church of England. The Revolution had not seemed to him 'Glorious', but bungled. Fortunately the spring of 1689 proved 'most seasonable', and free from the usual sharp easterly winds. More happily, by 8 June, Evelyn was sitting for his picture by Kneller, made for Pepys, 'holding my *Sylva* in my right hand'. It was placed in Pepys's library and its subject thought it masterly. It reveals him in his sixties, hard, worn, clever and anxious.

The coalition against France, William's main concern, was now becoming more formidable on the continent, and on 7 May war was declared by the English against France while the understanding between the United Provinces and the Empire, which would lead to the Grand Alliance, was being set in train; so the king had plenty on his mind as well as Ireland. But to Evelyn, so representatively English, Ireland was always a potentially serious threat, and he continued to complain that the new king had allowed James to master 'all Ireland' – 'a terrible beginning of more troubles'. A new oath of allegiance was also now 'fabricating' for the clergy, with penalties of loss of dignity and spiritual preferment if they refused it, and he now referred to the government as 'our new governors'. As a staunch Anglican, he deplored the rough and ready solutions of power politics, so painful to those tender consciences who had preached 'non-resistance' to the former king. Time, and economic interest would settle his representative doubts.

Meanwhile, the prospects of the succession appeared doubtful; the Princess Anne of Denmark's pregnancy (with the Duke of Gloucester who would die of water on the brain aged eleven) appeared 'a tympane only', so 'the unhappy family of Steuarts [seemed] to be extinguishing'; and then, Evelyn and his like asked, 'What government next? Regal or by Election?'

Through the summer the campaign in Ireland wore on; and by July Protestant Londonderry had been relieved, while in Scotland the Jacobite Claverhouse rising collapsed: Evelyn bade farewell to Lady Sunderland, now intent on rejoining her husband, still, 'with too much sense to continue a Papist', working his passage home in Holland. In Ireland Marshal Schomberg at last occupied Newry, that perennial bone of contention.

On 31 October 1689, Evelyn began his sixty-ninth year, blessing God for 'prolonging his years to this great Age', and praying elaborately for salvation in the world to come; but the campaign in Ireland, he felt, had been miserably mismanaged, and recorded that the Commons had appointed a committee to look into it, as well as into the lack of convoys for merchant shipping.

So in much gloom over public prospects after what still seemed an improvised sudden and uncongenial change of rulers, Evelyn and his household came up to winter in Soho Square: he appropriately concluded 1689 by describing an 'extraordinary wet season and stormy, great losses by sea, and much confusion and discontent among ourselves'. William's great strategic designs, of which his acceptance of the crown of England had only been one aspect, were in fact now coming slowly into shape on the continent; but to Evelyn, the royalist Anglican who had apprehensively lived through it, the 'sad', and in his opinion, inglorious, Revolution had not appeared propitious.

# CHAPTER TWENTY-ONE

# Heir to Wotton

It is significant of the increasing power of the early modern state that Evelyn who, like his father, had in youth wanted to keep clear of public employments, now, when the court aristocracy and gentry had accepted and were exploiting central government, and when a wealthier establishment were setting the social pace, found himself 'in want of some more lucrative office than any I yet have prospect of'. Such employment could come only through patronage of the great, and his appointment as Commissioner of the Privy Seal, though punctually paid, had lasted only for two years.

'Young' John had long been a burden, for on his marriage in 1680 Evelyn had allowed him £500 a year – the entire rents of Sayes Court – so that the years of comparative affluence seemed ending; it was of course out of the question for a gentleman of Evelyn's standing to go into trade or even make an auxiliary income from his pen; so he had to depend on the patronage of Godolphin both for himself and for his son. But in March 1690, Godolphin resigned from the Treasury through illness and, though he returned by November, he failed, fortunately, to secure the Sheriffdom of Jamaica for 'young' John. It was anyway worth only £200 a year. Perhaps to escape such mundane concerns, old John, long obsessed with his puritanical and gloomy beliefs, now became even more addicted to sermons, and his *Diary*, now designed in part to instruct his descendants, became swamped with longer and more laborious accounts of them.

## II

The year 1690 had begun badly with a storm so violent that it recalled the tempest before the death of Oliver: 'What this portends,' wrote Evelyn, 'time will discover. God avert the

Judgements we deserve.'[1] He was also concerned at the 'famous Infamous Tryal' of his nephew Montague, who had married Richard's heiress, then eloped with another man's wife and had to pay damages of £6,500 – 'the immense wrong this proflygate wretch did my Niepce, drawing justly on him this disgrace'.

Nor were politics much better. The campaign in Ireland was going badly, and Evelyn dilates on the exceeding neglect of the soldiers, perishing for want of clothes. Pepys, in retirement, deplored the state of the navy, now 'Govern'd by unexperienc'd men etc since the Revolution': we had been the first to build fast frigates, but to gratify the new gentlemen commanders, thrown away our advantage and gone back to building huge great ships vulnerable to fire ships and clumsy to handle.[2] Pepys in June read Evelyn his 'Remonstrance' on the 'Ignorance and incompetency' of the administration of the navy – 'of which he gave an accurate state, and showed his great abillitie'.

By late June 1690, when the king had at last landed in Ireland, Pepys and other prominent persons had even been committed to the Tower 'on suspicion of being affected to King James', and the French were 'braving our Coast to the very Thames mouth'. On 30 June they defeated an Anglo-Dutch force off Beachy Head, and in Ireland William was slightly wounded on reconnaissance – 'great expectations,' Evelyn writes ambiguously, 'from thence'.

He need not have worried. By 6 July news reached London that on 1 July King William had utterly vanquished James II at the battle of the Boyne. Soon Drogheda and Dublin were captured, James fled to France, and the now loyal Evelyn declared 'if K.W. be returning, one may say of him, as of Caesar, *Veni, vidi, vici*, for never was such a Kingdome won in so short an Expedition'.[3]

Pepys, released from the Tower, now dined with Evelyn, who at the Royal Society heard a discourse explaining that most hills and mountains came from subterranean eruptions. But the French still 'domineering' at sea, burnt 'Tinmuth' in Devon. William, meanwhile, was still slowly clearing up Ireland, and, as an extremely fine summer broke up in August in thunder and lightning, Limerick still held out: but Cork surrendered, and by October Kinsale had been captured, though Evelyn learnt that 'the poor Duke of Grafton, who came to take his leave of me just before he embarked for Ireland', was now dead of his wounds.

At the end of the month Evelyn joined 'young' John in Dover Street for the winter; but on 1 December he managed, in this 'ill conjunction of public affairs' to avoid accepting the presidency of the Royal Society. The year ended in a fever of apprehension of a French invasion and of disasters to the Coalition on the Continent. Then, early in January 1691, a plot was discovered for a general rising against the 'new' government; and though on the 16th William, with four millions voted from parliament for the war, left England for Holland for a major campaign, he returned, frustrated by the loss of Mons, at Easter.

At Whitehall, Evelyn records with relish, a great and terrible fire now consumed the appartment of the late Duchess of Portsmouth and the 'Lodgings of such lewd creatures who debauched both King Char: 2d and others'. He also enjoyed Dr Sloane's comprehensive collection of the *flora* of Jamaica, and a sermon at St James's on the madness of deferring repentance or 'putting it to adventur ... whether ther were any Heaven or Hell at all.'[4]

By way of good works, he regularly visited Lord Clarendon, held in the Tower on suspicion about the late plot, who asked him to stand in with his brother, Rochester, for bail, to which Evelyn agreed. Such was the plight of Queen Mary's and Princess Anne's uncle. Having also inspected the hospital and infirmary for 'emerited' soldiers, complete with refectory and chapel, Evelyn in mid-May returned to Sayes Court for the summer.

### III

Here on 22 May 1691, he had news which transformed his prospects. George's only surviving son, John, the heir to Wotton, had long been drinking himself to death by much wine and strong waters to 'comply with other young intemperate men', and in 1688 had suffered a 'fit' when celebrating the advent of the Prince of Orange. He had since contracted a palsy, and now a stroke had killed him. He was thirty-five. George Evelyn's only surviving children were now a daughter and three granddaughters, and John Evelyn became the heir of the paternal estate – 'far,' he wrote, 'from my least expectation, or desert'. 'The Lord God,' he concluded, 'render me and mine worthy of this Providence, that I may be a comfort to my Bro:.'[5] And, indeed, George wrote ' 'Tis my comfort that you and your son are still *in vivis.*' John attended the elaborate funeral at Wotton, with its gratifying concourse of coaches.

In London by early July archbishop Sancroft, as a 'non-juror', had been superseded by Dr Tillotson, who after Sancroft's nephew had been ejected by the Sheriff, briskly took possession of Lambeth. Evelyn, who knew both archbishops, thought that since no heresy was involved, the new appointments must be accepted, mainly to prevent a schism and a failure of succession.

From the distance came news of King William's gruelling battles in the Low Countries, of his relief of Liège, and of the slow subjugation of all Ireland. In the hot summer of 1691, John went down to Wotton to settle business with his brother, while Mary and the youngest daughter Susanna went to Bath. But the war at sea remained inconclusive, and by the end of September the battle fleet 'came in to lay up the great ships, nothing don at sea ...'. The king returned from the continent, and on 22 October parliament reassembled. Evelyn recorded at the end of the month, with his usual thankfulness and pious resolutions, that he was seventy-one.

The autumn was wonderfully warm and sunny far into November, and then drew out into 'a winter unwonted warme and calme'. Soon after Christmas, Evelyn recorded: 'Dined at Lambeth with the new AB [Tillotson], far politer than the old man': he was glad to see his own newly designed furnace for the archiepiscopal greenhouse at work; and the year's end coincided with the death of the great natural philosopher, the Hon. Robert Boyle, at whose funeral in January bishop Burnet of Salisbury made a philosophical discourse and eulogy, saying that he had combined scientific knowledge with piety and endowed preachers expressly to denounce atheists, libertins, Socinians (Unitarians) and Jews. Evelyn concurred that he had been a 'great and good man'.

In contrast, he considered Lord Marlborough, in fact dismissed on 20 January 1692 from all his offices on suspicion of Jacobite intrigues and excessive influence over Princess Anne, was not at all good, but had taken bribes and practised extortion from subordinates. Indeed, about the great Marlborough Evelyn is venomous; he had been advanced by King James II, entirely through the prostitution of his sister (Arabella) to the king; he was now 'disgraced; and by none pittied, being also the first who betrayed and forsooke his Master K James, who advanced him from the son of Sir Wi. Churchill, an officer of the Greene Cloth'.[6] Such was Evelyn's scorn for the new risen Churchills.

He was also vindictive about his sister-in-law, Richard's deceased widow of Woodcote, who had broken the entail on the estate for the benefit of the 'vicious' Montague and so defrauded George of Wotton of about £500 a year: he prayed, however, that God would forgive her. And by the spring of 1692 he was delighted when Richard Bentley, whom as a trustee he had appointed to give the Boyle lectures against atheism, brought him the brilliant text of *Matter and Motion Cannot Think*; *or a Refutation of Atheism, from the faculties of the Soul*. In electing the future Master of Trinity, the trustees had made a shrewd choice. Evelyn at once agreed that the lecture should be printed.


## IV


The country now again became rightly alarmed at the threat of a major French invasion. 'Greate talke of the French Invading; and of an universal rising: our Fleet begins to joyne with the Dutch, Souldiers march towards the Coasts etc'.[7] By May 1692, reports of an invasion had become so 'hott' that Court, City and people were exceedingly alarmed; suspected persons were imprisoned, more forces sent to the coast, and the fleet 'hastened out'. Fortunately an east wind favoured the English, and Evelyn recorded that on the 19th it had 'pleased Almighty God, to give us such a Victory at sea to the utter ruine of the French Fleete, Admirall and all their best men of Warr'.

The victory off Cape La Hogue was, in fact, the Trafalgar of the seventeenth century. The English admiral, Edward Russell (in 1697 created Earl of Orford), whose fleet had outnumbered the French by eighty-two to forty-five, had caught them in hazy weather before they had realized his superiority. By the time fog had closed in, the French centre had been enveloped and, when the fog had lifted, had taken refuge in the Bay of La Hogue west of Cherbourg. Here twelve of them and eight transports were burnt by an English cutting out expedition, though others escaped south through the race of Alderney.[8] This great naval victory restored English command of the Channel and destroyed the threat of a French invasion; and when on 9 June Namur, though not its citadel, capitulated to King William, even the campaign on the Continent appeared at last to prosper.

Evelyn's own prospects also seemed further enhanced when, George's daughter having just married Sir Cyril Wyche, secretary of state for Ireland, in mid-June George had confirmed to him the reversion, without revocation, of Wotton, the paternal estate; and that summer even 'young' John, through the influence of Godolphin at last secured an official position. True, it was unfortunately in Ireland and as a Commissioner for the

Revenue, but it was better than the Sheriffdom of Jamaica; and uncle George, in relief, generously fitted out his nephew to take it up. In August 'young' John, his wife and daughter sailed for Dublin, to live 'divided from the rest of the world', and there, increasingly bored, but resolved to be content with his inadequate pay, he would remain until 1696. So when at the end of July, Evelyn, Mary and Susanna all descended upon Eton, where 'young' John's son, Jack, now aged ten, had been placed, both public affairs and private prospects seemed more promising. Indeed, Jack, at Eton and Oxford, would become Evelyn's principal concern and interest and, unlike his father, manage to live up to expectations.

What was more, although George's daughter, now Lady Wyche,[9] was making mischief and difficulties at Wotton, by the spring of 1693 Susanna was making a good match. William Draper was the nephew and heir presumptive of Sir Thomas Draper of Sunninghill, Berkshire. Twenty-eight to her twenty-four, he already had £1,000 a year, with £600 in prospect and much greater expectations. Under her grandfather Sir Richard Browne's will, Susanna was to have a marriage portion of £4,000 from his estate, of which the Evelyns had been the heirs; now John, by the sale of land at Deptford, paid it into the marriage settlement. So on 27 April 1693 the marriage was festively celebrated; 'She is a good Child,' wrote John, 'religious, discreete, ingenious'. She had a talent for painting, spoke French, was well read in Greek and Latin, and was 'exquisitely shaped and of an agreeable countenance'. 'This Character,' he concluded, 'is due to her, though coming from her Father.'[10] In her new home the Evelyns were magnificently entertained, the appartments richly adorned, and for this model daughter, John heartily thanked providence.

That July, reverting to interests now being swamped by religion, John inspected the exiled Queen Mary's (of Modena) cabinets and china – 'wonderfull rich and plentifull': looking glass frames and stands, historic bas-reliefs and carved medals all of amber sent from the Duke of Brandenburg, Indian cabinets, screens, hangings, an extensive library, a cupboard of gold plate. He thought that it should all have been generously dispatched to her in her exile. For he was still uneasy over the 'sad' revolution, and at the slightest reverse, as when the French captured Huy or a convoy from Turkey off Cape St Vincent, he considered it a 'forerunner of destruction for our folly and precipitous Change etc: God avert the deserved consequence';[11] but he also much enjoyed a sermon on the effect of fervent and constant prayer in time of calamity.


## V


In March 1693 Evelyn, while still at Sayes Court, had enhanced the amenities of life when under his name, there appeared a translation of La Quintinye's *Instructions pour les jardins frutiers et potagers*. The real author, a subordinate colleague of the famous André le Nôtre who had revolutionized the fashions of grand gardening on the Continent, was in charge of the fruit and vegetables at Versailles, and his treatise, translated as *The Compleat Gard'ner* (London, 1693), found a large public. Switzer, the early eighteenth-century horticulturalist, thought it so well translated that 'gardening could' at last 'speak proper English'.

For it was not about the design of vast royal and noble gardens, but on 'discriminating the several kinds of fruits' by their leaf, taste and colour, so as not to be confused and taken in by exotic names bandied about by nurserymen. It made detailed and practical observations on how best to grow peaches, nectarines, grapes, pears, melons and plums, and how to choose the right kind of gardener by judging his temperament. Evelyn had merely supervised the translation, though he had allowed his name to appear as having made it; but he had in fact – the 'toile of meere translating being ungratefull' – arranged for most of it to be dealt with by George London, the King's gardener, who had worked in France. He had already greatly furthered London's career, as also that of Henry Wise, his collaborator, gardener to Queen Anne, and had added a section strongly recommending their work at their Brompton Park nurseries, Kensington.

The publication was a success. La Quintinye had made his name in an exacting profession – satisfying the enormous year-round appetite of Louis XIV for muscat grapes and pyramids of the very best nectarines and peaches, and the book dealt with the 'most useful though less pompous' part of horticulture; six years later, London and Wise brought out a condensed edition from which Evelyn's name was omitted, and though the supreme French expert remained Le Nôtre, who set the fashion for the royalty and nobility of most of Europe, Evelyn and his collaborators had greatly advanced the amenities of many an English mansion, manor house, farm and rectory.

# CHAPTER TWENTY-TWO

# 'A solemn Remove'

In 1694 the most important public event which Evelyn recorded was the foundation of the Bank of England – 'a publique Bank,' he wrote in April, 'of 140,000 pounds set up by Act of Parliament ... for mony to carry on the War', and in July finally 'put under the government of the most able and wealthy Cittizens of Lond, by which all who adventured any summs had 4 per Centum, so long as it lay in the banke'.[1] This innovation, long overdue, and following Dutch methods, at last contrived that the immense cost of the war could be financed by a funded National Debt, its interest secured on the public revenue, and provided far better security than the intermittent and precarious loans which had financed earlier Stuart governments. Moreover, it provided in government annuities a better haven for investment of the increasing capital that an expanding economy was now creating. It was now possible to obtain interest on capital otherwise than through rents from land, casual loans and mortgages to friends or relations, or through highly speculative ventures overseas.

The Evelyns had little share in this new prosperity: in fact, mainly through the expense of launching a family, their position had long been deteriorating, and from the affluence of his youth John was now harassed by financial anxiety. George's recognition that he was heir to Wotton had been decisive, but now there were difficulties. In January 1693 George had already invited John to live at Wotton, but Mary or 'Moll' Wyche, George's daughter, was still in residence there and set on mischief. She particularly detested 'young' John, and resented the innovations that Evelyn was suggesting, as for example, a conservatory for orange and lemon trees, or his criticisms of the excessive felling of timber on the estate.

John Evelyn therefore postponed moving to Wotton, while further difficulties built up. At Sayes Court both Evelyns had accumulated a large library, but at Wotton shelf-room would be insufficient. Evelyn therefore proposed that 'young' John's

French and law books be sold, a suggestion he strongly and rightly resisted; 'I would not but have it in my power to read sometimes. I was ever guilty of loading myself with books, and you will easily conjecture from whom I derive this laudable infirmity.'[2] Moreover, Lady Wyche's mounting hostility discouraged Evelyn from further interest even in the garden at Wotton, though George had done his best by writing 'harbour no such hard imaginations ... but go on to plant what you designed which my cousin your grandson may live to enjoy'.[3]

John, now seventy-two, increasingly dreaded the London winter, and Mary was surprised by her 'wont'd winter rheumatism', but Jack, their grandson, now twelve and a 'hopeful fine child', visited them from Eton, and the Drapers, Susanna being pregnant, came to keep Christmas. In January, 1694, the anniversary of King Charles I's martyrdom, was celebrated with an excellent discourse deriving government from Adam, though in February a chaplain at St James's upbraided the ingratitude of men as exceeding that of brutes, and Evelyn recorded one ill-effect of King William's apparent pacification of the Highlands, when a gigantic and supposedly tame Highland dragoon, called a coward by a Dutchman, decapitated his tormentor on the spot and split another one's skull.

But the tensions in the Evelyn family had now subsided, and after a phase of salutary neglect of Wotton, John resumed sending consignments of Scio fig trees and Frontiniac vines by the Dorking carrier.


## II


So at last, on 4 May 1694, occurred the great and final change in the Evelyns' lives: for economy and reinsurance they moved down to Wotton to share the house of which John was now the heir. 'I went this day,' he writes,[4]

with my Wife and 3 Servants from Says-Court, and removing much furniture ... books, Pictures, Hangings, bedding etc: to furnish the Appartment my Brother assign'd me; and now after more than 40 yeares, to spend the rest of my dayes with him at Wotton, where I was borne.

Sayes Court was not now what it had been; the dockyard had become larger and more obtrusive, and on Sundays and holidays crowds came out from London. If the Evelyns felt that leaving it was a wrench, John characteristically kept his feelings to himself. It was now, in effect, Mary's property, and they left it adequately furnished in the care of three servants for the Drapers to occupy for as long as they liked.

Predictably, John at first found the church services at Wotton unsatisfactory. One incumbent, put in by easy-going George upon the importunity of relations, already held another fat living and he had appointed a 'hireling' without spirit or vigour; in another living, George had placed a relative of his own second wife, and he, too, appeared slothfull and unfit. So John determined on reform. Fortunately his discontent subsided, as Mr Morus, the curate of Wotton, preached acceptably on the infinite compassion of God to repentant sinners, and, next Sunday, on faith, repentance and good works; then, Mr Wall, the curate of Abinger, proved sound on the Sermon on the Mount, and Morus made an honest discourse against atheistical scoffers at religion; while the rector of Albury discoursed on 'sitting loose to this present world and the use of things of this life, which are at best ... fading and unsatisfactory'.[5]

In the great world the war continued: when, in mid-July, admiral Lord Berkeley burnt Dieppe and Le Havre with bombs, Evelyn put the blame on the French who had begun this sort of warfare; but he thought it 'ruinous' and 'barbarous, especially falling on the poorer people'; nor, he concluded, did it hasten the end to the war, but rather tended to excite revenge. But when some 'clippers' were hung at Tyburn for clipping money, he recorded the necessary punishment without comment.

The usual perilous result of a seventeenth-century marriage occurred in September 1699, when Susanna, having given birth to a son who himself died within a year, became dangerously ill with puerperal fever: the Evelyns hastened to Sayes Court to help, even sacrificing church attendance for two Sundays. But by early October Susanna had visibly mended, with great hopes of recovery, and Evelyn took the opportunity of inspecting the progress of Wren's St Paul's – 'a piece of architecture without reproch'.

By December, after the death of Tillotson, Evelyn's friend, Dr Tenison, was translated from London to be archbishop of Canterbury, and at a lower level Evelyn was able to get the curate of Abinger transferred to another living in Surrey; vacant because the incumbent had unhappily been killed by reaching a gun at full cock 'to his son in a Tree, watching to shoot some rabbits', whereat, not surprisingly, the gun had gone off and miserably slain the clergyman himself.[6]

At the end of 1694 the Evelyns returned to Wotton through the worst winter John ever remembered, on the day after Queen Mary had died 'full of Spotts' of the prevalent and epidemic smallpox. She was only thirty-two, and the king 'seemed mightily afflicted, 'as indeed,' Evelyn comments rather acidly, 'it behoved him'. She had left her papers in meticulous order, with only very small debts, and Evelyn with exaggerated enthusiasm, thought her 'so Renowned a creature as if possible to outdo the Renown'd Q; Eliz. herself'. Her death, widely lamented, led at least to a reconciliation between William and the Princess Anne, now heiress apparent, and so to a lessening of internal political strife, but the only cheerful event Evelyn recorded was that Jack, home from Eton, had again spent Christmas at Wotton.

## III

In February 1695 Evelyn, now well into his seventies, was offered by Lord Godolphin the ill-paid position of treasurer to the newly founded Chelsea Hospital at £300 a year. But the commissioners included the archbishop of Canterbury, the Lord Privy Seal and other grandees; and Evelyn was also appointed to a committee which included Wren to make a survey at Greenwich. They reported that £6,000 would make it serviceable, and Evelyn prepared a *Preamble to the Subscriptions to Greenwich Hospital for Seamen*. He also inspected a comprehensive charity at Blackheath founded by Sir John Morden, a Turkey merchant, for 'merchants that had failed – a very worthy charity'. By July the Commissioners for Greenwich had already received about £8,000 of subscriptions, and on the 6th Evelyn dined with archbishop Tenison at Lambeth with 'much company and great cheere', the archbishop showing him over his house, furniture, and garden – all very fine. They discussed the difficult position of the Princess Anne, now accorded full royal honours, but still excluded from any say in government. On the 19th Evelyn left London with the Drapers for Wotton where, for once, the parson of Albury preached very well on the sin of calling vices by the name of virtues – 'as Intemperance, good fellowship, etc.'.

The Drapers' infant son, apparently so promising, now died suddenly of a 'convulsion fit at Nurse', to the general affliction; but by September Susanna had borne a daughter. It was a bitterly cold autumn, already by early October 'winter approaching apace', but Evelyn carried on with his useful minor reforms – as assisting Dr Bentley, now librarian at St James's, to obtain more room for the books. The year ended with parliament still 'wondrous intent on ways to Reforme the Coine', and on preventing the circulation of the notoriously clipped crowns and halfcrowns; but in January 1696, Evelyn had to record 'Greate confusion and distraction by reason of the clip'd mony and the difficulty found in reforming it';[7] nor was the curate at Wotton encouraging on the 'dreadfullness of the last Judgement and separation of the Sheepe, Goats etc.'. Moreover, the old *Royal Sovereign*, built in 1637 under Charles I, caught fire at Chatham, and there was an 'earthquake' or collapse of ground near the quarries on Portland, which set back the supply of stone for St Paul's. Evelyn, now in his seventy-fourth year and afflicted with kidney disorders and gravel, fell back on an even more meticulous chronicle of sermons.

Then suddenly a widespread conspiracy was discovered: nothing less than to assassinate King William on his return to Kensington from hunting, with King James ready at Calais on a signal from Dover to cross the Channel with an invading army. The militia was mobilized, regiments recalled from Flanders, and leading Catholic conspirators executed for high treason. The principal conspirator had been General Sir John Fenwick, a landowner in Northumberland, who had long, following a personal slight, been casually plotting against the king; arrested, he had implicated both Shrewsbury and, what was serious for Evelyn, Godolphin before his execution in January 1696. By an extraordinary coincidence, it would be Fenwick's horse, Sorrel, now acquired by King William, who, over six years later, stumbling on a molehill created by 'a little gentleman in black velvet', would throw the king so that he died.

The eclipse of Godolphin was also serious for 'young' John, who in April 1696 returned to Ireland disappointed of any increase in salary, so that when at the end of April Godolphin resigned from the treasury, both father and son lost a patron. Nor did Sunderland, at last rehabilitated, prove helpful to either of them.

Against this discouraging background, Evelyn decided to let Sayes Court for three years at £100 a year to Vice-Admiral John Benbow, then Master-Attendant at the Deptford dockyard. Benbow, the son of a tanner in Shrewsbury, had risen in the navy as a ship's Master, fought Algerian pirates off North Africa and

bombarded French ports, so, often in command at sea, he was
not precisely the character to 'keepe the garden in order etc.'. By
18 January 1697 Evelyn wrote fastidiously that he was daily
mortified at seeing 'much of his former labours and expenses
there impairing for want of a more polite tenant'. The vice-
admiral, more interested in battle, was then, that spring,
appointed commander-in-chief against the French in the West
Indies, where, in 1702, as admiral of the Blue, he would perish,
his legs shattered by a chain shot, but still indomitably on the
quarter deck.

In his absence, Evelyn was now landed with an even more
unsuitable sub-tenant: in 1678 the king took it into his head to
assign Sayes Court to Peter, the young Tsar of Muscovy, then
eager to visit and work in Deptford dockyard. 'The Czar Emp: of
*Moscovy*,' wrote Evelyn on 6 February, 'having a mind to see the
Building of Ships, hired my House at Says Court, and made it his
Court and palace, lying and remaining in it, new furnish'd for
him by the King.'[8] Evelyn, down at Wotton, wisely declined to
brave the winter cold to do the honours of his house, for the
Russians were far worse than Benbow. Strickland, Evelyn's
bailiff, describes them roundly:[9]

There is a housefull of people, and right nasty. The Czar lies next to
your Library and dines in the parlour next your study. He dines at 10
o'clock and at 6 at night, is very seldom at home a whole day, very often
in the King's Yard, or by water, dressed in several dresses. The King is
expected there to-day, the best parlour is pretty clean for him to be
entertained in. The King pays for all he has.

'Right nasty' was the word for the jovial conduct of the
Muscovites: they ruined Mary Evelyn's best sheets; they smashed
window panes, broke the furniture and damaged the pictures;
Evelyn's precious garden was 'damnified', fruit trees broken,
potholes made in the gravel, holly bushes broken. The Tsar and
his merry men even smashed wheelbarrows, so that, following
Evelyn's later reference to 'hedge breakers' in his 'now ruined
garden',[10] a muddled legend grew up, accepted by otherwise
fastidiously critical historians, that the Tsar, trundled in a
wheelbarrow, had crashed the nine-foot-high holly hedge
himself. There is, in fact, no evidence that Peter enjoyed such
masochism: his tastes were exclusively sadistic. But it was not
until 21 April that Evelyn could record with relief 'The Czar of
Mosco(vy) went from my house towards Russia etc.'; the damages
of the Muscovite occupation were assessed, jointly to Benbow
and Evelyn, at £300.

# IV

In spite of personal and public anxieties, Evelyn had been working on another long and loosely constructed book. In January 1697 appeared *Numismata*,[11] the treatise on medals and much else, by which he himself set little store. Though Bentley had vetted the opening chapters, Evelyn's propensity to ramble in recondite fields of learning had got badly out of hand, so that Horace Walpole would afterwards damn the book with malicious ridicule. But when Evelyn declared that he had attempted 'things beyond his force' in his 'dotage', he did himself injustice.

The book is dedicated in elegant Latin to that 'most noble youth' Francis Godolphin, son of Sidney and Margaret Godolphin, and the reader informed that for almost five years, finding so little written about medals in English and so much in French and Italian and most 'learned tongues', Evelyn has been making notes for such a work; and even after Dr Obadiah Walker's book on Greek and Roman coins and medals had appeared in 1692,[12] he had 'thought there was still some room to fill in'.

The *Numismata* was comprehensively designed: on the use of medals, whether for money or to commemorate worthy actions, relating to several nations, civil and barbarous; on persons and things; on inscriptions; on how to collect antiques and discriminate true from false; on mints and how to methodize medals for the cabinet, with some reflections – (very severe and topical) on the modern clipping and diminution of coin; on heads and effigies in prints and taille douce; and concluding with an extensive digression concerning physiognomy. There is an admirable index.

The main body of the book, mainly of interest to professional numismatists, can hardly here be summarized, but the concluding chapters, containing immense lists of those worthy of medals in history, are revealing of Evelyn's mind on the accepted English poets and great wits, and not least, on the travellers – Dampier, Mandeville Sherley – 'by no means forgetting our renowned leg stretcher Thomas Coriat of Odcomb etc'. And among 'the Ladies', 'how should one sufficiently value a Medal of the Famous Heroina Boadicia!'

We also celebrate the Incomparable Queen Elizabeth, knowing in all learned Tongues – Scaliger says that she spoke five languages – and Elizabeth of Bohemia 'to whom Des Cartes dedicates his workes [as] the only person that ever yet he had met with who properly understood and comprehended what he had published.

Our 'Sappho, Mrs Behn', also deserves a Medal. Then there are the illustrious strumpets, whose effigies would be interesting, such as Rosamund and Jane Shore.

Among the lesser men, Evelyn would 'see the faces of Scoggin (Henry VIII's Fool), Archee (James I's buffoon) and Hobson the 'merry Carter of Cambridge'. Then there is Wood the 'Great Eater, of Kent', and 'the Earl of Abensperg, who being the Father of Forty Children, brought two and thirty of them (all alive and all at once) to wait upon the German Emperor'. The freaks of age also deserve medals, as Old Par, and Dame Kerton, former abbess of Amesbury, who married after the dissolution of her nunnery and lived to be a hundred and forty.

Turning now to beyond England, Evelyn lists the athletic and gigantic men who deserve commemoration.

The noble Silesian who, hunting a vast wild Boar, taking him by the Snout Kill'd him with his sword, and could at dinner quaff a whole German *Ohm* of Rhenish. And now we speak of German Boars, I read of a Boor or Country Fellow of that Nation who, upon a wager devoured an Entire *Hog*, entrels and all, new and alive, beginning at the tail.

After a ramble among 'Zanis, farcers and the Dutch woman Tumbler', Evelyn proceeds to Physiognomy and the 'different Countenances of men who resemble Brute Animals', not only in their faces but their dispositions: 'Man is, after all, the *Compendium* of Nature'. Some with noses like hawks and eagles are of towering spirits; others are sheepish or hog-jawed, or rabbit mouthed, and their natures conform; some 'bird faced and bird witted'. Those who resemble goats or buffles are libidinous and stupid, while there was once an English sea captain at Venice who looked so like a lion that the Venetians called him *Capitano Lione*. And consider Mr Hobbs; 'those who remember him, as I perfectly do (and whose pictures are perfectly like him) might discover in his very looks 'supersilious, saturnine, opiniatrety'. Sir Francis Bacon, on the other hand, always looked upwards, and by 'standing up against dogmatists' was to 'emancipate and let free the long and miserably captivated philosophy which has since made such conquests in the territories of Nature'.

So after his oldfashioned but entertaining digression, Evelyn fetches up to a conclusion on the side of the moderns in this 'age of Wonders',[13] with praise of 'the men of genius who have made this age as great as any, by *experimental* knowledge'. This '(after all a-do), is really and indeed of all human knowledge the only true and valid learning', discovered by 'Persons, I say, of Equal Desert with any which past and former ages produced, as Good as Greeks and Romans' and as worthy of medals and effigies as any 'ambitious Potentates'. He concludes on a note of resounding if rueful good sense: 'the great Archimedes was barbarous slain by a rude and common soldier in the midst of his speculations, whose life was of more value than a thousand Syracusas and all the Conquests of Marcellus'.

## V

'Young' John's affairs had now become even more dilapidated. In May 1696 he had left Ireland, apparently suffering from sinus inflamation, in the vain hope of obtaining better treatment in London, and the vainer one of obtaining some equivalent post in England. 'We have many things before us not very pleasing,' wrote Mary Evelyn, 'my son gives me many melancholy hours: I pray God he may find a right cure'.[14] 'Young' John had also suffered ineffective treatment from the celebrated Dr Radcliffe, and in August had gone to Bath, where he found the grand company far too rich for him; and in the general shortage of money caused by the war, Evelyn himself did not even receive his own meagre salary as treasurer of Chelsea Hospital. 'What became of my Lord Godolphin?' he enquired of Draper, 'I would be glad you enquire what the meaning of the recess of his is and whether he be out of the Council?'

Early in 1697 'young' John was still in London, but refused £800 offered for his Irish post. Yet he was reluctant to leave England and his friends and relations – not least his own son Jack, now, at the large expense of £450 a year, doing well at Eton. In May uncle George had invited 'young' John, to whom he had already lent substantial capital, to stay at Wotton, but 'young' John had spent most of the summer in London, returning to Wotton only in September. Even at Wotton there was now again no tranquillity, for by the spring of 1698, when the Tsar was wreaking havoc at Sayes Court, George had been inveigled by the 'crafty serpent', the Rev Dr Fulham who had married Katherine, one of his granddaughters, into 'a new and unreasonable settlement of the Wotton estate'. This appalling blow both to Evelyn, 'young' John and Jack, struck at the whole accepted future of their branch of the Evelyn family, and resolutely and successfully Evelyn fought it.

In July 1698 he recorded, 'I came to passe the rest of the summer at my sonn's house in Berkly-streete, during my Brothers (or, rather, my Niepces and Dr Fullams) displeasure, because I could not assent to the alteration of a settlement of my Brother's gift freely to me: etc which I pray God to reconcile.'[15] Here 'young' John and his father, both out of sorts, worried at this family imbroglio, though in August Evelyn dined with Pepys and met Dampier, the 'famous Buccaneere', who two years earlier had written *A New Voyage round the World* – a 'Relation of very strange adventures'. Dampier, who had brought back from Mindanao a 'painted Prince' called 'Jolo' (he died in Oxford of smallpox), was soon to set out again: Evelyn thought him 'a more modest man, than one would imagine, by the relation of the Crue that he had sorted with'.[16] Moreover, Dampier brought a map, and assured them that all other ones extant were 'false as to the Pacific Sea', which, he pointed out, was in fact, particularly along the Peruvian coast, very tempestuous.

By September Evelyn was reduced to recording 'Nothing of Publique worth much notice', but that it was 'a very cold, wett, and winter-like season, little summer this quarter', and by October that 'Indisposition and paine of Gripes' kept him from church. In his late seventies he found it 'a very darke, rainy gloomy Autumn'. And George, that summer, had actually petitioned the House of Commons for a Bill to resettle the Wotton estate, and, when rejected, had even petitioned the Lords. Evelyn, however, on a warning from Godolphin, had realistically bought off Fulham, Lady Wyche and the granddaughters by increasing their legacies from £4,500 to £6,000 each in return for their recognition that the entire inheritance was unconditionally his, with no question of reversion to George's descendants. So by March 1699 he had saved Wotton for the Evelyn name.

But by the 24th a long impending blow fell: 'young' John, aged forty-four, died in London. 'To my exceeding griefe and affliction,' Evelyn recorded, 'after a tedious languishing sicknesse contracted in Ireland ... died my onely remaining son John; ... leaving me one Grandson, now at Oxon: whom I beseech A. God to preserve, and be the remaining support of the Wotton family.'[17] 'Young' John was interred in the family vault, his funeral merely 'accompanied by severall', and not by his father.

An amiable, bookish character, with a sense of humour, he had translated Rapinus, *Of Gardens*, Chassepol's *History of the Visiers*, and Plutarch's *Life of Alexander the Great*, but he had been casual in business, feckless about money, and too fastidious over intrigue.

## VI

In contrast to his unfortunate father, Evelyn's grandson Jack had always been promising. At Eton, which he had entered in 1692, Jack had developed into a clever and charming boy, and became the close, admiring friend of Francis Godolphin, the son of Sidney (now Lord) Godolphin, Evelyn's principal patron, and of his now deceased wife, Evelyn's adored Margaret. Eton, which still contained well under 400 boys, was then flourishing under an amiable schoolmaster (headmaster), John Newborough, assisted since 1693 by an 'usher' Stephen Weston, still commemorated by Weston's Yard. In 1695 Henry Godolphin, brother of Evelyn's friend and patron, had been appointed provost; the year before, the present Upper School had been completed, and under Godolphin (d. 1713), the elegant statue of Henry VI was put up in School Yard, so Jack was at Eton during a memorable time.

Evelyn now sent him to Balliol, his own college, recording in February 1799, 'My grandson went to Oxford with Dr Mander, the Master of Bal: Coll: where he was entered a fellow Commoner.'[18] Balliol under Mander's Mastership was emerging from its poverty and delapidation following the interregnum; indeed, old Dr Bathurst of Trinity had been observed on his garden wall throwing stones at those of the Balliol windows which had any glass 'as if happy to contribute his share to the appearance of ruin'.[19] But Dr Goode, soliciting endowments, had managed to obtain £20 from Evelyn 'in proof of good intentions', and Mander in 1692 had himself given the college the advowson of Bere Regis in Dorset, with its superb timber church roof. More important to Evelyn, the college, after its Puritan-radical phase, had now become thoroughly Tory, and he felt that young Jack's contemporaries were of the right political persuasion.

He was following his grandson's education with meticulous, untiring and potentially overwhelming attention: he pressed him to concentrate on the 'Moderns' – Bacon, Descartes, Gassendi – as well as keeping up the traditional Renaissance standards of a gentleman – in dancing, music and daily exercise. Not that he forgot Herodotus, Thucydides, Xenophon and Polybius – or to hold up as an example Jack's 'virtuous' friend and schoolfellow, Francis Godolphin Margaret's son, whose merits – and influence – by May 1699 had already made him one of the tellers of the Exchequer at £2,000 a year; an office, moreover, executed by deputy.

Jack took all this in good part. Urged to produce a Latin celebration of his friend's success, he did so with *éclat*, and, coached by his grandfather, wrote facetious epigrams for Pepys and his club at York Buildings. The perceptive old recipient approved his Latin, but rallied Evelyn for having 'made all' Pepys' 'geese swans'. Jack's own judgment, he shrewdly concluded, would 'rectify him, though yours won't'.[20]

In April Evelyn wrote, 'My grandson sent me a Latin Epistle from Oxon: giving me account of ... his studys there',[21] and of his first Easter communion. It was all very satisfactory. Fortunately Jack's adaptability and intelligence could accept the demands of his grandfather, and they both found a common and amicable interest in sorting out Jack's father's library when it arrived from Ireland, as well as in discussing how to counteract the recent depredations on the timber at Wotton.

# 'A sedate and amicable composure': *A Discourse of Sallets*

On 4 October 1699 George Evelyn of Wotton died in his eighty-third year. A wealthy and conventional country gentleman, he had been popular in his county, the oldest living member of parliament, who had kept open house in the ancient English tradition of lavish hospitality; and if under an 'eternal female Clack' he had wavered in keeping Wotton in the male line, he had finally left the estate to Evelyn, and to Jack as Evelyn's heir.

Unfortunately, though he had left the estate to his brother, he had appointed the turbulent Lady Wyche as an executrix, leaving to John, of his personal possessions, only his library and the portraits of their father, mother and sister Jane, who had married William Glanville. Lady Wyche arranged an extravagant funeral, as if, said John, George had been a nobleman, not a private gentleman, attended by over two thousand of the local gentry; and John, in pique, retired to London until 'my Lady should dispose of herselfe and family'; but on his seventy-eighth birthday he thanked God for deliverance out of the troubles of the past year. The essential inheritance had been secured.

After a very hot summer, the autumn of 1699 brought fog in London so thick that candles, lanterns and even torches were useless; John feared robbers, and drums were beaten along the banks to direct the Thames watermen to the landing stages. But the winter itself proved extremely mild, and by the end of January John again felt he could face Wotton, now unfurnished since Lady Wyche had sold or disposed of George's goods. And in March 1700, Susanna's husband William Draper inherited a fortune – £20,000 in land, money and plate, including a big house at Adscombe near Croydon. He also backed up John about moveables on the Wotton estate, getting a solicitor's opinion that fish in ponds and pigeons in dove houses always went with an inheritance, and that no fixed brewing vessels, coppers or cisterns were 'moveable'. But John had to buy in all the farm carts and utensils and enough stock to keep the farms going; indeed, he told Jack, he was forced to become 'a motley husbandman or farmer'. For 'Cocks, hen, hog and ducks are all flown already, so as we are to go as to a new plantation ... and there you have the state of our affairs for our improvement, of which you will have need of all your mathematics.'[1]

## II

Wotton was a large estate, estimated by Evelyn at 7,500 acres, with a rent roll of £1,150 a year; but money had to be raised at once to pay off outstanding debts and the portions agreed for Lady Wyche, Evelyn's nephew Glanville and the claim of Dr Fulham. So Evelyn sold off the outlying estates of Northstoke and Denton, raising £5,667, not counting timber sales from Wotton. He got no thanks from Lady Wyche, who reproached him in 'rude and undecent language in the street', and went about saying that George and Evelyn had 'used them like bastards'. Evelyn refers to her 'immodest and provoking passion' and 'envenomed tongue': 'Envy and avarice,' he concluded, 'make her lean.' Even his habitual reserve apparently broke down and he would complain to neighbours, 'My brother hath not left me estate enough to keep a coach: the executors, contrary to law, hath sold my brother's goods ... and left me an empty house.'[2]

But by May all the books and furniture from Sayes Court had arrived at Wotton, where, that summer, Evelyn wrote ruefully to Pepys, 'I pass the day in the fields among horses and oxen, sheep and cows, bulls and sows.'[3]

Evelyn, indeed, in spite of his concern with ploughs and implements, gardens and woods, scorned the actual farming which produced the income from Wotton, and preferred cultivating ornamental trees and flowers to improving the productivity of his land, just when, in spite of the Civil Wars, agriculture on the larger estates was getting better. He could be utterly subservient to obtain a post in the administration for Jack, when the equivalent income might well have been obtained by better farming: but, in spite of Evelyn's zeal and knowledge about forestry and gardens, the days of the eighteenth-century improving landlords had yet to come.

The topic, other than money, that still most passionately excited him was sin. In the spring of 1700 he was recording how in view of the profanity of the nation, religious persons had formed a 'fraternity' to attempt reformation; how the most eminent clergy were to preach quarterly sermons against atheism, and the king had made a declaration against the universal and growing wickedness, while bishop Burnet had preached a 'very pathetic discourse' before the Lord Mayor.

Meanwhile, parliament had sent commissioners to examine the disposal of the confiscated estates in Ireland, granted by William to 'great favorits of both sexes, Dutch and other', in the hope that at least some of the proceeds could be diverted to diminish the National Debt. More hopefully, in April Evelyn had accompanied Wren to Kensington to present the king with a model and engravings of the new hospital being built at Greenwich. With that, at least, William could be satisfied, though Evelyn considered that 'the Government of this nation being so equaly poised betweene King and Subject', there was such tension between Court and country parties in parliament that even money bills were but narrowly passed, and the nation seemed 'satisfied with nothing'. But since, he had commented, there is no perfection this side of heaven, both parties ought to be contented 'without straining things too farr'[4] – the perennial wish of the moderate in politics.

Political strife had indeed made it hard for William even to carry on government, and Evelyn had contended with his troubles at Wotton against a background of increasing political and economic anxiety; to add to his gloom, even a Fellow of All Souls, an acquaintance of Evelyn's who had published a translation of Lucretius and appeared to be of grave and solid temper, went and hanged himself, though besides his ample fellowship, he had a living worth £200 a year.

### III

In spite of a wonderfully warm spring, by the summer of 1700 John's age was beginning to tell: having moved down to Wotton in May, he had spent a month in bed with strangury and fever, and, though he recovered, thought that God had graciously warned him of his duty to prepare for his end, which could not now be far off, 'at this greate Age of mine'.[5] Fortunately the young Drapers came down for a fortnight's visit at Wotton.

But public anxieties continued. William, Duke of Gloucester, Anne's only surviving child, apparently full of promise and the heir to the throne, died aged twelve leaving, as John wrote ruefully, the succession to the crown on 'some Protestant Prince, the next, I think, being the Prince of Hanover, Grandson, to the Q; of Bohemia ... otherwise, I think, descending (if the P: of Wales be utterly excluded) on the Dutchesse of Savoy, daughter to the princess Henrietta, Sister to Charles the first. Wher the Crowne will now Settle', he rightly concludes, 'should the Princesse of Denmark breed no more to live, is matter of high speculation to the Politic:'.[6]

By August Jack had returned from Oxford for the vacation, the weather was seasonable and serene, and in spite of another bout of illness, Evelyn could record that in the one year of his long life for which he had been 'obliged to turn to ... plowing and sowing', it had pleased God to allow a most plentiful harvest, all safely gathered in the very day before the weather broke. And in September the Evelyns were well enough to stay with the Drapers at their new house at Adscombe. Save for the loss of another infant son, the Drapers were prospering; a help to both the old people, whom they accompanied on a visit to an elegant property at Marden, so well developed with intermingled timber and walks that it seemed almost foreign and pleasantly exotic.

Evelyn also visited his old friend Pepys at Clapham, in his 'very noble, and wonderfully well furnish'd house, especialy with all the Indys and Chineze Curiositys, ... the Offices and Gardens exceedingly well accommodated for pleasure and retirement'.[7] Now on 31 October, aged eighty, he could conclude a year that had ended in comparative serenity with 'sight hearing and other senses and facultys tollerable'.

And when, early in November, news arrived from Balliol that Jack was stricken with smallpox, Evelyn weathered the shock; diminished because the Master, with seventeenth-century disregard for infection, had taken the youth into his own household and even bedroom, and summoned his own physician. But Jack recovered, the Master remained impervious, and, following Tory victories in a general election, Godolphin returned to office as First Lord of the Treasury.

Henceforward, Evelyn's final objective was clear and so remained; to procure through Godolphin's influence a salaried position for Jack, and strengthen the ties with the Godolphins by a marriage between Jack and Anne Boscawen, daughter of Edward Boscawen and Jael Godolphin, Lord Godolphin's sister. These objectives Evelyn would now pursue with unflinching tenacity, while at last at Wotton he and Mary could enjoy a 'sedate and amicable composure'.

## IV

In 1699, in the previous October, had appeared Evelyn's *Acetaria, a Discourse of Sallets*. Unlike *Numismata*, it had been what the public had expected, and it had been well received. The diet of the well-to-do late seventeenth-century English had been ample, with great quantities of meat, game and fish, washed down with plenty of ale, while if already the upper classes preferred the 'white' bread, about which Evelyn's Dutch prisoners of war had complained, and from which the more nutritious contents had been removed, most of the people still ate the more nourishing 'wheaten' loaf. Unfortunately the medieval and Tudor popular prejudice against vegetables persisted, and sub-scorbutic conditions were still common.

In France, however, vegetables were now much better appreciated, and the gargantuan meals of Louis XIV already included salad, while William III's bad manners had shocked the English courtiers when, disregarding the queen, he had devoured a whole plateful of fresh green peas himself. François de la Varenne's *Le Cuisinier Français*, the first treatise on French classical cooking (1651) had particularly recommended mushrooms, asparagus and *bouquet garni*, while in England Robert May's *The Accomplisht Cook* (1660) had included recipes for spinach, asparagus, cucumbers and salads, elaborately composed.

So Evelyn's *Acetaria*,[8] with its characteristic mixture of easy modern exposition and pedantic mid seventeenth-century learning, had a wide public waiting, and based on the immense unpublished *Elysium Britannicum*, it is extremely thorough. It is dedicated with grovelling flattery to Lord Somers, Lord High Chancellor (1697–1700), and president of the Royal Society. Somers was a sagacious authority on Constitutional Law, who had defended the Seven Bishops in court and favoured the accession of William and Mary and the Declaration of Rights; he was a wealthy bachelor, a good linguist and patron, who had risen from minor gentry in Worcestershire. But it is a mark of changing times that Evelyn, as a young man so independent of patronage and central government, could now laboriously apologize for his subject, 'low and despicable tho' it appears', as a 'part of natural history', stress that he is but a 'very moderate eater of sallats himself'; and conclude 'but my Lord, whilst you read on (if at least you vouchsafe me that honour to read at all) I am conscious that I rob the publick of its most precious moments – the Chancellor's Time'. Somers, bibliophil and connoisseur, would afterwards, having survived attempted impeachment, combine with Evelyn's principal patron, Godolphin, to back Marlborough's wars in the reign of Anne.

Few modern readers would wish to linger over these preliminaries, extended into a preface which relates salads to the 'far-extended limits of the vegetable kingdom, so incomprehensible in its variety', and referring to an author (Evelyn) who 'for forty years has been gathering materials for an hortulan design'. But after citing Pliny, Columella, and Salmasius, Evelyn thoroughly lists the 'esculent plants and herbs improv'd by culture' employed in the salads of his day. '*Artichaux*' – 'a noble thistle' – are best at the end of meals, with orange juice and sugar: borage purifies the blood; Broom buds are good for spleen and scurvy; cabbage – Pompey's beloved dish – prevents intoxication, though only the Dutch eat it raw. Cauliflowers provoke eructations, and chervil is commended for the aged; nasturtium leaves quicken the torpid spirit and prevent scurvy, and cucumber cools the liver, while fennel expels wind and sharpens the sight.

Garlic, 'which southern people eat with almost everything', is indeed a charm against infection; but we think it only fit for 'our northern rusticks' and absolutely forbid it into our 'sallets' for its intolerable rankness – and 'for sure 'tis not for a ladies palate, nor for those who court them'. Leeks, of course, make people prolific – look at the Welsh, but the lettuce is more refined, the foundation of 'sallets'; it bridles choler, conciliates sleep and, unlike the leek, promotes chastity.

But melons, rather recently come in from Spain, are the paragons of the garden, and sliced or pulped with pepper and salt, not sugar, are then an excellent ingredient: mushrooms, on the other hand, generally banished from 'sallets', are only tolerable if chosen with the nicest circumspection. There is something malignant about them, and they sent the emperor Claudius to another world. Of course, onions, if boiled, give a 'kindly relish', and an honest laborious Italian countryman 'with good bread and salt and a little parsley, will make a contented meal with a roasted onion'; indeed, Egyptian onions were so luscious and tempting that the Israelites longed to return to Egypt to enjoy them. Oranges sharpen the appetite and discourage putrefaction, while rosemary is 'soverainly Cephalic', and good for the memory. Pepper is always excellent against flatulence, but 'next to flesh', nothing is more nourishing than

'*Sparagus*', quickly boiled; although, writes Evelyn wisely, 'I do not esteem the Dutch larger sort so sweet and agreeable are those of moderate size.' If you need an emollient laxative, spinach is good, boiled in its own moisture and served with lemon or butter.

After this illuminating catalogue, Evelyn concludes with a warning from the great naturalist John Ray (1627–1705), whose *Catalogus Plantarum Angliae* had appeared in 1690, that 'all persons should be caution'd upon unknown herbs', and cites Grillus, who by transmigration had become a beast, declaring that he had fed much better as an animal, as then better knowing what plants were most proper to him, than he did when he was again a man. But Evelyn carefully disowns being a vegetarian, 'preaching down hogs' puddings', even if Adam and Eve did feed on 'hortulan productions' before the 'fatal lapse'; and he prudently ends the subject 'with whatever is advanced in countenance of ante-diluvian diet we leave to be ventilated by the learned'.

# CHAPTER TWENTY-FOUR

# The Final Achievement

Early in 1701 Evelyn completed the sale of his mother's property of North Stoke near Arundel to pay off the portions to George's granddaughters; the climate, as usual, was appalling, alternating deep snow and frost with thaw and slush, and at the end of January a tempest 'threw down the chimnys, did great spoil at sea' and destroyed more than twenty trees at Wotton. Indomitably, in spite of 'agues' and somnolences, Evelyn continued to analyse the sermons, now his main intellectual interest.

But by 10 February he was back in London where a new parliament had been debating the royal succession, the Princess of Denmark being now 'not likely to have any child live'. On the Continent the outbreak of the war of the Spanish Succession (1701–13) was imminent; the English, in alliance with the Dutch and the Austrian emperor, were about to fight France, Spain and Bavaria for commercial supremacy and overseas empire in what they still term the 'Marlborough Wars'. The death of Charles II – Carlos the Bewitched – the last Habsburg king of Spain, in 1700 without a direct heir, and then that of the designated Joseph Ferdinand of Bavaria, had let in a Bourbon candidate, Philip of Anjou, a grandson of Louis XIV, as Philip V. The prospect of a combination of the Spanish and French military and naval power and empire had become extremely menacing, and the far-flung war would be decisive for the future of Great Britain. Evelyn thought the parliament quite unequal to its immense responsibilities; elected by perjury and bribery and filled with 'young, debauched boys and worthlesse members'.[1] He hoped that God would avert the sad fate which, as usual, he believed threatened all Christendom.

But by the end of February, as treasurer, he was well enough to lay before the Commons the accounts of the building of the marine college at Greenwich, and on the death of the parson of Wotton, he presented Dr Bohun, his friend and his grandson's tutor, to the living. From the Continent came rumours of the French king's preparations for war, unalleviated in April by a solemn fast in England to avert the consequences of the accession of Philip V; for the French continued to threaten the rest of Europe under pretence of Louis XIV's being his guardian. By May, the Dutch, invoking the treaty of 1678, were demanding reinforcements of 10,000 men. Having no regular means of calling ministers to account for indecision, all the Commons could do at this critical time was to impeach Lord Somers and three other ministers; whereat the Lords refused to participate, and far from punishing the accused, acquitted Somers and dismissed the impeachment; so with much animosity between Lords and Commons, parliament was prorogued.

On 8 July Evelyn and his household retired to Wotton, where they had a fine August, with excellent harvest weather. Abroad the French king made his intentions even clearer when in mid-September he formally recognized Prince James Edward (the 'Old Pretender') as king of Great Britain.

Evelyn, now eighty-one, continued to cultivate his garden: 'I planted,' he records 'the Elme walke in the back of the Meadow.' At the end of November he went to Dover Street in London for the winter, where in January 1702 a new parliament was unanimous in support of the king's joining the confederate allies against the French. But now a grave crisis blew up. On 21 February 1702 King William had been thrown when hunting a deer near Hampton Court, and on 8 March Evelyn recorded that, having broken his collar bone, and being already 'Aguish' with his 'long Cough', he died that morning at Kensington. The event threw the whole city into 'extraordinary disturbance' and jeopardized the interests of the whole nation in such a[2]

dangerous Conjuncture.... Matters both abroad, and at home, being in so loose a posture, and all Europe ready to breake out into the most dangerous Warr that it ever suffered, and this Nation especially being so unprovided of persons of the Experience, Conduct and Courage, just as we were concluding this Confederacy so long concerted with the Emp: and other Princes to resist the deluge of the French.

The event in fact made little impression on the ordinary people, who showed 'no sort of alteration or Concerne', only the shopkeepers complaining that the mourning of the quality had diminished trade. Queen Anne was proclaimed on the day of William's death; 'an English queen' as Mary Evelyn called her, 'with an English heart', and her coronation was on 23 April: her reign would see victories of a scale and consequence that the much-enduring William had never achieved.


## II

Down at Wotton during the winter and spring of 1702 workmen
had been thoroughly repairing and overhauling the house; and
in May Mary Evelyn, practical as ever, wrote that she had visited
every part of it, approved the dairy and the new chimney in
John's study, though the one in George's old room still let in the
rain. But the gardens were 'rough', – owing, said the gardener
from Sayes Court, to dry weather – and she had 'expressed her
dislike'. She 'wished John was there for the good air and the
quiet'.[3] The repairs, agreed as fair by John, had cost the very
large sum of £1,900. Meanwhile Evelyn and Mary kept in touch
with London on Wednesdays and Saturdays by what 'we call
Lecture Nights, when my wife and myselfe take turns to read the
packets of newes sent constantly from London which serves us
for discourse till fresh news comes'.[4]

But by the end of June the house was habitable enough for the
Evelyns, the Drapers and their households – in all thirty people –
to settle there for the summer in hay harvest weather. And
grandson Jack was now with them. In December 1701 he had
come down from Balliol in a shower of mutual compliments
with the dons, particular civilities to the Master and a 'guinea
extraordinary' to his tutor. Evelyn now concentrated on
promoting his career by a well paid sinecure and a rich marriage.

Since it was hard to obtain the marriage without the salary, it
was lucky that with the accession of Anne, Lord Godolphin had
come back to greater power as Lord Treasurer, with
Marlborough as Captain General; and Evelyn, now with £1,200 a
year from Wotton, at once solicited the Lord Treasurer's help for
Jack. He also, with more pertinacity and accuracy than tact, twice
petitioned for a refund of his expenses long ago incurred during
the Second Dutch War. Godolphin, with other things on his
mind, made no response.

The girl Evelyn intended as a wife for Jack was Anne, daughter
of Edward Boscawen, a Turkey merchant of an old Cornish
family long established on estates around the river Fal, and of
Jael Godolphin, Lord Godolphin's sister; but he had first to
convince Mrs Boscawen that Jack would have a sufficient
fortune. Evelyn made the best of his prospects – writing to Mrs
Boscawen that Jack could expect to inherit nearly £2,500 a year

after leases were determined and jointures paid off. She replied that, wanting to 'dispose of her daughter in a good family, a sober virtuous young man and a competent fortune',[5] she looked to meet these things in Evelyn's grandson; but since the girl was only seventeen and Jack twenty, they were both young enough to wait a little. If and when Evelyn could get some relief from the friend he relied on (Godolphin), she would be 'ready to enter into a closer treaty'.

So on 8 September 1702, the anniversary of Margaret Godolphin's death, Evelyn took occasion at last to send his patron a copy of the *Life of Mrs Godolphin*, written in 1684. The great man did not, apparently, acknowledge it.

So, early in 1703, he tried an official approach: again applying for a refund of his expenses in the Dutch war, imploring Godolphin 'not to abandon him', and promising still to pray for his lordship. He also again pressed on Mrs Boscawen the need for Godolphin to find Jack employment, and with an old man's pertinacity, again demanded payment of his expenses in the Dutch war.

His remaining intimates were now very old. When, on 14 May, Evelyn called on Pepys at Clapham he found him 'languishing with small hope of recovery', and was much affected. Twelve days later Pepys died of smallpox.[6]

This [day] dyed Mr Sam: Pepys, a very worthy, Industrious and curious person, none in England exceeding him in Knowledge of the Navy, in which he had passed thro' all the most Considerable Offices ... all which he performed with greate Integrity; when K: James the 2nd went out of England, he layd down his Office, and would serve no more. ... Mr Pepys had ben for ... neare 40 yeares, so my particular Friend, that he now sent me Compleat Mourning, desiring me to be one to hold up the Pall.

Broken by old age and anxiety, Evelyn was too ill to attend the funeral.

That summer, he still urged Jack's marriage upon Mrs Boscawen, and even wrote to Francis, Godolphin's son and Jack's Eton friend, to speak kindly of Jack to his father.

Nor was his urge to write yet defeated. He was working on a new edition of *Sylva* and of his impeccably orthodox *Account of Architects and Architecture*. With a nuance of donnish jealousy, Dr Bathurst, the aged president of Trinity, Oxford, remarked that if, at eight-four, his contemporary Evelyn could still put out new editions, he had 'little reason to complain'.

## III

Early in January 1704 Godolphin could at least appoint young
Jack to a minor post at £300 a year as receiver-general of the
Stamp Duties. It was not much, but it was a sign of favour. With
the tiresomeness of great age, Evelyn responded by again
demanding repayment of his vintage expenses: wherat the
Treasury, already at that level in recognizable form,
counterattacked with bureaucratic skill by alleging that in fact
Evelyn owed them £244, having long ago overcharged them for
expenses already paid. But Evelyn, with access to their master,
made the right response: he wrote to Godolphin that he was
much surprised that he should 'alone be singled out for a
precedence to others of somewhat inferior rank and credit to
serve at a cheaper rate'. He also pressed in vain for a refund of
the £6,000 which the Crown still owed the estate of Sir Richard
Browne. Godolphin could do nothing about that, but stayed the
Treasury's process against the old gentleman for the £244.

When, in his eighty-fourth year, Evelyn brought himself to
write *Memoires for my Grand-Son*,[7] the prosaic side of his mind
predominated. With old age he had reverted to the method, if
not the enterprise, of the business tycoon, his grandfather, and
his advice to Jack is comprehensively and relentlessly practical.
He begins, in the best manner of old gentlemen making wills, by
laboriously and at length explaining how he had put aside plans
for leaving part of the Wotton estate to his daughter, Susanna
Draper, and part to the local poor; then how since he *at present*
finds in Jack all those good and laudable inclinations which
nourish the hope that he will improve to become an honest,
religious and worthy man, he has left him the entire estate, as
freely as it was left to himself, without any reservations 'save
what is settl'd and express'd in [his] own Will and Testament'.

He then adjures him to endow six poor children from
Abinger, to say his private prayers regularly, and hold household
prayers daily before dinner, to instruct his own children in a
'familiar Reverence' which will make them prefer his company
to that of the servants, to instruct his wife in piety, and never to
live above his income. Indeed, he ought to lay up a third of it
every year to provide dowries for his daughters, whom he should
'match with honest worthy and prudent men', whose moderate
fortunes would be 'preferable to great Riches sordidly gotten' or
to 'nobleness of the family alone'. With this sober end in view,
the girls should be brought up good house wives, modest,

moderate and 'discreetly frugal'. As to the sons, they should be 'ever dutifully obedient', but able to make their livings 'in the Law, Physick, Merchand, or the Church'. Though the Evelyns were substantial armigerous gentry, they did not, in contrast to their French equivalents, have inhibitions about commerce for younger sons, who should also be well enough educated to 'rise by the dexterity of their pens' through serving magnates in public office.

Jack, himself, when squire of Wotton, should be decently hospitable, but without ostentation, and not waste money on building or over-rich furniture, but invest it in 'gardening, groves and walkes', and in planting oak, ash and elm on the estate. He should use double entry book-keeping, pay his servants punctually at the half-year, and inspect all broken wheels, harness and implements himself, while keeping the spare parts locked up 'to prevent imbezzlement'; he should, of course, keep meticulous inventories and appoint a reliable steward, with whom they would be regularly checked. Coach and stables should be often inspected and 'Armor, gunns, carbines, pistols, swords or buff coats' regularly cleaned, to avoid their owner's being reported by the Muster Master and fined by the Deputy Lieutenant. He should keep all powder dry and aired, and never let a servant have a fowling piece without special leave or he will poach game. Evelyn's distrust of servants was ineradicable.

With a grasp of detail entirely unimpaired, he then advises that 'your boate be lock'd and chain'd up' for the winter and fastened at both ends; clear the gutters and spouts every spring, clean the hog pens, poultry houses and pigeon house, and see that your wife regularly inspects all apartments and the contents within the house 'To prevent imbeziling by Chare women'. It is cheaper to use coal than wood for the kitchen, laundry and Brewhouse, and even worth making 'trial of peate'.

Given a well-run household, 'a regular economy in the country is the best condition'. Here you must win the esteem both of your neighbours and of the poor; 'to your Tennants be not strange or ridgid', difficult or exacting, and use field sports only in moderation 'without the slavery of keeping Dogs, especially Hounds, Hauks, Race-Horses etc'. Enjoy your recreations with others of your own rank rather casually, and 'as seldom as you can', though you must always be 'strict on Poachers'.

Jack having had an education 'something above that of most ordinary country gents, who commonly unlearne and abolish all they have learned at schole university etc, when they come to their estates', he will need to keep up his reading, 'seasonably and moderately taken as by the way'. He should make 'a well digested common place book', not allow his Latin, French and Italian to get rusty, and of course, besides re-reading Bacon, Ralegh, Selden, Grotius, and the classics, continue to study the scriptures and the church fathers. His library should be carefully catalogued. Finally, as the foundation of his way of life, Jack should preserve the records and the Court Rolls of the estate in tin boxes, and all relevant loose papers should be kept in order.

Evelyn then instructs his heir to burn his own personal loose papers, 'the tiresome (laborious) exercise of Sundays and Holydays', or 'the marks of Time indiscreetly lost and fit only to be abolished ... and by me seriously repented of'.

The *Memoires* conclude by *Promiscuous Advices* – or short aphorisms, of uninspired and characteristic homespun commonsense, of which the liveliest are 'Suspect', for example, 'anything that is too prosperous'; 'Be not cheated out of virtue for Bread'; and 'Do your Duty and let people talk.'

Written in his eighties, when his carefully navigated ship had at last come into harbour, the *Memoires* and *Advices* display an exhausted but tenacious mind; the lively comprehensive curiosity of youth and maturity are whittled down to the essentials of prudence, management and property. Indeed, Evelyn seems almost to anticipate the smugness of an eighteenth-century landowner, and the deliberate self-effacement, so baffling to strangers, of the modern Wykehamist. The panache of the man of fashion is discarded; and his grandson is heavily exhorted to a deliberately unpretentious life; he should be casually and amiably conventional, with a wary and methodical eye on the property which, great and small, was to be the mainspring of his existence.

So fortified, the prudent Jack was to be launched into a career that would more than fulfil his grandfather's expectations.[8]


## IV


While his grandson's marriage and advancement were pending, Evelyn still observed public affairs with a penetrating eye. In December 1702 he had chronicled how vice-admiral Benbow, once his tenant at Sayes Court, had been wounded in battle with the French in the West Indies, and how he had fought on, only to be deprived of a great victory by the cowardice of his commanders who had been afterwards tried and executed. But as old age wore him down, Evelyn's interests grew more limited, and he recorded how the bishop of Lincoln's wife, 'a melancholy woman', had flung herself out of a window and died, as well as his own cumulative infirmities, as kidney disease gripped him, bringing uraemia, drowsiness and pain. As very old people with fading memory will read and re-read the same familiar books, so Evelyn continued to record sermons on the old subjects – as the prodigal son, the dangers of death-bed repentance, the supersession of the Mosaic Law by the Gospel. He also chronicled the misfortunes of others, recording in the spring of 1703 how the Duke of Marlborough after his prosperity, riches and glory, 'lost his onely son, who died at Cambridge of the small pox';[9] but how, undaunted, 'Marbarrow', having buried his son at King's, took ship to the Low Countries to command as Captain General. But while Marlborough was organizing the diplomatic and military prelude to the campaign of 1704 which would culminate at Blenheim, Evelyn, having stumbled in his garden, was immobilized by a broken shin and, when convalescent, even slept through a sermon on the Ingratitude of the 9 Lepers, 'through my owne fault in eating too much'. And in July he was prostrated by severe fits of a 'quartern Ague', and extremely annoyed with Dr Bohun, his particular tame clergyman, for preaching violently against pride and luxury of apparel, since the indictment could only apply to Mary and Susanna, the only people of quality in the church. Dr Bohun took his reproof very ill; nor had he said a word of the pride of the clergy, with their 'long powdered peruks and silk cassocks', though in his next sermon he turned to the safer theme of the evils of intemperance.

Tormented now by piles, Evelyn was let four ounces of blood – perhaps too much, he rightly considered – but felt no relief, and sustained another aguish fit. So on his birthday, aged eighty-three, he prayed that God would make his infirmities tolerable and prepare him for a better [future] life; but in November God sent a terrible tempest which wrought havoc on his precious Wotton farms and woods. The hurricane had struck the whole country and done immense damage in the New Forest and the Forest of Dean, and when, for the winter of 1703–4, Evelyn and his household moved to Dover Street, they were shocked at the devastation on the way; worst, oddly, in villages and valleys.

Evelyn had now not much to record but sermons and illness, and gloom increased when Dr Bathurst of Trinity, ('I think the oldest acquaintance now left me in the world'), deaf, blind and his memory gone, died, aged eighty-six, his death gave Evelyn 'serious alarm'. But on the Continent Marlborough was making his historic march to the Danube, and in early July the English and their allies beat the Bavarians at Schellenberg; then on 10 August came news of the stunning victory at Blenheim. It had been brought to the queen by Daniel Parcke, one of Evelyn's distant American cousins, and though too brief to describe the victory in detail, it set off triumph and joy in the City, reinforced by the capture of Gibraltar.

Godolphin, chosen Knight of the Garter, was now at the height of his power, and already in mid-March Evelyn had made a decisive move in his own tenacious campaign. 'I waited on my L. Treasurer to whom was proposed my G-sons marriage to his Neipce which he much approved of.'[10] Well he might, for Evelyn was improving the prospects of Jack's marriage settlement. He borrowed £9,000 on mortgage from his affluent son-in-law Draper, secured on the Wotton estate, and could now pay off the £5,000 due to his nephew Glanville, so that apart from paying off the mortgage, Jack would inherit an unencumbered estate. So Anne Boscawen's mother now also approved of Jack as a man of sufficient property, and even desired 'to finish an affair which had been now a good while depending, in case you and Mrs Evelyn approve it, and that the young people should like the conclusion as well as the old'.

What was more, on 5 July Evelyn had at last recorded that 'My L. Treasurer made my Gr-son one of the Commissioners of the Prizes, the sallary 500 pounds per Annum.' By September, the master plan, so long worked for, had succeeded.

Though again and worse afflicted by renal illness which he attributed to the stone, Evelyn in very hot weather managed to 'creep' to church and receive communion, and in August he wrote that Jack's marriage settlement with Anne Boscawen was now 'finished', staying only for the examination of the deeds and seal. By the 23rd it had been 'given to be Ingrossed, giving him my Intire Estate, reserving only possession during my life'. 'The lease and intire furniture of my house in London,' he concluded, 'I give absolutely to my dear wife.'[11] Finally on 6 September he made the entry, not without pride, 'Were sealed the Writings etc, by which I settled my Estate on my Grandson, in order to his Marriage with Ann, Daughter to Mrs Boscawen, sister of my L:

Godolphin, L High Treasurer of England.'[12]

On 18 September 1704 Jack Evelyn and Ann Boscawen were married by Evelyn's old friend Dr Tenison, now archbishop of Canterbury, in Lambeth Chapel. It was a small family ceremony including the Evelyns, Jack's widowed mother, and his sister Elizabeth, the Drapers, Mrs Boscawen and the bride's uncle, Henry Godolphin, Provost of Eton. The entertainment, wrote Mary, was great and plentiful – 'quietly and kindly performed: We left the young couple in bed'.[13]

## V

With immense and devious tenacity in his eighty-third year Evelyn had obtained his objective; the enhanced status and affluence of the family name. He had rescued the Wotton estate from George's ill-judged attempt to disrupt it and secured the succession to the Evelyn male line; and he had married his grandson into eminent Cornish families – the Godolphins, who had already gained an earldom and the Boscawens who would become Viscounts Falmouth.[14]

These worldly objectives Evelyn's grandfather, who had launched the family, would have approved; indeed, his businesslike qualities, latent in the young aesthete who had first travelled on the Continent, had formidably developed in the grandson's old age.

But John now had less than six months to live; with added interest he clung to sermons, and recorded one which elaborately declared that the day of judgment could not last a mere twenty-four hours, since, from Adam onwards, so many people had to be judged, with witnesses; and on his last birthday, with touching faith and humility, John could still write 'Lord teach me so to number the days to come that I may apply them to wisdom better than hitherto I have done, for J. C. sake.'[15]

During a hard winter in London he was failing; his old infirmities closed in, and on 27 February 1706, at his house in Dover Street, John Evelyn died aged eighty-five. He was buried at Wotton, where his memorial remains. Mary survived him until 7 February 1709.

# Notes

## Sources of the *Diary*

1 Now in the Geffrye Museum, Bethnal Green; made in Paris in 1652, exhibited in November 1979 at the Art Treasures Exhibition at Somerset House.
2 The story is cited in E. S. De Beer's definitive edition of the *Diaries*, Oxford, 1955, vol. I, pp. 53–4.

## Introduction

1 For the prevalence of such beliefs, see Keith Thomas, *Religion and the Decline of Magic*, London, 1971, ch. 4, pp. 78–112.

## 1 Origins and Upbringing

1 John Evelyn, *Kalendarium. My Journal etc. 1620–1649, The Diaries of John Evelyn*, now first printed in full from the manuscripts belonging to Evelyn, ed. E. S. De Beer, Oxford, 1955, vol. II, p. 1.
2 *Victoria County History of Surrey*, vol. II, p. 306.
3 *Ibid.*, vol. II, p. 306.
4 Evelyn, *Kalendarium, Diaries*, vol. II, pp. 1–2.
5 *Ibid.*, p. 3.
6 *Ibid.*, p. 9.
7 Evelyn, *Kalendarium, Diaries*, vol. II, p. 11.
8 He wrote the famous lines on James I's daughter Elizabeth, Queen of Bohemia:

> You meaner beauties of the night
> That poorly satisfy our eyes
> More by you number than your light,
> You common people of the skies,
> What are you when the Moon arise?

## 2 Balliol and London

1 John Evelyn, *De Vita Propria*, Pars Prima, *The Diaries of John Evelyn*, ed. E. S. De Beer, Oxford, 1955, vol. I, p. 12.
2 John Evelyn, *Kalendarium, Diaries*, vol. II, p. 16.
3 'Being the first from the Leape Year composed for the Meridian of the famous Towne of Shrewsbury, and generally for all Britaine, by Thomas Langley, *Faelix qui potuit rerum cognoscere causas*', London. The *Almanack*, bound up with others from 1636 to 1640, is in the library of Balliol College, Oxford. They are small pocket books, the equivalent of modern engagement books.
4 Evelyn, *De Vita Propria, Diaries*, vol. I, p. 13.
5 H. W. Carless Davis, *History of Balliol*, revised H. W. C. Davis and Richard Hunt, supplemented by H. Hartley, Oxford, 1963, p. 104.
6 Evelyn, *De Vita Propria, Diaries*, vol. I, p. 13.
7 *Ibid.*, p. 15.
8 Zanchius, *Opera*, 3 vols; Granadus (S. J.) on Thomas Aquinas, 3 vols; the *Electa Sacra* of Novarinus and the *Anthologia Sacra* of Cresollius – all very scholastic.
9 The admission of Fellow Commoners almost collapsed during the Civil War, to be revived, along with the power of the nobility and gentry, after the Restoration.
10 Davis and Hunt, *History of Balliol*, p. 113.
11 Evelyn, *Kalendarium, Diaries*, vol. II, p. 21.
12 *Ibid.*, p. 22.
13 Evelyn, *De Vita Propria, Diaries*, vol. I, p. 18.
14 *Ibid.*, p. 18.
15 Dr Kettle was president 1599–1643. John Aubrey, *Brief Lives*, ed. Oliver Lawson Dick, London, 1950, pp. 181–7. Aubrey went up to Trinity in 1642, then, forced to retire to Wiltshire in the following year, did not return to Oxford until 1646.
16 Evelyn, *Kalendarium, Diaries*, vol. II, p. 26.
17 Most vividly described in the *Letters and Journals of Robert Baillie*, Principal of the University of Glascow, ed. David Laing, 3 vols, who had a sharper eye for detail. See also John Bowle, *Charles I*, London, 1975, pp. 183–7.
18 Evelyn, *Kalendarium, Diaries*, vol. II, p. 28.

## 3 Holland and the Spanish Netherlands

1 John Evelyn, *Kalendarium. My Journal etc. 1620–1649, The Diaries of John Evelyn*, ed. E. S. De Beer, Oxford, 1955, vol. II, p. 41.
2 Richard Browne (1550–1633) had preached against bishops in Cambridge and at Norwich, where he had founded an 'Independent' sect. He had then migrated to Walcheren and Scotland and ended in the local gaol at Northampton. This fiery

eccentric, who advocated a new reformation by a new 'elect', had obtained a considerable following which spread to America.

3 Evelyn, *Kalendarium, Diaries*, vol. II, p. 46.

4 *Ibid.*, vol. II, pp. 46–8.

5 Thomas Howard, Second Earl of Arundel (1585–1646). Educated at Westminster School and Trinity College, Cambridge, he was granted his father's forfeited titles, but not his estates, by James I. He recouped his fortunes by marrying the heiress of Gilbert Talbot, Earl of Shrewsbury, and in 1613 escorted the newly married Princess Elizabeth and the Palsgrave to Heidelberg, whence he proceeded to Italy. Brought up a Catholic, he turned Protestant in 1616, and became a Privy Councillor. He served, in vain, for Charles I in 1636 on a mission to the Emperor Ferdinand II on behalf of the Elector Palatine, and as Lord High Steward had presided at Strafford's trial. In February 1642 he would escort Queen Henrietta Maria to the Netherlands and avoid the Civil War by settling at Padua, where Evelyn again encountered him and where he died. He became the first great art collector among the English nobility. His collections were inherited by his descendant, Henry, sixth Duke of Norfolk (d. 1684), who was persuaded by Evelyn to present the Arundelian Library to the Royal Society and the Arundelian Marbles to Oxford University.

6 Evelyn, *Kalendarium, Diaries*, vol. II, p. 63.

7 Though most of it was burnt down in 1718, it was depicted by W. S. von Ehrenburg, and the interior is reproduced in H. R. Trevor-Roper's admirable *Princes and Artists, Patronage and Ideology at Four Habsburg Courts*, London, 1976, p. 146.

8 Evelyn, *The State of France as it stood in the Ninth Year of the present Monarch Louis XIV, written to a friend by J.E. (1652)*, reprinted in *The Miscellaneous Writing of John Evelyn Esq. F.R.S.*, ed. William Upcott, London, 1825, p. 45.

9 Evelyn, *Kalendarium, Diaries*, vol. II, p. 79.


## 4 Evelyn in France

1 John Evelyn, *Kalendarium. My Journal etc. 1620–1649, The Diaries of John Evelyn*, ed. E. S. De Beer, Oxford, 1955, vol. II, p. 81.

2 Reprinted in *The Miscellaneous Writings of John Evelyn Esq. F.R.S.*, ed. William Upcott, London, 1825; see p. 42.

3 As from de Varenne's *Le Voyage de France*, or Varenne's own source, the *Itinerarium Galliae* of Jodocus Sincerus (Justus Zinzerling), both now mainly of interest to professional art historians. (See Evelyn, *Kalendarium, Diaries*, vol. II, bibliographical note, pp. 571–3.)

4 *Ibid.*, vol. II, p. 94.

5 *Ibid.*, vol. II, p. 106.

6 *Ibid.*, vol. II, p. 137.

7 *Ibid.*, vol. II, p. 140.
8 *Ibid.*, vol. II, p. 151.
9 *Ibid.*, vol. II, pp. 158–9.
10 *Ibid.*, vol. II, pp. 163–80.
11 *Ibid.*, vol. II, p. 165.

## 5 Evelyn in Italy

1 John Evelyn, *Kalendarium. My Journal etc. 1620–1649, The Diaries of John Evelyn*, ed. E. S. De Beer, Oxford, 1955, vol. II, p. 173.
2 *Ibid.*, vol. II, p. 175.
3 In 1655 he published a translation of an Italian *History of China* by Samedo, 'to which was added a history of the late invasion of the florrishing Kingdom of the Tartars'. His papers for the Royal Society included one on saltpetre and one on gunpowder, subjects on which he had presumably consulted Evelyn.
4 As from Pflaumern's *Mercurius Italicus* (1628), and John Raymond, *An Itinerary contayning a voyage made through Italy in the year 1646 and 1647* (1648), with material from François Schott's *Itinerarii Italiae rerumq. Romanorum libri tres* (1600), itself, scholars may be reminded, heavily derived from S. V. Pighius, *Hercules Prodicius*, which includes an account of a tour by a German prince in 1574–5. See Evelyn, *Kalendarium, Diaries*, vol. II, bibliographical note, pp. 573–4.
5 *Ibid.*, vol. II, p. 195.
6 'Because it is here, my lord is here dead', for he had commanded his servant to ride ahead and mark where the best wine was by *Est*, 'it is here', and then drunk far too much of it.
7 Evelyn, *Kalendarium, Diaries*, vol. II, p. 213. He is said to have become a Protestant and accompanied Penn's expedition to the West Indies in 1655, where he died (see the *Dictionary of National Biography*).
8 Evelyn, *Kalendarium, Diaries*, vol. II, p. 214.
9 *Ibid.*, vol. II, p. 221.
10 *Ibid.*, vol. II, p. 229.
11 *Ibid.*, vol. II, p. 233.
12 *Ibid.*, vol. II, p. 255.
13 Still famous from his portrait as a younger man by Velasquez.
14 Evelyn, *Kalendarium, Diaries*, vol. II p. 326.
15 *Ibid.*, vol. II, p. 330.
16 *Ibid.*, vol. II, p. 354.

## 6 Venice and Switzerland

1 'Felix qui patriis aevum transegit in agris,
Ipsa domus puerum quem videt, ipsa senem'.

2 Evelyn, *Kalendarium. My Journal etc. 1620–1649, The Diaries of John Evelyn*, ed. E. S. De Beer, Oxford, 1955, vol. II, pp. 387–8.

3 *Ibid.*, vol. II, p. 448.

4 *Ibid.*, vol. II, pp. 468–9.

5 *Ibid.*, vol. II, p. 511.


## 7 Marriage: England and Paris: *The State of France*

1 It is a small dark red leather-bound book with Evelyn's coat of arms on the binding, but the lettering is so faded by the damp at Wotton that it is mainly illegible. What can be read does not suggest any startling revelations to be 'kept under lock and key'. Evelyn was naturally aware of the grosser aspects of sex, as witness his outspoken advice to his son on marriage (see page 176), but does not appear to treat of them here. The book is among the Evelyn Papers (MS 149) at Christ Church, Oxford.

2 *Diaries and Correspondence of John Evelyn F.R.S.*, ed. W. Bray, London, 1857, vol. III, p. 16.

3 Bray, *op. cit.*, vol. III, p. 30.

4 Bray, *op. cit.*, vol. III, p. 9.

5 Evelyn, *Kalendarium. My Journal etc. 1620–1649, The Diaries of John Evelyn*, ed. E. S. De Beer, Oxford, 1955, vol. II, p. 545.

6 Bray, *op. cit.*, vol. III, p. 35.

7 François de la Motte le Voyer, 1588–1672, Author of *De la Vertu des Paysans* (1642) and other writings.

8 Evelyn, *The Miscellaneous Writings of John Evelyn Esq. F.R.S.*, ed. W. Upcott, London, 1825, p. 1.

9 See my *Hobbes and His Critics*, London, 1951, pp. 17–21.

10 I hope this tedious author may not inspire a thesis.

11 Evelyn, *Kalendarium, Diaries*, ed. De Beer, vol. II, p. 547.

12 *Ibid.*, vol. II, p. 553.

13 Bray, *op. cit.*, vol. III, pp. 52–3.

14 Upcott, *op. cit.*, p. 52ff.

15 *Ibid.*, p. 66.

16 *Ibid.*, p. 78.

17 Ravaillac, the assassin of Henri IV.


## 8 Paris: Sayes Court

1 Evelyn, *Kalendarium. My Journal etc., The Diaries of John Evelyn*, ed. E. S. De Beer, Oxford, 1955, vol. III, pp. 3–4.

2 *Ibid.*, vol. III, pp. 4–8.

3 *Ibid.*, vol. III, p. 14.

4 *Ibid.*, vol. III, p. 16.

5 *Ibid.*, vol. III, pp. 58–9.
6 John Evelyn, *Mundus Muliebris, or the Ladies Dressing Room unlock'd ... together with the Fob Dictionary Compiled for the use of the Fair Sex*, London, 1690. Part of this facetious pamphlet is written by Evelyn's daughter, Mary.
7 Evelyn, *Kalendarium, Diaries*, vol. III, p 63.
8 *Ibid.*, vol. III, p. 80.
9 *Ibid.*, vol. III, p. 87.
10 *Ibid.*, vol. III, p. 93.

## 9  A Tour in England

1 Evelyn spells his name impartially Seymor, Seamore and Seymour, the last being the now accepted version.
2 John Evelyn, *Kalendarium. My Journal etc. 1620–1649, The Diaries of John Evelyn*, ed. E. S. De Beer, Oxford, 1955, vol. III, p. 114.
3 Termed by Evelyn, following the Wiltshire accent, '*Darneford Magna*', and then the property of Edward Hungerford, Mary's uncle by marriage.
4 Evelyn, *Kalendarium, Diaries*, vol. III, p. 115.
5 *Ibid.*, vol. III, pp. 115–16.
6 *Ibid.*, vol. III, pp. 128–9.
7 *Ibid.*, vol. III, pp. 145–6.
8 The son of a Cambridge barber, he had been Perse Fellow of Gonville and Caius, then, through Laud's patronage, a Fellow of All Souls at Oxford, chaplain to Charles I and rector of Uppingham. In 1655 Cromwell again had him imprisoned at Chepstow, but he was again in London in Evelyn's circle before retiring to Lisburn, Co. Antrim. After the Restoration he obtained his Irish bishopric, where he complained of the intransigent Ulster Presbyterians on whom his elegant Anglican tolerance was lost.
9 Evelyn, *The Diaries and Correspondence of John Evelyn F.R.S.*, ed. William Bray, London, 1957, vol. III, p. 219.
10 *Ibid.*, p. 220.
11 Evelyn, *Kalendarium, Diaries*, vol. III, pp. 149–50.
12 Reprinted in *The Miscellaneous Writings of John Evelyn Esq. F.R.S.*, ed. William Upcott, London, 1825, pp. 148 ff.
13 Evelyn, *Kalendarium, Diaries*, vol. III, p. 224.

## 10  The Restoration

1 John Evelyn, *Kalendarium. My Journal etc. 1620–1649, The Diaries of John Evelyn*, ed. E. S. De Beer, Oxford, 1955, vol. III, p. 234.
2 *Ibid.*, vol. III, pp. 237–8.

3 *The Miscellaneous Writings of John Evelyn Esq. F.R.S.*, ed. William Upcott, London, 1825, pp. 169–92.
4 *Ibid.*, pp. 194–204.
5 Evelyn, *Kalendarium, Diaries*, vol. III, p. 242.
6 Upcott, ed., *op. cit.*, pp. 194–204.
7 *Kalendarium, Diaries*, vol. III, p. 246.
8 *Kal. op. cit.*, vol. III, p. 271.
9 *Miscellaneous Writings of John Evelyn*, ed. Upcott, *op. cit.*, pp. 258–336.
10 For a full discussion of Rupert's contribution, see Patrick Morrah, *Prince Rupert of the Rhine*, London, 1976, pp. 392–9.
11 The full title is *A Panegyric to Charles the Second, presented to his Majestie the XXIII April being the day of the Coronation, MDCLXI*, ed. Geoffrey Keynes, pp. 82–5.

## 11 The Royal Society: *Fumifugium*: *Tyrannus*

1 *Fumifugium*, London, 1661, p. 8.
2 Thomas Parr, celebrated by John Taylor the 'Water Poet' as 'The Old, Old, very Old, Man', was said, though not proved, to have been born in 1483, and spent his life as a small leaseholder at Alderbury in Shropshire. Evelyn's friend, Lord Arundel, collected him to London in 1635 and presented him to Charles I. When the monarch rather coldly remarked, 'You have lived longer than other men, what have you done more than other men?' Parr replied rather coarsely, 'I *did penance* when I was an hundred years old' (for getting a bastard). But London proved too much for him, and he died at Lord Arundel's house that November. Harvey, the famous physician, reported after an examination that Parr's death had been due mainly to the change from the healthy Shropshire air to the air of London. Evelyn may well have repeated the report of this opinion.
3 *Fumifugium*, p. 69.
4 John Evelyn, *Kalendarium. My Journal etc. 1620–1649, The Diaries of John Evelyn*, ed. E. S. De Beer, Oxford, 1955, vol. III, p. 296.
5 *Ibid.*, vol. III, p. 310.
6 *Ibid.*, vol. III, p. 300.
7 *Tyrannus*, London, 1661.
8 Evelyn, *Kalendarium, Diaries*, vol. III, p. 321.
9 *Ibid.*, vol. III, p. 331.
10 *Ibid.*, vol. III, p. 347.

## 12 *Sylva* and the *Gard'ner's Almanack*

1 Cited in the account in *The Garden*, vol. 102, part II, November 1977, of Sandra Raphael's publication of the manuscript then in preparation.

2 I quote from the revised and expanded second edition of 1670, to which is annexed 'Pomona or an appendix concerning Fruit-Trees, in relation to Cider: the making and several ways of ordering'. The third edition, of 1679, was further enlarged.
3 See Lindsay Sharp, 'Timber, Science, and the Economic Reform in the Seventeenth Century', *Forestry*, vol. XLVIII, no. 1, 1975, p. 60.
4 William Lawson, who wrote *A New Orchard and Garden, or the best way for Planting, Grafting, and to make any ground good for a Rich Orchard, particularly in the North of England*, 1618.
5 First published London, 1664; reprinted in William Upcott, ed. *The Miscellaneous Writings of John Evelyn Esq. F.R.S.*, London, 1825, pp. 420–95.
6 There is an elaborate drawing of one with a subterranean furnace and complete ventilation annexed to the *Almanack*.
7 John Evelyn, *Kalendarium. My Journal etc. 1620–1649, The Diaries of John Evelyn*, ed. E. S. De Beer, Oxford, 1955, vol. III, p. 371.
8 *Ibid.*, vol. III, p. 382.
9 *Ibid.*, vol. III, p. 387.

## 13 The Second Dutch War and the Plague of London

1 John Evelyn, *Kalendarium. My Journal etc. 1620–1649, The Diaries of John Evelyn*, ed. E. S. De Beer, Oxford, 1955, vol. III, p. 387–8.
2 Reprinted in William Upcott, ed., *The Miscellaneous Writings of John Evelyn Esq. F.R.S.*, London, 1825, pp. 351–424.
3 Evelyn himself wisely thought French bread 'by general consent' far the best.
4 Evelyn, *Kalendarium, Diaries*, vol. III, p. 404.
5 *Ibid.*, vol. III, p. 413.
6 The Duke of York had told Evelyn that 'his dog sought out absolutely the very securest place in all the vessel, when they were in fight'.
7 Evelyn, *Kalendarium, Diaries*, vol. III, p. 417.
8 *Pepys's Diary*, ed. J. P. Kenyon, London, 1963, p. 94.
9 *Ibid.*, p. 93.
10 Evelyn, *Kalendarium, Diaries*, vol. III, p. 421.

## 14 The Fire of London

1 John Evelyn, *Kalendarium. My Journal etc. 1620–1649, The Diaries of John Evelyn*, ed. E. S. De Beer, Oxford, 1955, vol. III, p. 429.
2 *Ibid.*, vol. III, p. 439.
3 *Ibid.*, vol. III, p. 441.
4 *Ibid.*, vol. III, pp. 451–3.
5 *Pepys's Diary*, ed. J. P. Kenyon, London, 1963, p. 126.

6　Evelyn, *Kalendarium, Diaries*, vol. III, ·p. 457.
7　*Ibid.*, vol. III, p. 465.
8　*Ibid.*, vol. III, p. 484.
9　*Ibid.*, vol. III, p. 486.
10　Sir Arthur Bryant, *Samuel Pepys, The Man in the Making*, London, 1933, p. 248.
11　Evelyn, *Kalendarium, Diaries*, vol. III, p. 494.
12　In *The Miscellaneous Writings of John Evelyn Esq. F.R.S.*, ed. William Upcott, London, 1825, pp. 501–52.
13　Evelyn, *Kalendarium, Diaries*, vol. III, p. 502.

## 15　Politics, Encaenia and 'a rare Discovery'

1　The *Miscellaneous Writings of John Evelyn Esq. F.R.S.*, ed. William Upcott, London, 1825, pp. 555–62.
2　*Diary and Correspondence of John Evelyn F.R.S.*, ed. Wm. Bray and re-edited H. B. Wheatley, London, 1857, vol. III, pp. 435–56. The whole of this letter is well worth perusal.
3　John Evelyn, *Kalendarium. My Journal etc. 1620–1649, The Diaries of John Evelyn*, ed. E. S. De Beer, Oxford, 1955, vol. III, p. 525.
4　*Ibid.*, vol. III, p. 536.
5　*Ibid.*, vol. III, p. 549.
6　*Ibid.*, vol. III, p. 559.
7　*Ibid.*, vol. III, p. 567.
8　*Ibid.*, vol. III, p. 573.
9　Nell Gwyn, who came from Hereford, had already borne a son to the king, Charles Beauclerk (ironically named, for his mother could not write), who became Duke of St Albans. Originally an orange wench, she had made a hit on the restored stage, and Pepys had admired 'Little Nelly' as 'mighty pretty'. When she smiled 'her eyes almost dissappeared', and the Monarch had been so smitten by her acting in a 'coach wheel hat' that he had promptly carried her off to supper. Mistaken in Oxford for a French rival, she had remarked, 'Pray, good people, be civil: I am the Protestant whore'. Mindful of Charles's dying behest 'Let not poor Nelly starve', James II, who possessed a painting of her nude with a cupid, which could be concealed by a shutter, would pay off her large debts and settle an estate upon her with reversion to St Albans.

## 16　Foreign Plantations: *Navigation and Commerce*

1　John Evelyn, *Kalendarium. My Journal etc. 1620–1649, The Diaries of John Evelyn*, ed. E. S. De Beer, Oxford, 1955, vol. III, p. 579.
2　*Ibid.*, vol. III, p. 589.
3　*Ibid.*, vol. III, p. 589.

4 *Ibid.*, vol. III, pp. 589–90.
5 *Ibid.*, vol. III, p. 597.
6 *Ibid.*, vol. III, p. 610.
7 *Ibid.*, vol. III, p. 614.
8 *Ibid.*, vol. III, p. 619.

## 17 Romantic Friendship: the *Life of Mrs Godolphin*

1 John Evelyn, *Kalendarium. My Journal etc. 1620–1649, The Diaries of John Evelyn*, ed. E. S. De Beer, Oxford, 1955, vol. IV, p. 7.
2 *Ibid.*, vol. IV, p. 78.
3 *Ibid.*, vol. IV, p. 80.
4 *Ibid.*, vol. IV, p. 110.
5 *Ibid.*, vol. IV, pp. 136–7.
6 *Ibid.*, vol. IV, pp. 148–51.
7 It remained unpublished until 1847, when it appeared edited by Samuel Wilberforce, bishop of Oxford, afterwards famous for his controversy with T. H. Huxley over Darwin's theory of evolution.
8 *The Life of Mrs Godolphin* 'by John Evelyn of Wooton Esq., now first published and edited by Samuel, Lord Bishop of Oxford, Chancellor of the most noble Order of the Garter', London, 1848. It was dedicated by Evelyn to Lady Sylvius, wife of Sir Gabriel Sylvius, Hoffmeister to the Prince of Orange and envoy to Denmark, and left unpublished, on the list of 'things I would write out faire and reform if I had the leisure'.
9 Fellow of All Souls, 1774.

## 18 The Popish and Protestant Plots

1 John Evelyn, *Kalendarium. My Journal etc. 1620–1649, The Diaries of John Evelyn*, ed. E. S. De Beer, Oxford, 1955, vol. IV, p. 153.
2 *Ibid.*, vol. IV, p. 154.
3 *Ibid.*, vol. IV, p. 158.
4 *Ibid.*, vol. IV, pp. 176–7.
5 *Ibid.*, vol. IV, p. 185.
6 The eighteenth-century Stonehouse mansion now forms part of the principal building at Radley College.
7 Letter to J. Evelyn junior, 1679, cited in W. G. Hiscock, *John Evelyn and his Family Circle*, London, 1955, p. 122.
8 Evelyn, *Kalendarium, Diaries*, vol. IV, pp. 194–5.
9 *Ibid.*, vol. IV, p. 201.
10 *Ibid.*, vol. IV, p. 230.
11 *Ibid.*, vol. IV, p. 269.
12 Born at Farley, Wiltshire, he became MP for Salisbury and Paymaster General to the army and 'pewed the body of the

Cathedral Church at Sarum'. He was grandfather to Charles James Fox, a less provident character.

13 Evelyn, *Kalendarium, Diaries*, vol. IV, p. 331.

## 19 'Le Roi est Mort: Vive le Roi'

1 John Evelyn, *Kalendarium. My Journal etc. 1620–1649, The Diaries of John Evelyn*, ed. E. S. De Beer, Oxford, 1955, vol. IV, p. 347.
2 Among the Evelyn MSS at Christ Church, Oxford.
3 Evelyn, *Kalendarium, Diaries*, vol. IV, pp. 389–90.
4 *Ibid.*, vol. IV, p. 409.
5 *Ibid.*, vol. IV, pp. 405–11.
6 In 1688 Oates got a bedmaker in prison with child, and next year, pensioned by William and Mary, regained his freedom. He became a Baptist, but expelled as usual in 1701, survived until 1705.
7 H. Ellis, *Original Letters*, London, 1824, vol. III, p. 346.
8 Evelyn, *Kalendarium, Diaries*, vol. IV, pp. 456–7.
9 *Ibid.*, vol. IV, p. 472.
10 *Ibid.*, vol. IV, p. 475.
11 *Ibid.*, vol. IV, p. 481.
12 She retired, under pressure, to Ireland, on the £5,000 a year which the king had provided, and in 1696 married Sir David Colyear, afterwards Earl of Portmore.
13 Evelyn, *Kalendarium, Diaries*, vol. IV, p. 511.
14 *Ibid.*, vol. IV, p. 530.
15 *Ibid.*, vol. IV, p. 542.
16 *Ibid.*, vol. IV, p. 554.
17 *Ibid.*, vol. IV, p. 586.

## 20 'A sad revolution to this sinfull Nation'

1 John Evelyn, *Kalendarium. My Journal etc. 1620–1649, The Diaries of John Evelyn*, ed. E. S. De Beer, Oxford, 1955, vol. IV, p. 603.
2 *Ibid.*, vol. IV, p. 605.
3 Cited by L. von Ranke, *A History of England principally in the Seventeenth Century*, Oxford, 1875, vol. IV, pp. 459–64.
4 Evelyn *Kalendarium, Diaries*, vol. IV, p. 616.

## 21 Heir to Wotton

1 John Evelyn, *Kalendarium. My Journal etc. 1620–1649, The Diaries of John Evelyn*, ed. E. S. De Beer, Oxford, 1955, vol. V, p. 2.
2 *Ibid.*, vol. V, pp. 9–10.
3 *Ibid.*, vol. V, pp. 28–9.

4 *Ibid.*, vol. V, p. 50.
5 *Ibid.*, vol. V, pp. 54–5.
6 *Ibid.*, vol. V, p. 86.
7 *Ibid.*, vol. V, p. 97.
8 Characteristically, the English public demanded, and briefly enforced, the resignation of Russell for not doing better; but he was reinstated and, by 1695 in command of a Mediterranean fleet, blockaded the French in Toulon.
9 Evelyn, *Kalendarium, Diaries*, vol. V, p. 101.
10 *Ibid.*, vol. V, p. 138.
11 *Ibid.*, vol. V, p. 148.

## 22 'A solemn Remove'

1 John Evelyn, *Kalendarium. My Journal etc. 1620–1649, The Diaries of John Evelyn*, ed. E. S. De Beer, Oxford, 1955, vol. V, pp. 177 and 185.
2 Letter of John Evelyn junior to John Evelyn, February 1693, quoted in W. G. Hiscock, *John Evelyn and his Family Circle*, London, 1955, p. 168.
3 *Ibid.*, p. 173.
4 Evelyn, *Kalendarium, Diaries*, vol. V, p. 179.
5 *Ibid.*, vol. V, p. 185.
6 *Ibid.*, vol. V, p. 199.
7 *Ibid.*, vol. V, p. 228.
8 *Ibid.*, vol. V, p. 284.
9 Evelyn MS 12, pp. 485–6.
10 In *Sylva*, 1706 edition, p. 182.
11 *Numismata*, 'A Discourse of Medals Ancient and Modern, together with some account of Heads and Effigies of Illustrious and Famous Persons in Sculps and Taille Douce of whom we have no medals extant, and of the Use to be derived from them, to which is added a Digression concerning Physiognomy by John Evelyn Esq F R S', London, 1697.
12 Obadiah Walker (1616–99), Master of University College, Oxford, 1676–88, who, having turned Catholic under James II, was imprisoned in the Tower, and spent his declining years supported only by his former pupil, Dr Radcliffe. His *Education, especially of young Gentlemen* (1673) is still worth reading, and the full title of his last book is *The Greek and Roman History Illustrated by Coins and Medals*. He is perhaps best remembered by an Oxford rhyme:

> Oh, Old Obadiah
> Sing Ave Maria
> But so will not I a ...

13 *Numismata*, London, 1697, pp. 340–1.
14 Hiscock, *op. cit.*, p. 187.
15 Evelyn, *Kalendarium, Diaries*, vol. V, p. 292.

16 *Ibid.*, vol. V, p. 295.
17 *Ibid.*, vol. V, p. 318.
18 *Ibid.*, vol. V, p. 314.
19 R. H. C. Davis and R. Hunt, *A History of Balliol College*, Oxford, 1963, p. 146.
20 Hiscock, *op. cit.*, p. 210.
21 Evelyn, *Kalendarium, Diaries*, vol. V, p. 322.


### 23 'A sedate and amicable composure': *A Discourse of Sallets*

1 Cited in W. G. Hiscock, *John Evelyn and his Family Circle*, London, 1955, p. 215.
2 *Ibid.*, p. 216.
3 *Pepys's Private Correspondence*, ed. J. R. Tanner, vol. II, cited in Hiscock, *op. cit.*, p. 217.
4 John Evelyn, *Kalendarium. My Journal etc. 1620–1649, The Diaries of John Evelyn*, ed. E. S. De Beer, Oxford, 1955, vol. V, pp. 402–3.
5 *Ibid.*, vol. V, p. 420.
6 *Ibid.*, vol. V, p. 421.
7 *Ibid.*, vol. V, pp. 427–8.
8 *Acetaria, a Discourse of Sallets* by J.E. F.R.S. author of *Kalendarium Hortense*, London, 1699, reprinted in William Upcott, ed., *The Miscellaneous Writings of John Evelyn Esq. F.R.S.*, London, 1825, pp. 771–88.


### 24 The Final Achievement

1 John Evelyn, *Kalendarium. My Journal etc. 1620–1649, The Diaries of John Evelyn*, ed. E. S. De Beer, Oxford, 1955, vol. V, p. 446.
2 *Ibid.*, vol. V, p. 491.
3 W. G. Hiscock, *John Evelyn and his Family Circle*, London, 1955, p. 222.
4 Evelyn, *Diaries*, Introduction, vol. I, p. 89.
5 Cited in Hiscock, *op. cit.*, p. 228.
6 Evelyn, *Kalendarium, Diaries*, vol. V, pp. 537–8.
7 London, 1661.
8 In 1713 he would be made a baronet; he not only catalogued Evelyn's books but built a library at Wotton for them, and when he died, in 1763, his grandson, Sir Frederick, would live at Wotton until 1812. Childless, he would transfer the estate to a cousin, descended directly from the original George, the founder of the family's affluence, and the baronetcy would last until 1848.
9 Evelyn, *Kalendarium, Diaries*, vol. V, p. 530.
10 *Ibid.*, vol. V, pp. 587–8.
11 *Ibid.*, vol. V, p. 606.
12 *Ibid.*, vol. V, p. 607.

13 Cited in Hiscock, *op. cit.*, p. 237.
14 As well as producing Anne's nephew, the famous Admiral the Hon. Edward Boscawen, victor of the battle of Lagos, Portugal, and known to his sailors as 'Old Dreadnought'. Woken one night at sea with the words, 'Sir, there are two large ships which look like Frenchmen bearing down on us, what are we to do?' he replied, 'Do? Do? Damn 'em. Fight 'em'. Evelyn and Pepys would surely have approved.
15 Evelyn, *Kalendarium, Diaries*, vol. V, p. 614.

# Index

Gardening, comments on, 2, 4, 9, 122–3; in England, 123; fruits, 214; interest in, 28, 72, 81, 90, 113–14, 228; continental, 113; in Paris, 34, 72; tools, 114; water gardens, 31; at Wotton, 31, 81, 228; year's tasks, 122–3
Garlic, effect, 232
Geneva, illness at, 61–2; inspects city, 62
Gennep, fortress, siege of, 22
Genoa, visits, 39, 40–1; churches, 41; development, 160–1; journey to, 39, 40; Plazzo Doria, 41; treasures of, 40, 41; violence in, 41
Gentleman Commoners, at Oxford, 13, 14
Geology, Royal Society on, 209
George, Prince of Denmark: appearance, 184; marriage, 184
Ghent, visits, 27
Gibbons, Grinling, discovers, 2, 149–50
Gillingham, inspects, 157
Glanville, Jane (sister) 77, 227
Glanville, William, 196, 227, 228, 242
'Glorious Revolution', 200, 205, 207
Gloucester, visits, 88
Goats, chased by Wray's dog, 60
Goddard, Jonathan, 133
Godfrey, Sir Edmund Berry, 173–4
Godolphin, Francis: and Jack Evelyn, 163, 225, 226, 237; birth, 167; Margaret's concern for, 171; Numismata dedicated to, 221; career, 226
Godolphin, Henry, 225, 243
Godolphin, Jael (later Boscawen), 230, 236
Godolphin, Margaret: meets, 163; visits Paradise Transplanted, 163–4; legal

advice, 164, 165, 166, 168; court service, 164, 169–70; marriage, 163, 165–6, 170–1; acts at court, 165, 170; visits Paris, 165; furnishes apartments, 166; childbirth, 167; death, 168, 172; funeral, 168; Life of, 168–72, 237
Godolphin, Sidney, 1st Earl of Godolphin, 190; marriage, 163, 165–6, 170–1; wife's funeral, 168; at Treasury, 186, 196, 208, 219, 223, 230, 236, 242; and Prettyman lawsuit, 196; negotiates with William of Orange, 201; as patron, 208, 212, 218, 219, 223, 224, 230, 232, 236; downfall, 219; and Jack's marriage, 230, 237, 242
Godstone, gunpowder mill, 5, 6
Goffe, Col. William, 93
Gondolas, describes, 56
Gonzalvo de Córdoba, 50
Goode, Dr, 225
Gorges, Fernando, 154
Goring, George, 22, 29
Goring House, visits, 129
Gosterwood, Evelyn property, 8
Gothic architecture, 56, 59, 127, 148
Government: choice of, after James II, 203–4
Government service, 2, 144, 208: Commission on Hackney Coaches, 124; Commission on Mint, 124; Commission for Privy Seal, 190, 192, 193, 194, 195, 208; Commission for Sick and Wounded Mariners, 24, 126, 129, 131–2, 133, 138, 157–8; Council for Foreign Plantations, 150–1; Commission on Supply of Saltpetre, 134; Latin Secretary, 148; remuneration for, 208, 218, 223, 236, 237, 238; report on Swedish

ambassador's reception, 109; surveyors of St Paul's, 134; Treasurer of Chelsea Hospital, 218, 223
Grafton, Dukes of, see Fitzroy
Grand Alliance, 206
Grand Condé, 70, 72, 76
Gravel, afflicted with, 219
Gravesend: uses port, 71; visits wounded, 157, 159
Great, the: included in, 146; medals of, 221–2
Great Durnford, visits, 87
Great Fire of London, 134–6; monument to, 180
Greenwich Hospital, survey for, 218; plans, 229
Greenwich, Naval College, 234
Greenwich Park, king plants elms in, 123
Gregory XV, Pope, 47
Grenadiers, first sees, 167
Grotius, Hugo, escapes, 23; on the sea, 161
Guildhall, dines at, 126
Gunpowder: comments on, 7; manufacture, 5–7
Gunpowder Plot, 184, 192
Gun shops, in Brescia, 59
Gwyn, Nell, 151, 186, 187

Haarlem, church, 24
Hackney coaches, Commission on, 124
Hague, The: visits, 22; Prinzenhoff, 23; orders armour, 24
Hair washing, annual, 3, 84
Halifax, Marquess of, see Savile
Hampton Court: visits Charles I at, 66; Catherine of Braganza at, 133; visits Charles II at, 133
Hanging, views on, 65, 83
Hare coursing, 6, 87
Harrow, Evelyn family at, 5
Hartlib, Mr, 93; on planning, 115
Hawking, 166
Hawthorn hedges, 118
Health: illnesses: ague, 15,

*Numismata* (1697), 231;
synopsis, 221–3
Nymegen, Peace of, 165

Oak: hollow, as prison,
120; qualitiies of, 4, 116
Oates, Titus: and Popish
Plot, 173–5, 182; at
Stafford's trial, 179; trial
of, 188
Oblivion, Act of, 81
Observation, talent for, 17,
240
October, gardening tasks,
123
Offley, Mary (afterwards
Evelyn), 66, 81; dies, 123
'Old Salvatico', *see*
Salvatico, Benedetto
Old Testament, interest in,
102
Olivares, Conde Duque de
San Lucar, 50
Onions, 232
Opera: in Milan, 59; in
Venice, 57
Operations, watches, 58,
76, 157
Orange, Princes of, 21, 23;
*see also* William III
Oranges, effect of, 232
Orford, Earl of, *see* Russell,
Edward
Orleans, visits, 35–6, 62, 63
Ormond, Duke of, *see*
Butler, James
Orrery, Lord, *see* Boyle,
Roger
Osborne, Sir Thomas, Earl
of Danby, 78, 144; in
Tower, 185; and James
II, 196; and William III,
204
Ossory, Lord, *see* Butler,
Richard
Ostende, visits, 27
Otter hunting, 110
Owen, Sir John, visits, 70–1
Oxford, Charles II at, 133,
180; supports William of
Orange, 201; visit, 86–7,
124; Parliament at, 180
Oxford University:
Arundel Marbles, 140;
attends, 10, 12, 13–15;
Encaenia, 2, 147; helps,

2, 140, 225; honorary
doctorate, 147; son John
attends, 138, 146, 158;
grandson Jack attends,
225–6, 230, 236
Oysters, eats at Murano, 57

Paddington, Abinger,
Evelyn estate, 15
Padua, visits, 57–8; enters
university, 57–8; elected
to *Syndicus Artistarum*, 57;
illness in, 58; studies
anatomy, 58
Pageant, river, attends, 112
Painting, *see* Art
Palais Cardinal, 72
Palais d'Orléans, 78
Palladio, Andrea, 57
Palmer, Barbara, Duchess
of Cleveland, and
Charles II, 152, 155, 176,
185, 187
Palmer, Sir John, 69
Pamphili, Gian Battista
(Innocent X), 44, 49
Panama, capture of, 154–5,
165
*Panegyric*, presents to king,
103
*Paradise Transplanted and
Restored*, exhibition,
163–4
Parcke, Daniel, 242
Paris: visits: 1643, 31, 33–4,
35; 1646, 63, 64–5; 1649,
71–80; married in, 64;
architecture, 33–4;
English exiles in, 71, 78;
Fronde riots, 69–70, 71,
76; Louvre, 34, 128;
Margaret Godolphin
visits, 165; Notre Dame,
34; Pont Neuf, 33; smell,
33; Sorbonne, 34;
Tuileries, 34; Ville de
Venize, 33
Parkhurst, John, 12, 13–14
Parks, continental, 113
Parliament: 'Short'
Parliament (1640), 16;
'Long', (1640–1), 20;
*Grand Remonstrance* (1641),
28; Civil Wars, 29, 31,
66–7; Pride's Purge, 67;
Rump, 96, 97; Monck
dissolves, 97;

Convention Parliament,
105; after Restoration,
105, 142, 143–5;
'Cavalier', 105, 175;
Fasts, 130, 137, 179;
attacks Clarendon, 142;
party politics, 144–5; and
Popish Plot, 173–5, 179;
James II addresses, 188;
prorogues, 194, 196; and
William III, 203–4; on
clipped money, 219;
George Evelyn petitions,
224; Commissioners to
Ireland, 229; and
succession, 234
Parliament Act (1649), 70
Parr, Thomas, death of,
108
Passes, travelling, 20, 25,
31, 59–60, 77, 81, 142
Patronage, need of, 208; *see
also* Godolphin, Sidney
Pedantry, 107, 120–1, 141,
161, 231
Pelican, first sees, 23;
examines in St James's
Park, 128–9
Pembroke, Lord, 86
Penguins, comments on,
129
Penruddock, rising, 84, 91
Pepper, effect of, 232
Pepys, Samuel: personality,
1–2, 3; popularity, 1; and
apiary, 87, 113; Dutch
Wars, 131; on Evelyn,
131, 146; collaborates
with, 131; Fire of
London, 135; has stone,
147; wife dies, 147; and
Lord Sandwich, 158;
Master of Trinity House,
166, 189; in Tower, 175,
209; on shipbuilding,
181; visits Portsmouth,
190; and religion of
Charles II, 191; hears
eunuch sing, 196; JE's
portrait for, 205; retires,
209; deplores state of
navy, 209; dines with
Dampier, 224; Jack
Evelyn writes for, 226; at
Clapham, 230; death,
237
Perrault, Claude, 128